THE NOT-SO-SECRET SERVICE

AGENCY TALES from FDR to the Kennedy Assassination to the Reagan Era

VINCENT MICHAEL PALAMARA

THE NOT SO SECRET SERVICE: AGENCY TALES FROM FDR TO THE KENNEDY ASSASSINATION TO THE REAGAN ERA
COPYRIGHT © 2017 VINCENT MICHAEL PALAMARA

Published by:
Trine Day LLC
PO Box 577
Walterville, OR 97489
1-800-556-2012
www.TrineDay.com
publisher@TrineDay.net

Library of Congress Control Number: 2017936715

Palamara, Vincent Michael
—1st ed.
p. cm.

Epud (ISBN-13) 978-1-63424-121-2
Mobi (ISBN-13)978-1-63424-122-9
Print (ISBN-13) 978-1-63424-120-5
1. United States. -- Secret Service -- Officials and employees. 2. Secret service
-- United States. 3. Presidents -- Protection -- United States. 4. History/United
States/State & Local/General 5. United States. -- Secret Service. 6. Presidents
-- Protection. I. Palamara, Vincent Michael II. Title

FIRST EDITION
10 9 8 7 6 5 4 3 2 1

Printed in the USA
Distribution to the Trade by:
Independent Publishers Group (IPG)
814 North Franklin Street
Chicago, Illinois 60610
312.337.0747
www.ipgbook.com

In the heart the loom of feeling,
In the head the light of thinking;
In the limbs the strength of willing.
Weaving enlightening,
Enlightened strengthening;
Strengthened weaving.
Lo! This is man.

– Rudolf Steiner, 1923

TABLE OF CONTENTS

Introduction

REASONS AND LITERARY TRIBUTES

People often ask me, "Vince, what got you interested in the Secret Service, in general, and the JFK assassination, in particular?" Well, it all goes back to when I was around the age of 12 in 1978. As a precocious pre-teen during the height of the second major investigation into President Kennedy's murder, the House of Representatives Select Committee on Assassinations (HSCA), I was fascinated by all the news stories on the nightly news with their frequent updates about the progress of the committee, as well as the seeming pro-conspiracy nuggets of information they spoke of. At the same time, as both a stamp and coin collector, I came across many an image of JFK that prompted me to ask questions of my parents, who were and still are big admirers of President Kennedy (even owning a beautiful color photo of Kennedy that fascinated me as a youngster), recalling vividly the shocking news of his death, as well (that generation's 9/11, also akin to the previous generation's Pearl Harbor and the death of FDR).

At the same time this was all going on, I also became hooked on reruns of a classic fictional television program about the Secret Service of the 19th century, *The Wild, Wild West*, complete with its fictional plots to kill President Grant and other intriguing espionage. The Secret Service seemed very heroic to an impressionable boy like myself. The show remains my favorite to this day, but I digress.

However, it wasn't until the 25th anniversary of the assassination 10 years later in late 1988 that my interest really took off with regard to Kennedy, the assassination, and the Secret Service. By the time the turn of the decade happened in 1990, I knew I had to do original research on the subject. My choice? To study the Secret Service in the context of the Kennedy years, of course. The next year, in 1991, I gave my first conference presentation in front of 60 authors and researchers, many of whom could have been, age-wise, my father (or, in a few cases, my grandfather). The overwhelmingly positive response I received by these veteran sleuths made me realize I was onto something. Thus began my quest to do as much primary research as possible and interview as many former Secret Service agents as I could find, quite a challenge in those pre-internet times.

9/27/92 is a date which will live in infamy for myself: the day I contacted former #1 agent for JFK, Gerald Behn, who told me President Kennedy never ordered the agents off his limousine, among other interesting items. Coming from such an authority and sounding so definitive on the matter, this left quite an impression on me, a still impressionable 26 year old at the time. The fact that Behn passed away on 4/21/93 made my conversations with him that September day even more poignant.

Thus began an obsession to uncover the REAL story of President Kennedy's security- or lack thereof- in Dallas and my first book *Survivor's Guilt* in 2013. Along the way (starting in 1998, to be exact), I also began a peripheral interest in the medical evidence, corresponding and interviewing many former Parkland Hospital doctors and nurses, as well as many former Bethesda personnel, culminating in my second book *JFK: From Parkland to Bethesda* in 2015. A personal highlight for me in this arena was interviewing on video tape x-ray technician Jerrol Custer in 1991 and 1998, respectively (Custer passed away in 2000), but I again digress a bit.

Now to the current volume in your hands.

People sometimes ask me, in some form or fashion, "Vince, I like your work, but why are you always picking on the Secret Service?" In point of fact, I am not. Truth be told, I am an ardent admirer- a true fan- of the Secret Service, America's oldest law enforcement agency. There is much to admire with these gallant men and women- they have helped prevent assassinations of President-Elect Franklin Roosevelt, President Truman, President Ford (twice) and President Reagan, among others... and that is just what we know of. There are countless under-reported or "kept-confidential" threats and assassination attempts that have been thwarted by the Secret Service. So, why do I get this comment? The answer is simple:

I am also a huge critic of their performance on November 22, 1963, when President Kennedy was assassinated.

My first book *Survivor's Guilt: The Secret Service and the Failure to Protect President Kennedy* addresses this issue in great detail, based on many interviews with former agents and years of dogged research. My second book *JFK: From Parkland to Bethesda* is a methodical compendium of the JFK assassination medical evidence, also drawing on many interviews and correspondence with principals in the case. I am very proud of those books.

So why a third volume? The answer, again, is a simple one:

There is more to me than just my interest in the JFK assassination.

That said, there are some important loose ends and corroborative details that did not make the first book that are presented here at length for the first time, while my research into most of the other important presidents of the modern era of the 20th century- FDR, Truman, Ike, LBJ, Nixon, Ford, Carter, and Reagan-needed to be brought to light here, again based on my many interviews and correspondence with former agents-and years of research- that perhaps ended up on the "cutting room floor", so to speak, or were somewhat overshadowed by my previously necessary narrow focus on Kennedy's murder.

For the Bush 41, Clinton, and Bush 43 years, I decided not to reinvent the wheel and heartily recommend former agent Dan Emmett's personal memoir *Within Arm's Length* (2012; 2014)[1] and, for including the Obama years, former agent Dan Bongino's *Life Inside The Bubble* (2013) and *The Fight* (2016). For personal former agent memoirs I feel responsible for "inspiring", there are Gerald Blaine's (very) disappointing blame-the-victim tome *The Kennedy Detail* (2010) and Clint Hill's infinitely better (well, minus a page or two*) Mrs. Kennedy & Me* (2012). I spoke to and corresponded with both former agents, they "contributed" (by default) to my first book and this one, and they have mentioned my work, more than once, on television.[2] Hill also came out with the forgettable and repetitive picture book *Five Days In November* (2013) and the improved *Five Presidents* (2016). All four of the aforementioned books were co-authored by Lisa McCubbin, a woman I have had some contentious correspondence with.

For enjoyable yet somewhat tabloid-style works on the Secret Service, there are the two Ronald Kessler[3] books, *In The President's Secret Service* (2009) and largely repetitive *The First Family Detail* (2014), *Confessions of An Ex-Secret Service Agent* (the late agent Marty Venker story) by George Rush (1988), and the late former agent Dennis V.N. McCarthy's *Protecting The President* (1985), the latter 2 books (actually, all 4) considered an embarrassment to the agency, as former agent's Robert Snow, Darwin Horn and Walt Coughlin conveyed to myself. A prominent Secret Service

---

1. I am mentioned as a Secret Service expert on the cover of the 2012 edition of Dan's book and he contributed a little to my first book. I consider him a friend.

2. See chapters one and ten of my first book *Survivor's Guilt*.

3. I corresponded with Kessler- see chapter one of *Survivor's Guilt.* He wrote: "I actually tried to find you early on but was not successful, so you are not mentioned in the book." How could he not find me-my online footprint is large! He also wrote: "I am aware of your work and have read a lot of it." (E-mail, 6/6/2009)

book I am mentioned in several times is the late Professor Philip Melanson's[4] definitive overview-warts and all- of the Secret Service from 1865-2005 entitled *The Secret Service: The Hidden History of an Enigmatic Agency* (2003; updated 2005), which is actually an updated version of a book he wrote back in 1984 called *The Politics of Protection*.

For good, straightforward agent memoirs, the following are quite useful: *Standing Next To History* by former agent Joseph Petro (2004), *In The Secret Service* by the late former agent Jerry Parr[5] and his wife Carolyn Parr[6] (2013), *Riding With Reagan* by former agent John Barletta[7] (2005), *The Echo From Dealey Plaza* by former agent Abraham Bolden[8] (2008), and *20 Years in the Secret Service* by the late former agent Rufus Youngblood[9] (1973). In addition, I highly recommend three historical treasures that contain a potpourri of Secret Service interviews and information (again, no reason for me to reinvent the wheel on these subjects): the definitive book on the 3/30/81 Reagan assassination attempt, *Rawhide Down* by Del Wilber[10] (2011), the definitive book on the 11/1/50 Truman assassination attempt, *American Gunfight* by Stephen Hunter and John Bainbridge, Jr. (2005),[11] and the definitive book on the 9/22/75 Ford assassination attempt, *Taking Aim at the President* by Geri Spieler[12] (2008) (to date, there has been nothing real definitive on the 9/5/75 attempt on Ford's life by former Charles Manson follower Lynette "Squeaky" Fromme, although it is mentioned in numerous books, magazines and documentaries). In addition, there are definitive books out there on the assassinations (attempted and successful) of Presidents Lincoln, Garfield, McKinley and Teddy Roosevelt that are interesting, from a Secret Service perspective,

---

4. I spoke to and corresponded several times with Melanson who passed away 9/18/2006.
5. I spoke to Parr once in 1995. Parr passed away 10/9/15.
6. I have corresponded with Carolyn via Twitter and Facebook.
7. I corresponded several times with Barletta.
8. I have corresponded and spoken to Abe Bolden many times starting back in 1993 up to the present time. Now, with the advent of Facebook, I also have corresponded with his wonderful family. I consider Abe a friend and he was a prominent part (including one whole chapter) of my first book *Survivor's Guilt*. In fact, I would like to think, and I may be right, that I inspired him to write his own book, based on having a copy of an early draft of my book (which he greatly admired) way back in 1993.
9. I spoke to Youngblood twice. Youngblood passed away 10/2/96.
10. I corresponded with Wilber several times and had one nice long conversation. In addition, one agent I did later correspond with, Robert DeProspero, told me: "I should have spoken to you instead of Del."
11. I did speak to two of the three surviving principal agents involved in the protection of the president that day, Vince Mroz and Floyd Boring, both now deceased. The other agent, the late Stu Stout, was covered via much correspondence with Stout's surviving family.
12. Spieler reached out to me before publication and we have corresponded a few times. She said I am "the most knowledgeable person about the Secret Service outside the agency." (E-mail, 4/20/2009)

only in a tangential way, at best. Since these works cover events of a much earlier time, I chose not to delve into them here.

For "the rest" (often dry and clinical books that, nevertheless, often contain valuable information), in no particular order: *Out From The Shadow* (about the late agent Charlie Gittens) by Maurice Butler (2012); *Walking With Presidents* by former agent Michael Endicott (2008); *Get Carter* by former agent Bill Carter[13] (2006); *Breaking Tecumseh's Curse* by Jan Marie Ritter and former agent Bob Ritter[14] (2013); *Dar's Story* by former agent Darwin Horn[15] (2002); *Criminals & Presidents: The Adventures of a Secret Service Agent* by former agent Tim Wood (2016); *Special Agent in Charge* by former agent Forrest Guthrie (2014); *Secret Service Chief* by the late former Chief U.E. Baughman[16] (1962); *Reilly of the White House* by the late former agent Mike Reilly[17] (1946); *Starling of the White House* by the late former agent Edmund Starling[18] (1946); *Special Agent* by the late former Chief Frank Wilson[19] (1965); *American Secret Service Agent* by the late former agent Don Wilkie [son of Chief John Wilkie] (1934); *The United States Secret Service in the Late War* by the late former agent LaFayette Baker and *Death To Traitors* (about Baker) by Jacob Mogelever (1960); *Looking Back and Seeing the Future* by the AFAUSSS, the Association of Former Agents of the United States Secret Service[20] (1991); *The Secret Service Story* by Michael Dorman (1967); *The Story of the Secret Service* (1971) and *The Secret Service in Action* (1980) by the late former agent Harry Neal; *Transitions* (2002) and *Not On The Level* (2006) by former agent Mike Maddaloni[21]; *Undercover* (1971) and *In Crime's Way* by the late former agent Carmine Motto; *The United States Secret Service* by Walter Bowen and the late former agent Harry Neal (1960); *Secret Service: History, Duties, and Equipment* by C.B. Colby (1966); *What Does A Secret Service Agent Do?* By Wayne Hyde (1962); *The Story of the Secret Service* by Ferdinand Kuhn (1957); *The United States Secret Service – What It Is, What It Does* by the late former Chief U.E. Baughman (1956); *Whitewash II- the FBI-SS Cover-up* by the late Harold Weisberg[22] (1966);

13. I corresponded with Carter.
14. I corresponded with the Ritters.
15. I corresponded numerous times with Horn.
16. Baughman passed away 11/6/78.
17. Reilly passed away in June 1973.
18. Starling passed away 8/3/44.
19. Wilson passed away 6/22/70.
20. I was fortunate to receive a photocopied version of this rare, out of print and largely agents-eyes-only book via the late former agent Frank Stoner. As for the AFAUSSS itself, I contacted/ corresponded with former Executive Secretaries (the late) Hamilton Brown and Donald Stebbins.
21. I corresponded several times with Maddaloni.
22. I corresponded with Weisberg. Weisberg passed away 2/21/2002.

High Interest Books: Secret Service by Michael Beyer (2003); *To Be A U.S. Secret Service Agent* by Henry Holden (2006); *The U.S. Secret Service* by Ann Graham Gaines (2001); *Extreme Careers- Secret Service Agents* by David Seidman (2003); *Know Your Government: The U.S. Secret Service* by Gregory Matusky & John Hayes (1988); *A Million Miles of Presidents* by the late former agent George McNally[23] (1982); *The Death of a President* by the late William Manchester[24] (1988 edition); *The Day Kennedy Was Shot* by the late Jim Bishop (1992 edition); *Mortal Error* by Bonar Menninger, based on the work of the late Howard Donahue[25] (1992/2013) and further elaborated upon by Colin McLaren[26] in *JFK: The Smoking Gun* (2013); *Unsung Heroes: The Story of the U.S. Secret Service* by Jack Roberts (2014); *Hunting The President* by Mel Ayton (2014); *Near Miss: The Attempted Assassination of JFK* (2014) by Steve B. Davis; *Behind The Shades* by former agent Sue Ann Baker (2015); Gary Byrne book *Crisis of Character* (2016) and AFAUSSS book *Guardian of Democracy* (2016); and *A Career as a Secret Service Agent* by Therese Shea (2015).

Finally, for definitive Secret Service television documentaries, these are highly recommended: *The Secret Service* (History Channel, 1995; VHS); *Inside The Secret Service* (Discovery Channel, 1995; VHS); *Inside The U.S. Secret Service* (National Geographic, 2004; DVD); the bonus DVD to the great 1993 Clint Eastwood movie *In The Line of Fire*; *Dangerous World – The Kennedy Years* (ABC, 12/4/97; VHS); *Secrets of the Secret Service* (Discovery Channel, 2009); various Secret Service related Sixth Floor Museum oral histories (2003-2011); *Top Secrets – Presidential Assassins* (National Geographic, 2013); *Secret Service Secrets – Campaign Nightmare, Home Front, On Enemy Soil* (2012); *America's Book of Secrets-Presidential Assassins* (2013); *Kennedy's Suicide Bomber* (2013); *JFK- The Smoking Gun* (2013); and, believe it or not[27], *The Kennedy Detail* (Discovery Channel, 2010).

Agent Larry Newman saw me on the History Channel program *The Men Who Killed Kennedy* in 2003 and thought I was "some 20 year old kid" (actually, I was 36 at the time!). Agent Tony Sherman highly recommended a book that mentioned me several times, Philip Melanson's 2005

---

23. I have corresponded several times with McNally's grandson Reid McNally, as well as other relatives. George McNally passed away 8/11/70.
24. I spoke to Manchester in 1993. Manchester passed away 6/1/2004. I have also researched his archives at Wesleyan University.
25. I spoke to and corresponded with Donahue. Donahue passed away in 1999.
26. I corresponded with McLaren and have a brief mention in his book.
27. Despite some falsehoods and propaganda, it is a brilliant production with great photos and films, as well as several JFK era agents interviewed.

work *The Secret Service: The Hidden History of an Enigmatic Agency*, while another agent, Don Cox, told me that "I ran into your name again as I am reading some of Melanson's stuff." Agent Dan Emmett sought me out to read and critique his then as-yet-unpublished book *Within Arm's Length* (I ended up with a nice mention on the front cover) ... so I get around.

One of the leading authors and researchers in the Kennedy assassination field, Robert Groden, a man who has appeared on television many times and was also a consultant to the HSCA in the late 1970's, was once asked about the Secret Service. He had no substantive response to the questioner, responding with a witty "I guess that is why they call the Secret Service secret."

Presented in this volume are tales from the now not so Secret Service.

CHAPTER ONE

ONE OF JFK's SECRET SERVICE AGENT DRIVERS DIED SHORTLY *BEFORE* THE KENNEDY ASSASSINATION

Secret Service agent Thomas B. Shipman

P onder this incredible thought for a moment: out of literally thousands of Secret Service agents who have come and gone since the inception of the agency in 1865, encompassing part or all of three different centuries (the nineteenth, twentieth, and twenty first, to be precise), only 36 operatives/agents/personnel have died in the line of duty.[1] Fortunately for all concerned, this is an extremely small number of unfortunate souls who made the ultimate sacrifice for their country. However, what makes this tiny sampling even more powerful is the fact that, as I discovered in 1997, one very special agent, Thomas B. Shipman, one of three agents who drove President Kennedy or his Secret Service follow-up vehicle on many trips between Election Night 1960 and the Fall of 1963, died 10/14/63 of an alleged heart attack at (of all places) Camp David, the month before the Kennedy assassination

I made this shocking discovery when perusing a passage buried in Col. George J. McNally's obscure and non-indexed book entitled, *A Million*

---

1. See the AFAUSSS website: https://www.oldstar.org/index.php/in-memoriam

Miles of Presidents.[2] The relevant passage reads, "One of the President's drivers, Tom Shipman, died suddenly." I cannot convey how amazing this bit of information was back in 1997 (and still is today), as no other book, article or website ever even hinted of an agent from Kennedy's own detail passing away shortly before the assassination. In the chronology of McNally's narrative, after discussing the death of baby Patrick Kennedy (Aug. 1963) and the 11-state "Conservation Tour" (late September 1963), this would seem to indicate a time period of around Sept. 1963 for Shipman's death. McNally also mentions the death of Administrative Officer Frank Sanderson who died in May 1963, as verified by a quick internet search at *Ancestry.Com* and other sites. Strangely, no death for a "Tom" or "Thomas" Shipman was listed at the time for 1963. However, Secret Service SA (Special Agent) Tom Shipman was on the "Conservation Tour," as Office-of-the-Naval-Aide records for this trip reveal. In fact, Shipman rode on Helicopter #2 from the South Lawn of the White House on the way to Andrews Air Force Base on 9/24/63 with Ken O'Donnell, SA Gerald Blaine, SA Paul Burns, and SA William Greer.

Also, Shipman is listed in the Protective Survey Report (written 9/20/63) for the 9/24/63 Milford, PA stop. Previously, Shipman had been on JFK's 3/23/63 trip to Chicago, IL, driving the follow-up car.[3] Secret Service agent Sam Kinney told me on 4/15/94: "[fellow agent/driver] Deeter B. [Flohr, Ike's driver] and I were buddies – traveled a lot together; Tom Shipman, Deeter B., and myself." Former agent Darwin Horn wrote to me on 2/25/04: "Shipman was a driver for many years with Dick Flore [sic] and Morgan Gies."

If that weren't enough, it also appears that there were two new additions to the regular White House Garage (chauffeur) detail in Oct.-Nov.

2. Col. George J. McNally was the first commanding officer of the White House Army Signal Agency, and its successor, the White House Communications Agency (WHCA) from 1941 until his retirement in 1965. Before that, McNally was an agent of the United States Secret Service (1935-1941). McNally was in the midst of finishing a book when he died of a heart attack on 8/11/70 (he is interred in Arlington National Cemetery). The name of McNally's book, not released until 1982 (with the help of his widow and the 1600 Communications Assoc.), is *A Million Miles of Presidents*. Among countless other trips (Truman-Johnson), McNally was on the Texas trip, working closely with Chief Warrant Officer Arthur W. Bales, Jr. and Ira Gearhart, a.k.a. The Bagman (these two men rode near the end of the motorcade in the White House Signal Corps car.) For his part, McNally stayed behind at the Love Field terminal to have lunch and to check on the upcoming Austin part of the trip to see if the communication lines were working. McNally was interviewed 4 times for Manchester's *The Death of a President* and appears on one page of Bishop's *The Day Kennedy Was Shot*. In addition, McNally's name appears several times during agent Robert Bouck's JFK Library Oral History, as McNally played a critical role in the White House taping system. Finally, McNally was one of the original members of founder Floyd Boring's Association of Former Agents of the United States Secret Service in 1969.

3. Secret Service documents in the author's collection.

1963: SA Henry J. Rybka[4], attending Treasury School from 11/1/63 to 11/8/63 and who would go on to be called away from Kennedy's limousine[5] by Agent Emory Roberts at Love Field, and SA Andrew M. Hutch, who did not join the detail until 11/18/63, having previously been a White House Policeman.[6] They joined veterans SA Samuel A. Kinney; SA George W. Hickey; SA William R. Greer; Special Officer (SO/Uniformed Division) William C. Davis[7]; WH Policeman James M. Carter, and SAIC Morgan L. Gies. From the record, then, it appeared Shipman died suddenly sometime between October 3 and November 1, 1963.

It would be nice to have the travel logs for this period, but the Secret Service destroyed them in January 1995. From the *Final Report of the Assassination Records Review Board*, page 149: "In January 1995, the Secret Service destroyed presidential protection survey reports for some of President Kennedy's trips in the fall of 1963. The Review Board learned of the destruction approximately one week after the Secret Service destroyed them, when the Board was drafting its request for additional information. The Board believed that the Secret Service files on the President's travel in the weeks preceding his murder would be relevant."

Why the destruction? No satisfactory answer was ever given, although many hold deep suspicion.

Where is Shipman's death certificate? At present, it is unavailable and, without an exhumation and toxicology tests, at this late juncture, a verdict of "heart attack" is a country doctor 'catch-all' that is unsatisfactory and inconclusive, given the subject at hand (a presumably fit Secret Service agent who had to pass annual physicals and perform the rare honor of driving several presidents).

This was the extent of my knowledge from 1997 until 1999, when I came across an online website dedicated to fallen officers that, for the first time ever, listed Shipman's death and his middle initial[8] and, most importantly,

---

4. Rybka was a Special Officer and member of JFK's Inaugural Detail: Protective Survey Report dated 1/16/61 Re: Inaugural Activities of the President on January 20, 1961, conducted by SAIC James M. Beary (1-15 [Washington Field Office]) and SA H.S. Knight (1-16 [WHD]), in the author's collection.
5. Along with fellow agent Donald Lawton.
6. Secret Service Shift Reports for November 1963 in the author's collection.
7. Steve Davis, son of the late William C. Davis, wrote to me on 1/12/14: "[My father] was assigned to the White House, upon our return from France, in 1961. In March of 1963, he retired from the Army and transferred over to the Secret Service...the garage was located at 1222 22nd Street NW, that's where they keep all the limos...my dad picked up the limo at Andrews Air Force Base and drove it back to the garage [on 11/22/63]. He was responsible for cleaning the car after the Dallas trip. [Before the assassination] He [his dad] had been alerted to go to Dallas, but Agent Greer recovered from his sickness on the morning they were supposed to leave." From a 12/31/13 e-mail: "My dad also drove the lead car in the funeral motorcade, from the capitol to Arlington."
8. Not long after the author's discovery, the website could no longer be accessed.

on 7/26/01, when I discovered, once again via the internet, The Association of Former Agents of the Secret Service's website (the organization goes by the abbreviation AFAUSSS).[9] It listed 33 (now, 36) agents and personnel who have died in the line of duty since the Secret Service was established. The only JFK-era agent listed is White House Garage/Chauffeur Special Agent Thomas B. Shipman: "October 14, 1963: Died of a heart attack while on a presidential protective assignment at Camp David, Maryland." It was not until 2013, thanks to the help of researcher Deb Galentine, that an obscure news article was found that mentioned the death of Shipman (*The News*, Frederick, Maryland, 10/16/63). After a coroner's report furnished the day after his death, Shipman was quickly buried only two days later. Obviously, no toxicology tests were performed. In the last couple of years, I have discovered similar newspaper articles, more data, and new information from surviving members of Shipman's family. More on this to follow.

Shipman's death meant fellow agent Bill Greer very ineptly drove JFK to his death in Dallas[10] and Shipman's immediate replacement, Henry J. Rybka, fresh from Treasury School, was recalled at Love Field by the aforementioned Emory Roberts. Former agent Gerald Blaine told me on 2/7/04 that Kinney, Shipman, and Greer were "the three consistent ones" that drove JFK's car (commenting that Greer "usually" did), adding that Shipman and Kinney also drove the follow-up car. Former agent Winston Lawson wrote to me in a letter dated 1/20/04: "Tom Shipman, also a driver, died of a heart attack while up at Camp David, prior to retirement. I don't know the year and couldn't find out. I believe Sam Kinney found his body. They would have roomed together in one of the cabins up there."

Shipman's passing just a month before Dallas puts him in very special and tragic company: three agents who have died in the 21st century; the six who died tragically in the 4/19/95 Oklahoma City bombing; five other agents who died in the 1990's; eight in the 1980's; two in the 1970's (including J. Clifford Dietrich, who died in a helicopter crash on 5/26/73); another one in the 1960's, Thomas Wooge, on 10/17/68 (he also briefly guarded JFK); Leslie Coffelt, the Uniformed Division officer who died on 11/1/50 during the Truman assassination attempt involving a few agents who later guarded JFK; one in the 1940's; four in the 1930's; two in the 1920's; and two in the period from 1900-1910. That's a very small and sad group, indeed.[11]

9. https://www.oldstar.org/index.php/in-memoriam. Here is another great source of information online: http://www.aorp.org/deceasedsort.html
10. See my entire chapter dedicated to Greer, chapter 8, in my first book *Survivor's Guilt: The Secret Service & the Failure to Protect President Kennedy* (2013, Trine Day).
11. *High Interest Books: Secret Service*, a 48-page book for young people written by Mark Beyer in 2003 (Children's Press, a Division of Scholastic Incorporated), states on p. 33: "Over thirty people

JFK and LBJ advance man Marty Underwood, on the ill-fated Texas trip, told author Harry Livingstone: "There were a couple of suicides in the thing, with the Secret Service and everything ... " When Livingstone asked "Do you remember who committed suicide?" Underwood responded: "I don't remember. I think there were a couple ...," only to be cut off by Livingstone.[12] Also, an unnamed agent took his own life "in the late Sixties, in Washington, with his own weapon. There were signs he was beginning to buckle," as former agent Chuck Rochner explained to fellow former agent Marty Venker.[13] Former agent Darwin Horn wrote to me in an e-mail dated 3/2/04: "I cannot recall the name of the SA who killed himself in the late 60's. I seem to recall something of that nature occurring though."

The above is a very good updated summation of what I presented in my first book. Since publication, more information and evidence has flown forth to add to the mystery. Former agent Gerald Blaine has a photo of Shipman in his 2010 book *The Kennedy Detail*, yet, strangely, although he is much aware of my writings online (after all, as I have strenuously argued, his entire book is a reaction *to* my work), he does not actually mention Shipman once (or even address his untimely death) in the actual text of his book; the same goes for Clint Hill's multiple books or, for that matter, all other books out there to date! Researcher Tyler Newcomb, the son of author Fred Newcomb of *Murder from Within* fame, wrote to me on 2/5/14: "I got a private eye to try and look into any information on him (Shipman). He apparently died of a heart attack and his widow Jacqueline just plain disappeared from what I found. No trace whatsoever after the funeral. Shipman had 2 brothers I believe and both are deceased." While I found several similar contemporary news articles mentioning Shipman's death (all only available after paying a fee and searching the archives), Tyler was kind enough to forward this information on to me, as well:

> From the Associated Press, "White House Chauffeur Dies at Camp David," *Washington Post,* October 16, 1963, p.C9
> "Thomas Shipman, 51, one of President Kennedy's Secret Service drivers, died Monday at the presidential retreat at nearby Camp David. The cause of death was not immediately determined pending a coroner's report.
> Mr. Shipman, a native of Washington, was a District policeman from 1936 until 1950 when he transferred to the White House po-

have died while working as Secret Service agents."
12. *High Treason 2* by Harrison Livingstone (1992, Carroll & Graf), p. 439; I also spoke to Underwood.
13. *Confessions of an Ex-Secret Service Agent* by Johann Rush (1988), pp.216-217.

lice force. He became a Secret Service agent in 1954.

Mr. Shipman occasionally drove the President's limousine, but, more normally, drove the carload of Secret Service agents who follow directly behind the President.

He is survived by his wife, Jacqueline, of the home address, 3817 Van Ness St. NW."

Buried VERY quickly, indeed – no toxicology tests were performed (this very obscure article was only found in 2013, courtesy of Deb Galentine):

Page 22 **THE NEWS, Frederick, Maryland**
Wednesday, October 16, 1963

Camp David Man Had Heart Attack

WASHINGTON (AP)—A heart attack caused the death of Secret Service agent Thomas Shipman Monday at Camp David Md., the presidential retreat near Thurmont.

Shipman 51, drove Secret Service cars, and occasionally President Kennedy's limousine.

A coroner's report Tuesday gave a coronary attack as the cause of his death.

Funeral services will be held Thursday morning at St. Ann's Rectory at Wisconsin Avenue and Yuma Streets, N.W. Burial will be in Ft. Lincoln Cemetery.

Shipman was a native of Washington, D.C., and a member of the District of Columbia police force, then of the White House police detail before becoming a Secret Service agent in 1954.

Researcher Deb Galentine, whose father was a former police detective *and* CIA operative who guarded JFK, wrote to me in February 2014: "I, too, think Shipman had a heart attack. I think it's probable he was 'heart attacked' [intelligence method of assassination that, ostensibly, leaves the victim as a "natural cause" statistic]. I think if he was 'heart attacked,' it was because he refused to do what Greer did – slow down to a near stop as soon as the signal happened.

Shipman's death could have been a "natural early death." It happens. But the records show JFK was at the White House, so why the Secret Service were at Camp David needs to be addressed." Here is what Galentine is referring to:

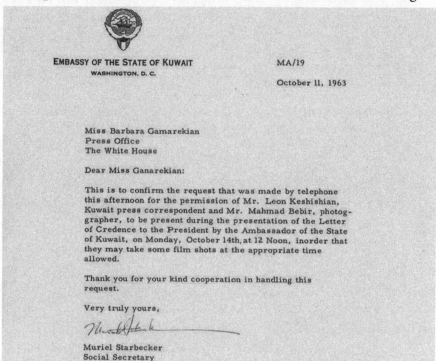

EMBASSY OF THE STATE OF KUWAIT
WASHINGTON, D. C.

MA/19

October 11, 1963

Miss Barbara Gamarekian
Press Office
The White House

Dear Miss Ganarekian:

This is to confirm the request that was made by telephone this afternoon for the permission of Mr. Leon Keshishian, Kuwait press correspondent and Mr. Mahmad Bebir, photographer, to be present during the presentation of the Letter of Credence to the President by the Ambassador of the State of Kuwait, on Monday, October 14th, at 12 Noon, inorder that they may take some film shots at the appropriate time allowed.

Thank you for your kind cooperation in handling this request.

Very truly yours,

Muriel Starbecker
Social Secretary

Galentine added: "That letter sets up an appointment, a time for photos with the President, an ambassador, and photographers. Noon. 10/14/63. The letter was written on the 11th."

10/14/63 Stanley Tretick photo: JFK Jr, under dad's desk during serious Oval Office discussion. [14]

14. http://store.jfklibrary.org/its-okay-to-smile-jfk-and-john-jr-poster/paaaaagilleikfdc/product

President Kennedy Babysits This Weekend 10-14-63

THURMONT, Md. (AP) — President Kennedy was baby-sitting again over the weekend. But it wasn't too tough a chore. With Mrs. Kennedy vacationing in the Eastern Mediterranean, her husband and two youngsters, Caroline and John Jr., spent a second consecutive weekend at Camp David on a ridge of the Catoctin Mountains.

But there were ponies at the camp and Caroline loves to ride. And there were swings and other jungle gym contraptions for her and John.

There's a heated swimming pool for everybody, including the President. Also available for grownups were movies which can be shown in the main lodge of the camp. And there are fa-cilities for trapshooting and for limited golfball-hitting if Kennedy was so inclined.

When the chief executive is tied up on the telephone to Washington or busy with papers dug out of his briefcase, nurse Maude Shaw and several Secret Service agents are around to amuse and keep an eye on the children.

No statement from JFK or the White House about the death of Shipman!

82

10 October 1963 (cont.)
OFFICE 1532
POOL 1959
OFFICE 2031
HOUSE 2033
THEATER 2117
HOUSE 2133

11 OCT 1963
OFFICE 0911
POOL 1327
HOUSE 1347
OFFICE 1600
EAST RM. 1616
OFFICE 1633
POOL 1932
OFFICE 2002
HOUSE 2005

12 OCTOBER 1963
OFFICE 0935
HOUSE 1033
OFFICE 1036
AIRBORNE SOUTH GROUNDS 1129
ARRIVE CAMP DAVID 1201

13 OCT 63
AT CAMP DAVID

14 OCTOBER 1963
DEPART CAMP DAVID 1655
ARRIVE SOUTH GROUND 1723
OFFICE 1725
POOL 1925
HOUSE 2000
THEATER 2124
HOUSE 2136

Actual handwritten records of President Kennedy's schedule, obtained via the JFK Library – again, no mention of the death of Shipman.

Pat, Julie in Greenwich For Funeral of Agent

GREENWICH (AP) — Mrs. Richard Nixon and her daughter, Julie Nixon Eisenhower, today brought a personal expression of sympathy from President Richard M. Nixon to the family of one of his Secret Service agents killed in a helicopter crash over the weekend.

They arrived by presidential jet at Westchester County Airport in New York and were driven by the Secret Service to Greenwich where they went directly to a funeral home to pay respects to the family of J. Clifford Dietrich, 25.

The First Lady, wearing a blue suit, and Mrs. Eisenhower, in a white skirt with a black jacket, then made their way past 400 people gathered on the street outside St. Mary church where they attended a Mass of the Resurrection.

Mr. Dietrich, born in Greenwich, was found dead Saturday by Navy divers off Grand Cay, Bahamas, where the helicopter crashed. He and several other agents were on their way to relieve another contingent of agents guarding the President at a Grand Cay hilltop villa.

Mr. Dietrich and his wife, Junet, had been living with their two young daughters in Woodbridge, Va., a Washington suburb.

Mr. Dietrich served in the New Canaan Police Department and started his Secret Service career in the New Haven field office.

Among those at the funeral were 100 policemen from the Greenwich, Hartford and New

(Continued on Page Two)

The curmudgeonly President Nixon expressed his sympathies to this fallen agent's family in 1973, even sending the First Lady and their one daughter to pay their respects at the funeral…yet nothing whatsoever was said or done by either President Kennedy or his staff in 1963 about Agent Shipman? Is this even believable?

Secret Service Agent Killed

Helicopter Crash Probed

By FRANCES LEWINE

KEY BISCAYNE, Fla. (AP) — A military investigation was begun Sunday into the crash of an Army helicopter carrying secret service agents off Grand Cay Island in the Bahamas, killing one agent and injuring nine other men slightly.

President Nixon ordered the probe after he was informed of the crash Saturday night. The helicopter, with an Army crew of three, was ferrying seven secret service agents from Key Biscayne, Fla., to presidential guard duty at the private island where Nixon and his family were spending the night.

The helicopter, a two engine turbine Sikorsky VH3A, crashed into the Atlantic Ocean about a quarter - mile off the island while coming in for a night landing.

* * *

The helicopter remained afloat after the crash, but turned over in the water.

The dead agent, J. Clifford Dietrich, 25, of Woodbridge, Va., married and the father of two girls aged four years and two months, was trapped in the water - filled helicopter. The Dade County, Fla., medical examiner said he died of asphyxia due to drowning. He had been in the secret service about three years.

White House photographer Ollie Atkins, who was waiting at the oceanside helipad to be picked up for a flight to a near - by Bahamian island, heard the helicopter make "a splash of very short duration, the engine cut off, and then just a long silence."

He said it had made a normal pass over the helipad a few minutes before and went down in pitch darkness.

The White House said the helicopter pilot, Army Chief Warrant Officer Ronald C. Bean, 37, of Dale City, Va., assisted the agents in getting out of the overturned aircraft and launched a rubber raft. The nine men were able to climb on top of the overturned helicopter to await rescue boats. The injured men received emergency treatment from White House Dr. William Lukash at Grant Cay and were helicoptered to Homestead Air Force Base Hospital in Miami, where they were treated for shock and kept overnight for observation.

President Nixon went to the island early Saturday afternoon, accompanied by his wife, Pat, daughters, Julie Eisenhower and Tricia Cox, their husbands, and Florida friend C. G. Bebe Rebozo. The island is owned by Nixon's friend, Robert Abplanalp.

The helicopter crash occurred at 10:10 p.m. (EDT) Saturday.

"The President expressed deep sadness and sympathy for the family of agent Deitrich," the White House said, and "expressed concern for the agents and crewmen."

The Nixons returned by helicopter to Key Biscayne early Sunday afternoon and were to conclude their Memorial Day weekend stay here late today.

New information was gleaned from unsolicited contacts from Shipman's family in 2015. Christine Jones, Shipman's niece, wrote to me on 10/3/15:

> Thank you for your coverage of Tom Shipman, my uncle. I just discovered your site and thought that you may find the following information helpful.
>
> Jacqueline was my mother's older sister and went by "Jackie." She grew up in Pittsburgh, and her maiden name was Maglaughlin. Her parents lived at 7004 Meade Place in Pittsburgh until her mother, Marion E. Maglaughlin died in July of 1975.
>
> Uncle Tom and Aunt Jackie had a daughter named Laura, who was approximately five years old when her dad died. Jackie and Laura later moved to Colorado where Laura still lives and works under the name Laura Shipman-Hamblin. Jackie was Tom's second wife. Laura knew Tom's children from his first marriage, and I guess that they are in their 60's or 70's.
>
> Tom and my mother were going to meet for dinner the day that JFK came to Dallas. (My mom and dad moved to Texas in 1950 and Dallas was our home.) Prior to the scheduled dinner with my mom, Tom expressed concern to her that JFK refused to use the protective bubble for the car to ensure his safety. During their phone conversation, Tom said that he was prepared to pull quickly out of the motorcade and do whatever was necessary to protect JFK if anything was to happen.
>
> When my mom received the call that Tom had died, she was shocked. According to Aunt Jackie, Tom had received a clean bill of health for his annual physical the month before his death. Aunt Jackie told my mom that after Tom had eaten lunch at Camp David, he told others that he did not feel well and went to take a nap. Sometime during the nap, he suffered a heart attack. The fact that no autopsy was ordered, and that Aunt Jackie was encouraged to bury Tom quickly, seemed strange.
>
> Aunt Jackie and my parents are deceased now so I can only share what I remember my mom telling me about Uncle Tom's death. I hope that this information is helpful to your ongoing research.

In a follow-up message the next day, Christine Jones wrote:

> I am happy to clarify the highlighted areas in your e-mail message. Please note that the information that I shared was based on conversations that my mother, (Josephine) shared with me as an adult. Unfortunately, she passed away 9 years ago.

The following information is what I remember from conversations with my mother, Josephine Maglaughlin-Leonard:

Tom Shipman called his sister-in-law, Josephine Maglaughlin-Leonard (*Jackie Shipman's younger sister and only sibling*) when he found out that he would be in Dallas with JFK. The exact date of that phone call is not known but it was before Tom went to Camp David. It was during this same call that Tom expressed his concern to Josephine about JFK refusing to use the protective bubble and that he was prepared to quickly pull out of the motorcade if anything was to happen.

Josephine was looking forward to meeting Tom for dinner when he was in Dallas since she had not seen him in 10 years.

Jackie called her sister, Josephine to tell her that Tom died at Camp David. During that conversation, Jackie told Josephine that there would not be an autopsy and that she was encouraged to bury Tom quickly. My mother (Josephine) said that Tom had received his annual physical a month earlier and received a clean bill of health. (*I can't verify the timing of Tom's annual physical.*) Josephine stated that Tom's death came as a shock to her and her sister, Jackie.

The details that I outlined in the e-mail was information that Josephine (*my mother*) shared with me when I was an adult. I did not ask my mother for specific dates or timing regarding the circumstances she described to me. Also, I never met my uncle and only learned about him through my mother, Josephine. She held Tom Shipman in high regard and said that JFK would have survived if Tom had been the driver that day in Dallas.

I hope that this information is helpful and provides some clarification.

On 10/6/15, I had a nice conversation with Laura Shipman, Tom Shipman's youngest daughter. She corroborated and did not dispute anything her cousin Christine Jones (her father's niece) had to say; no wet blankets. She also said her older sister always criticized Greer. Their father has a box of items that she was going to look through and scan for me, as well. In addition, her brother said her dad thought that JFK would be killed one day! It is true that Tom Shipman knew of JFK's upcoming Dallas trip, had planned to be part of it, and arranged a dinner meeting with his sister in law Josephine who lived in Dallas since 1950. Josephine was Christine Jones' mother. One more thing – she also views it as suspicious that her father was quickly buried and corroborates Christine that her mother was *urged* to bury him quickly! She also said that, when her father passed away, Kennedy's personal physician, Dr. George Burkley, took care of everything.

Some would add that Dr. Burkley "took care of everything" after observing Kennedy's body at both Parkland and Bethesda Hospitals...

Postscript number one: interesting tributes given to Shipman at the law enforcement online memorial:

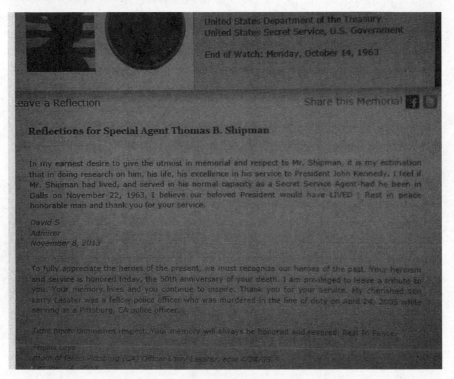

United States Department of the Treasury
United States Secret Service, U.S. Government

End of Watch: Monday, October 14, 1963

Leave a Reflection   Share this Memorial

Reflections for Special Agent Thomas B. Shipman

In my earnest desire to give the utmost in memorial and respect to Mr. Shipman, it is my estimation that in doing research on him, his life, his excellence in his service to President John Kennedy, I feel if Mr. Shipman had lived, and served in his normal capacity as a Secret Service Agent-had he been in Dallas on November 22, 1963, I believe our beloved President would have LIVED. Rest in peace honorable man and thank you for your service.

David S
Admirer
November 8, 2013

To fully appreciate the heroes of the present, we must recognize our heroes of the past. Your heroism and service is honored today, the 50th anniversary of your death. I am privileged to leave a tribute to you. Your memory lives and you continue to inspire. Thank you for your service. My cherished son Larry Lasater was a fellow police officer who was murdered in the line of duty on April 24, 2005 while serving as a Pittsburg, CA police officer.

Time never diminishes respect. Your memory will always be honored and revered. Rest In Peace.

Phyllis Loya
mom of fallen Pittsburg (CA) Officer Larry Lasater, eow 4/24/05

Postscript number two: Shipman's final motorcade – driving at the Mary Pinchot Meyer estate on 9/24/63–Shipman dies 10/14/63. Mary Pinchot Meyer, Kennedy's lover and the ex-wife of CIA officer Cord Meyer: dies 10/12/64. In addition, Camp David, formerly known as Shangri-La by FDR, also served as a training ground for the OSS, the forerunner of the CIA.[15]

---

15. From *Reilly of the White House*, page 67: "With the coming of war Shangri-La served him well. We had a good deal of trouble finding this vacation spot which met with his demands that it be within a reasonable driving distance of Washington and our insistence that it provide him a secure home. Shangri-La was in a state park on Catoctin Mountain, near Thurmont, Maryland. Originally there had been three separate camps there. They had been built for underprivileged children for use in the summer. Colonel Wild Bill Donovan's "cloak and dagger" boys had taken over one camp for training. The Marines had another for the same purpose, and the Boss had the third. The OSS men were training in sabotage and other weird and unpleasant phases of underground warfare, and their camp was necessarily rather overloaded with dark and myste-

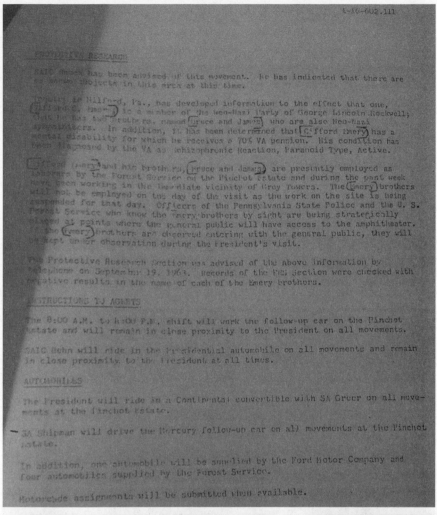

6/4/63 SA Thomas B Shipman, military aide, SAIC Behn, President Kennedy and guest from India:

rious foreigners. However, we didn't worry too much, because we had plenty of Marines around."

THE PRESIDENT'S APPOINTMENTS
WEDNESDAY, OCTOBER 16, 1963

9:30 –   (TV Tape)   OFF RECORD

10:00 –   His Excellency Dirk U. Stikker,
                              Secretary General of NATO
                         Honorable John Getz, Director of Office
                              of Secretary General
                         Honorable Thomas K. Finletter,
                              U. S. Ambassador to NATO
                         Mr. J. Robert Schaetzel, Deputy
                              Assistant Secretary of State for European Affairs

                         John Getz   *Christopher Van Holland*

11:00 –   OFF RECORD MEETING

                                             Mrs
11:45 –   (Mr. Calvin Horn)   OFF RECORD

                         Lee Anderson ✓

                                          LUNCH

4:00   *Sec Ball*
           Sec Martin
           Richard Helms
           Jit King
           Richard Helms
           Cord Meyer

5:15 –   The President will attend reception
                         in his honor given by Prime Minister
                         of Ireland and Mrs. Lemass (Mayflower Hotel)

✓ 6:00 PM   Justice Douglas – S. W. Gate   5:55 PM
✓ 6:30 PM   Bill Thompson – Diplomatic River
                                  S W Gate
                                  Lincoln & 20

10/16/63 – CORD MEYER OF THE CIA and others have lunch with JFK (Secret Service log via JFK Library) [Secret Service agent Thomas Shipman is buried on this date]:

Left: SA Thomas Shipman driving JFK and Jackie in Palm Beach, FL. Right: SA Thomas B Shipman, sitting next to ASAIC Floyd Boring – photo identified by Agent Winston Lawson (his hand writing, addressing my question mark as to the identity of the driver)

```
   ... MAY 1961                          - 12 -

   Assigned to Mr. and Mrs. Robert S.                  SA Henne
   Shriver, Jr.

   Assigned to Mr. and Mrs. Peter Lawford.             SA Holmes

   Assigned to Mr. and Mrs. Steve Smith.               SA Jones

                                                       SA Newman
   Reports to 3307 N Street, N.W., and upon
   departure of the President-elect will
   supervise the transfer of household
   personnel and personal effects to the
   White House.  Following this, SA assumes
   Post 35.

   Driver of lead car; then on standby duty            SA Shipman
   at White House Garage until relieved.

   On roof of Lafayette Building, H St. and            SA Dobish
   Vermont Ave., N.W., with portable radio             SA Strong
   and binoculars, to be assumed after                 SA Wagner
   President has passed their positions on
   parade route.

   On roof of Miatico Building, Connecticut            SA Blaine
   Avenue and H Street, N.W., with portable            SA Lockwood
   radio and binoculars, to be assumed after           SA Morrow
   President has passed their positions on
   parade route.


       POST ASSIGNMENTS - MAYFLOWER HOTEL

   Outside South entrance to ballroom.
                                                       SA Mullady

   Main Lobby entrance - Check point.
                                                       SA Weinstein
```

Shipman drove the lead car during the Kennedy inaugural parade:

CHAPTER TWO

THE SECRET SERVICE IS BOSS, NOT THE PRESIDENT! JUST ASK TRUMAN, KENNEDY, JOHNSON ... AND CLINTON

Secret Service agents Roy Kellerman, SAIC Gerald Behn and John Campion with President Kennedy Oct. 1962.

I t is a common but very understandable misconception that the President of the United States is the boss of his own security. After all, he *is* the President, the leader of the free world, and the commander in chief of the armed forces of America. It would be hard to fault anyone for thinking that this is true.

However, it is not. In fact, it is just this misconception that has been deliberately used as a platform to blame President Kennedy for his own tragic death. Time after time, in news articles, online journals, books (especially *The Kennedy Detail*), and television programs through the years, the blame-the-victim mantra has been used in a cowardly and disgusting attempt to switch the blame from some specific agents in charge of JFK's security toward the victim who can no longer defend himself.

A recent classic example of the Secret Service blame game:

"What continued to torment Agent [Clint] Hill as he replayed these images in his head, decades later, was the fact that he'd been pushed away. "If we had been in proximity, where we should have been," he explained, "the event would not have happened as it did." [Note: notice that Hill admits they should have been there – no later-day excuses about the speed of car, lack of spectators in the plaza, entering the freeway, etc.]Had Hill been allowed to do his job, a human shield would have been formed between the unseen shooter and President Kennedy, creating a near-impossible shot.

With the lights in the conference room still dimmed, [then-Secret Service Director Lew] Merletti cut to a rarely seen television interview with Clint Hill by Mike Wallace, filmed in the 1970s, after Hill's premature retirement from the Secret Service. The forty-three-year-old Hill chain-smoked cigarettes and choked up with emotion as he spoke of failing to protect the president that day in Dallas and of allowing himself to be pushed away by the president. "It was my fault," said Hill, crying as he stared into the camera. "I'll live with that till my grave."[1]

Merletti added the coup de grace: "He was prevented from doing his job by the president."[2]

My first book, *Survivor's Guilt: The Secret Service and the Failure to Protect President Kennedy*, goes a long way towards righting this wrong and correcting history, as well as placing the blame back where it belongs: the aforementioned specific agents of the Kennedy detail who failed miserably to protect the life of the president when shots rang out in Dealey Plaza. This view holds up whether one believes in Lee Oswald acting alone or a conspiracy.

As with buildings being guarded, I believe this important finding was largely overlooked by well-meaning readers who have a conspiracy bent and were searching for more grist for the mill, so to speak (it is hard to fault them for this). It is understandable that some of the "sexier" aspects of the book would be focused upon (prior threats, evidence of conspiracy, etc.). That said, even more evidence has been found to back up this very important finding of agency responsibility.

On page 19 of *The Kennedy Detail*, former JFK agent Gerald Blaine[3] begins to (using a lawyer's term) "lay the foundation" for blaming the victim,

---

1. *The Death of American Virtue: Clinton vs. Starr* by Ken Gormley (2010), pp 423-25.
2. Ibid page 427.
3. A very important article about Blaine titled *Gerald Blaine and the Kennedy Detail – Was the Secret Service 'Stood Down' in Dallas?"* can be found here: http://www.sott.net/article/269016-Gerald-Blaine-and-the-Kennedy-Detail-Was-the-Secret-Service-Stood-Down-in-Dallas

JFK and, in the process, stabs him in the back with baseless allegations. Blaine writes, "The Secret Service was not authorized to override a presidential decision." On page 397, he further alleges: "The president is not legally bound to follow the directives of the Secret Service"

This is ridiculous. Ample proof to the contrary abounds.

This news article from 1947 (Truman era) is plain and simple:

> The Milwaukee Journal – May 25, 1947 Brows
> is one.
> It makes no diffrence whether the president likes this protection or not. Where his safety is concerned, the secret service is "boss." Congress gave it that responsibility after the assassination of President McKinley in 1901.

Chief James J. Rowley testified under oath to the Warren Commission: "No President will tell the Secret Service what they can or cannot do."[4]

> there at that particular time.
> Mr. ROWLEY. No President will tell the Secret Service what they can or cannot do.

In fact, Rowley's predecessor, former Chief U.E. Baughman, who had served under JFK from Election night 1960 until he was fired ("retired") by the Kennedy brothers in September 1961, had written in his 1962 book *Secret Service Chief*, "Now the Chief of the Secret Service is legally empowered to countermand a decision made by anybody in this country if it might endanger the life or limb of the Chief Executive. This means I could veto a decision of the President himself if I decided it would be dangerous not to. The President of course knew this fact."[5]

> in at him through the window.
> Now the Chief of the Secret Service is legally empowered to countermand a decision made by *Anybody* in this country if it might endanger the life or limb of the Chief Executive. This means I could veto a decision of the President himself if I decided it would be dangerous not to. The President of course knew this fact.

4. Warren Commission Volume 5, page 570 (hereafter notated in this format: 5 H 570).
5. *Secret Service Chief* by U.E Baughman (1962/1963), p. 70.

Baughman further told the press:

> **Baughman said the law plainly states that the president's official bodyguards can order him not to endanger his own life.**

Indeed, an Associated Press story from *November 15, 1963* stated, "The [Secret] Service can overrule even the President where his personal security is involved."

> **The Secret Service, charged by law with protecting the person of the President, would say nothing. The service can overrule even the President where his personal security is involved.**

President Harry Truman agreed, stating, "The Secret Service was the only boss that the President of the United States really had."[6] This was brought up during Chief James Rowley's LBJ Library oral history:

> Mr. Truman, I believe it was, was quoted in last Sunday's paper in an article about your organization as saying that the Secret Service was the only boss that the President of the United States really had. Is there a good deal of truth in that?
>
> He did say that but he was trying to make a point at the time actually to demonstrate that the reason he couldn't do this or that is because the Secret Service was opposed to it, you know, from a security standpoint.

---

6. Rowley oral history, LBJ Library, January 22, 1969, p. 2. See also *Extreme Careers: Secret Service Agents: Life Protecting the President*, by David Seidman, p. 11. Rowley himself said, "Most Presidents have responded to our requests ...."

In fact, Chief Rowley heard this exact sentiment again repeated by none other than LBJ:

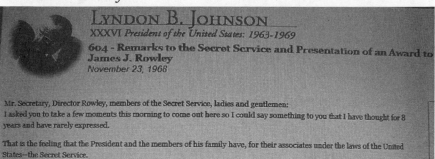

LYNDON B. JOHNSON
XXXVI *President of the United States: 1963-1969*
604 - Remarks to the Secret Service and Presentation of an Award to James J. Rowley
November 23, 1968

Mr. Secretary, Director Rowley, members of the Secret Service, ladies and gentlemen:
I asked you to take a few moments this morning to come out here so I could say something to you that I have thought for 8 years and have rarely expressed.

That is the feeling that the President and the members of his family have, for their associates under the laws of the United States—the Secret Service.

President Harry Truman once said that the Secret Service is the only boss the President really has. I think he meant in addition to Mrs. Truman.

President Bill Clinton also used Truman's words as a reference before a gathering of Secret Service officials (including former directors Eljay Bowron, John Magaw and Stu Knight, as well as SAIC Larry Cockell) and other dignitaries for the dedication of the United States Secret Service Memorial Building on 10/14/99: "Harry Truman once said, the Secret Service was the only boss he had as President, with the exception of Mrs. Truman. And even when I don't like it, *I have to admit that's true* (emphasis added)."[7]

In an 11/23/63 UPI story, titled "Secret Service Men Wary of Motorcade," based in part on "private conversations" with unnamed agents, Robert J. Serling wrote, "*An agent is the only man in the world who can order a President of the United States around* if the latter's safety is believed at stake ... in certain situations *an agent outranks even a President*" (emphasis added).

In addition, Democratic National Committee advance man Jerry Bruno, who played a role in planning the Texas trip, wrote, "[The Secret Service's] word on security was final. They could by law order a President not to go some place, on security grounds, and he was bound to obey them."[8]

for me. The same
—for the Secret Service. But still, their word on security was final. They could by law order a President not to go some place, on security grounds, and he was bound to obey them.

7. Citation: William J. Clinton: "Remarks Dedicating the United States Secret Service Memorial Building," October 14, 1999.
8. *The Advance Man* by Jerry Bruno & Jeff Greenfield, p. 91.

Former Agent George McNally, also on the Texas trip, among many others, wrote, "Legally the Secret Service could forbid a President to do such and such or go to this or that place."[9]

Former Agent Mike Reilly, the SAIC for FDR, wrote: "Incidentally, every schoolboy knows that the White House Secret Service boss can order the President of the United States not to go here or there if he chooses… presidents usually accept the laws of the land and follow Secret Service advice with little or no question."[10]

Former JFK Secret Service agent Bill Carter wrote, "The Secret Service still had absolute authority … complete authority when it came to a presidential visit."[11]

This article, which came out soon after the assassination, also stated that Kennedy cooperated with the Secret Service:

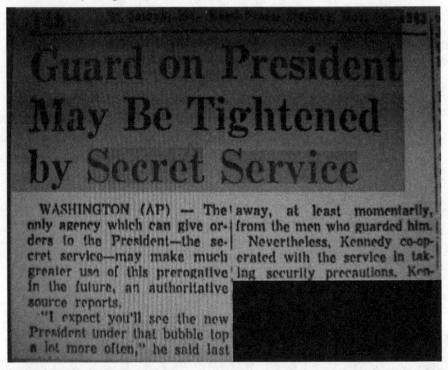

Guard on President May Be Tightened by Secret Service

WASHINGTON (AP) — The only agency which can give orders to the President—the secret service—may make much greater use of this prerogative in the future, an authoritative source reports.

"I expect you'll see the new President under that bubble top a lot more often," he said last away, at least momentarily, from the men who guarded him. Nevertheless, Kennedy cooperated with the service in taking security precautions. Ken-

During former Kennedy era agent Clint Hill's 11/19/10 Sixth Floor Museum oral history, the former agent revealed the full, unvarnished truth about JFK: he did not order the agents to do anything; they did what they wished to do, security-wise: "He can tell you what he wants done and he can tell you certain things but that doesn't mean you have to

9. *A Million Miles of Presidents*, p. 110.
10. *Reilly of the White House* by Mike Reilly (1947), pages 13-14.
11. *Get Carter* by Bill Carter, pp. 34-35.

do it. What we used to do was always agree with the President and then we'd do what we felt was best anyway."

Special Agent in Charge of the JFK detail, Gerald Behn, told me on 9/27/92: "I don't remember Kennedy ever saying that he didn't want anybody on the back of his car."

Assistant Special Agent in Charge of the JFK detail, Floyd Boring, told me the same thing on three different occasions between 1993 and 1997: "[JFK] was a very easy-going guy ... he didn't interfere with our actions at all. He was a very nice man; he never interfered with us at all. President Kennedy was very cooperative with the Secret Service." Boring also told the JFK Library on 2/25/76: "Of all the administrations I worked with [FDR-LBJ], the president and the people surrounding the president were very gracious and were very cooperative. As a matter of fact, you can't do this type of security work without cooperation of the people surrounding the president." (In my interviews with Mr. Boring, he was adamant that he never spoke to William Manchester and denounced the substance of the made-up quote attributed to him [the whole "Ivy League charlatans" nonsense attributed to JFK]. Ironically, none other than Gerald Blaine himself went on record stating that Boring was never interviewed by Manchester![12] The archivist of the entire collection of Manchester papers wrote to me: "I can confirm that there is no transcript of an interview with Floyd Boring in the papers."[13] I have always suspected – as I spelled out in my first book – that Gerald Blaine was the source for the quote in Manchester's book attributed to Boring. Blaine's good friend Frank Badalson wrote in an online review contesting my book: "Could it mean that Manchester simply confused the men?" Oh, really? This was my suspicion all along – Blaine, who was interviewed for the book instead of Boring, was the source of this made-up quote, just as Blaine submitted handwritten notes to the National Archives that were clearly written long after 11/22/63, as well as writing about a meeting that never occurred: as a fellow former agent said, it is "horseshit"![14]

Winston G. Lawson, the lead advance agent for the Dallas trip, wrote to me in a letter dated 1/12/04: "I do not know of any standing orders for the agents to stay off the back of the car...it never came to my attention as such."

Shift Leader Art Godfrey, also on the Texas trip, told me on three different occasions between 1996 and 1997: "President Kennedy never or-

12. https://www.youtube.com/watch?v=LxZVgPlt05o
13. E-mail from Leith Johnson 11/22/13.
14. See chapter one of *Survivor's Guilt*.

dered us to do anything. He was a very nice man ... cooperative...President Kennedy never asked me to have my shift leave the limo when we were working it."

Agent Sam Kinney, the driver of the follow-up car on the Florida and Texas trips (among many others), told me on three different occasions between 1992 and 1994: "[the idea that JFK ordered them off the limo] is absolutely, positively false ... no, no, no: he had nothing to do with that ... No, never – the agents say, 'O.K., men, fall back on your posts' ... President Kennedy was one of the easiest presidents to ever protect; Harry S. Truman was a jewel just like John F. Kennedy was ... 99% of the agents would agree ... [JFK] was one of the best presidents ever to control – he trusted every one of us...for the record of history that is false – Kennedy never ordered us to do anything. I am aware of what is being said but that is false." (Sam believed there was a conspiracy and knew the back of JFK's head was missing, corroboration for a shot from the front, as he had the piece in his hand and put in a phone patch aboard the C-130 to Dr. Burkley. What became of this specific fragment is a mystery. Sam's grandchild contacted me, telling me that Sam's wife Hazel believed LBJ was involved in JFK's death!)

Agent Bob Lilley conveyed to me on four different occasions between 1992 and 1996:"JFK was very cooperative with us once he became President. He was extremely cooperative. Basically, 'whatever you guys want is the way it will be'".

Agent Don Lawton told me on 11/15/95 that he agreed with his friends Sam and Bob, above: "It's the way Sam said, yes. You can take whatever information [Bob Lilley] passed on to you as gospel. JFK was very personable ... very warm. Everyone felt bad. It was our job to protect the President. You still have regrets, remorse. Who knows, *if they had left guys on the back of the car* ... you can hindsight yourself to death (emphasis added)." In fact, in new information from an obscure local news article (*Idaho State Journal* 11/24/13) that was totally overlooked by everyone on the 50th anniversary of the assassination comes some explosive new information regarding Lawton and his feelings on the matter at hand:

"Former Marine officer Jacquee Alvord is convinced the theory that Lee Harvey Oswald acted alone in the assassination of President Kennedy 50 years ago *is false. Her skepticism is born from intimate knowledge about the military and CIA and the fact a good friend of hers was a Secret Service agent in Dallas that fateful day. His name was Donald Lawton and his job* with the Secret Service was how they met.... 'Don had a personal like for the man,' Alvord said. 'He said Kennedy had a great personality and was easy to talk to.'" A few days before Kennedy's Nov. 22 visit to Dallas, she talked to Lawton about his duties in Florida where the president had just visited. Lawton talked about how he had ridden on the rear platform of the presidential limousine just behind the president. It was a job requiring balance and concentration that Lawton had perfected [note: Lawton also rode on the rear of the limo 3/23/63 in Chicago].

"He told me he was going to Texas next," Alvord said ... "He said his job had been to secure the airport in Dallas and that he had not been with the motorcade." [Right after the assassination] I asked him if he was OK and he said, 'No,'" Alvord said. "He said, 'I should have been there.'"

It wasn't until February of 1964 that Alvord was able to meet Lawton again in person. She said he was nervous because he was going to be interviewed by lawyers with the Warren Commission. The commission was a group of government officials, led by Chief Justice Earl Warren, charged with investigating the Kennedy assassination. There was some concern that Secret Service agents had been out drinking late the night before the fatal shooting and might not have been completely fit to protect the president. But Alvord said something else was bothering Lawton and he wouldn't talk about it.

"I knew he felt guilt," Alvord said. "That's why he kept saying, 'I should have been there.'"

It wasn't until later that Alvord realized the significance of Lawton's statements. She watched the documentary film "Four Days in November" and saw Lawton at Love Field in Dallas as the president's motorcade was preparing to depart. He was running alongside the rear of the car with his hand behind the president. It was a position he had mastered before jumping aboard the platform at the rear of the limousine. It was something Lawton had done in Florida and Chicago during presidential parades earlier in 1963.

Suddenly, someone pulled Lawton away from the car. The motorcade proceeded without him or any agent manning the rear platform on the president's limousine. To this day, it's a mystery to Alvord and others why there were no Secret Service agents on the back of that limo.

"If Don had been standing there, he would have been killed or prevented it," Alvord said. "That's why he kept saying, 'I should have been there.'" (Lawton passed away in 2013. His nephew, Richard James Lawton, wrote to me and thanked me for the information I had about his uncle).

Presidential aide Dave Powers, President Kennedy's best friend and political helper, who rode in the Secret Service follow-up car in Dallas and was on many other trips, wrote to me on 9/10/93:" [The agents] never had to be told to 'get off' the limousine." For the record, Agent Bob Lilley endorsed Mr. Powers' view: "Dave would give you factual answers." Frank Vamos wrote me on 12/6/10, "I developed a friendship with Dave Powers, and he told me that the President never asked the agents to get off of the limo." Assassination Records Review Board (ARRB) Director Tom Samoluk told me in 1996 that JFK's longtime friend and Presidential Aide Dave Powers, "agreed with your take on the Secret Service," based on a lengthy interview Samoluk had with the gentleman.

Researcher Will Ruha wrote to me on 11/11/13 concerning his in-person interview with Dave Powers:

> "Zboril, Blaine, et al, are full of it in their sorry refusal to accept responsibility and properly expiate for their failure in Dallas. What is so pathetic, indeed so meretricious about their current spate of lies is that they now choose to posthumously assault the very victim their past actions managed to help assassinate. And this I know to be true because shortly after the JFK Library opened, I was invited by JFK's aide, Dave Powers, to meet privately with him in his office, wherein we engaged in an almost hour-long discussion of JFK, his career, presidency, and alas, the assassination. Dave had been with Jack as a trusted aide and companion since Kennedy first ran for political office in 1946, and he was with him during countless motorcades, including right behind his vehicle in Dallas. Perturbed by Manchester's claim that JFK was irked by SS agents being too close, I asked him whether the president ever ordered agents away from his vehicle. Dave told me, "No. Not to my knowledge. He respected them and their performance of duties and left the matter of his security and personal safety entirely to their well-trained expertise. I know of no time that he ever ordered agents away from their assigned positions in his security detail."

I mentioned to him early reports that JFK outpaced or tried to avoid Secret Service agents after his election, to which he replied, "Well, you have to understand. He was 43, the youngest elected president in history – following the oldest. So it was natural that the Secret Service may have found it more difficult to keep up with him than Eisenhower. But I can tell you, that almost three years in office and after numerous threats, the president pretty much stuck to their security directives. He believed in them."

I won't go into all that we talked about, but Dave, you, and I all know that JFK would have never ordered Secret Service agents away in the fall of

1963 for the very fact that he was aware of numerous death threats and plots. Increasingly, he had begun to openly speak about the possibility of his assassination – to Jackie, Bobby, Dave, Kenny, Paul Fay Jr., authors like Jim Bishop, and even, with gallows humor, to Secret Service agents assigned to his protection. A few Sundays before his death, he teased one agent about the possibility of an assassin shooting him from the church's choir balcony, asking him if he would actually leap forward to throw himself over his president.

Jack was deploying his self-deprecating humor as a way of "acting out" what seemed to be almost an inevitability. At one point that season, alighting from the yacht, *Honey Fitz*, behind Jackie and Anita Fay, Jack acted out his being shot, grabbing his chest and falling to the pier before the mock horrified eyes of Paul Fay. The entire episode was filmed. Jackie was not amused. It was Kennedy's way of trying to deal with the stress and tension under which he had increasingly been thrust following his back-to-back addresses on detente and civil rights in June. Animosity toward him had spiked and with it, death threats sharply escalated.

In November, he repeatedly expressed reluctance to travel both to Florida and Texas in no small part for this very reason – especially to Texas. Senator Smathers (then, the only US. Senator named in the burgeoning Bobby Baker scandal) heartily encouraged him to travel to both places. Bill Fulbright strongly advised him not to go. So did numerous others. On the night of his departure, Kennedy family members and friends were celebrating Bobby's 38th birthday, but the Attorney General was anything but festive. He was dour, worried, and highly anxious about his brother's trip to Texas. And during JFK's stops and talks during the journey – particularly, the evening before his assassination, those behind the podium noticed how violently his hands trembled as he addressed the audience. Some attributed this to his medication, others to his essential reticence before a crowd, but in truth it was his foreboding that somewhere there in Texas he was to be targeted.

On the morning of November 22, 1963, perusing the Dallas newspaper, he noticed the black-bordered ad taken out by right-wing extremists and commented on it. Everyone in the room was concerned, very worried. Noticing this, Jack did what he always did in similar circumstances, he showed courage. "If anyone wanted to shoot me," he explained, "It wouldn't be that difficult. All he would need would be a high-powered rifle fired from a tall office building and there would be nothing anyone could do about it." He said this to show that, in almost three years, it hadn't happened yet, and then he reassured them by telling them not to worry, that the Secret Service would do their jobs. But his comment wasn't so much prophetic as it was simply based on what he had discovered to be foiled plots against him elsewhere. They hadn't materialized and so he simply hoped to get through Dallas to LBJ's ranch and then back home to Washington.

And to help ensure this, he assuredly did NOT order any agents away from his car. No way. It never happened."

Rufus Youngblood, Vice President Johnson's lead agent in Dallas who rode in the same limousine as LBJ, told me on more than one occasion between 1992 and 1994: ""President Kennedy wasn't a hard ass ... he never said anything like that [re: removing agents from limo]."

Press Secretary Pierre Salinger conveyed to a colleague of mine that JFK had a good relationship with the Secret Service and, more importantly, did not argue with their security measures.[15]

Cecil Stoughton, the White House photographer on both the Florida and Dallas trip (among many others), wrote me the following:" I did see a lot of the activity surrounding the various trips of the President, and in many cases I did see the agents in question riding on the rear of the President's car. In fact, I have ridden there a number of times myself during trips ... I would jump on the step on the rear of the [Lincoln] Continental until the next stop. I have made photos while hanging on with one hand ... in Tampa [11/18/63], for example...I would just jump on and off [the limo] quickly – no routine... As for the edict of not riding there by order of the President – I can't give you any proof of first-hand knowledge."

Michael W. Torina, Chief Inspector of the Secret Service on 11/22/63 who wrote the Secret Service manual[16], and to whom I corresponded twice in 1997 and 2003, contributed significantly to a book about the Secret Service written in 1962, in which it is plainly stated, "Agents of the White House Detail ride in the same car with the President. Others will walk or trot alongside, while still others ride in automobiles in front of and behind the Presidential car."[17] Indeed, agent Mike Reilly, the SAIC of the FDR detail, wrote in his book: "There were two inviolate rules. The man running or riding at the President's shoulder never left that position unless relieved. The other, if a situation got out of hand,

---

15. This was based on the author's correspondence with noted journalist Roger Peterson in 2/99, from Peterson's very recent conversations with Salinger. Peterson and Salinger have since passed away.
16. *The United States Secret Service* by Walter S. Bowen & Harry E. Neal (New York: Chilton, 1960), page 209.
17. *What Does A Secret Service Agent Do?* by Wayne Hyde (New York: Dodd, Mead, and Co., 1962), page 28 (and acknowledgments) On the same page is a picture of agents walking right by JFK's car.

empty all cars and get as much Secret Service flesh between the crowd and the Boss as possible."[18]

Former agent Sam Sulliman, on the Florida and Texas trips (among many others), told me on 2/11/04 that agents were frequently on the back of the limousine. When told of Art Godfrey's comments on the matter, the former agent agreed with his colleague. Regarding the notion that JFK ordered the agents off the car, Sulliman told the author twice, "I don't think so."

Agent Frank Stoner, a PRS agent during the Kennedy era, told me on 1/17/04: JFK was "very personable. He was an old Navy man. He understood security. He wouldn't have ordered them off the car."

Agent Gerald W. "Jerry" O'Rourke, also on the Texas trip, told me on 1/15/04: ""Did President Kennedy order us off the steps of the limo? To my knowledge President Kennedy never ordered us to leave the limo." The agent added, "President Kennedy was easy to protect as he completely trusted the agents of the Secret Service."

Agent Vincent Mroz, famous for protecting President Truman on 11/1/50 and who also went on to protect Presidents, from Eisenhower to Nixon, told me on 2/7/04 that President Kennedy was "friendly, congenial – he was really easy to get along with ... just like Truman." When asked point blank, if JFK had ever ordered the agents off the car, Mroz said forcefully, "No, no – that's not true." When asked a second time, the former agent responded with equal conviction: "He did not order anybody off the car."

JFK Agent Larry Newman told me on 2/7/04 that there was "no policy" regarding the use of agents on the rear of Kennedy's car, further adding that the question was "hard to answer: it depends on the crowd, the threat assessment, and so forth. There was not a consistent rule of thumb." Newman phoned me unexpectedly on 2/12/04 to say that "there was not a directive, per se" from President Kennedy to remove the agents from their positions on the back of his limousine.

Agent Jim Goodenough, on the Texas trip, told me on 3/16/04 that "President Kennedy was a pleasant and cooperative person to work for."

JFK agent Lynn Meredith wrote to me on 3/9/04: "I do believe if agents had been riding on the rear of the limo in Dallas that President Kennedy would not have been assassinated as they would have been in Oswald's line of fire.... To elaborate a little more on the assassination in

---

18. *Reilly of the White House*, page 24.

Dallas, I have always believed that the following adverse situations all contributed to the unnecessary and unfortunate death of President Kennedy: (1) No Secret Service agents riding on the rear of the limousine. Meredith wrote to me again on 5/22/05: "I do not know first-hand if President Kennedy ordered agents off the back end of his limousine."

Agent Darwin Horn told me on 1/30/04: "You asked about Kennedy. I have worked him primarily in Los Angeles on several occasions … and never heard him tell the agents to get off of the car. Agents on the rear of JFK's car might have made a difference. They may have been hit instead of the President. That would have been all right with all of us. Agents normally would have been on the sides [of the car]."

Robert I. Bouck, SAIC of PRS/Intelligence Division, told me on 9/27/92 that having agents on the back of the limousine depended on factors independent of any alleged Presidential "requests": "Many times there were agents on his car." On 4/30/96, the ARRB's Doug Horne questioned Bouck: "Did you ever hear the President personally say that he didn't want agents to stand on the running boards on his car, or did you hear that from other agents?" Bouck: "I never heard the President say that personally." The former agent also told the ARRB that JFK was the "most congenial" of all the presidents he had observed (Bouck served from FDR to LBJ).

DNC Advance man Martin E. "Marty" Underwood, on the Texas trip, told me on 10/9/92 that JFK never ordered the agents off the rear of the car.

JFK Agent Abraham W. Bolden, Sr. told me, in reference to Kennedy's alleged "requests," on numerous occasions from 1993-1996 and beyond to the present day that he "didn't hear anything about that … I never believed that Kennedy said that [ordering removal of agents]."

Maurice G. Martineau, SAIC of Chicago office, joined his colleagues in refuting the Manchester claim that JFK ordered the agents off the rear of the car. Martineau said this to the author in two telephone interviews conducted on 9/21/93 and 6/7/96, respectively.

Agent Walt Coughlin, also on the Texas trip, told me on several occasions between 2003 and 2004: "In almost all parade situations that I was involved with we rode or walked the limo. We often rode on the back of the car."[19] During his 2/18/11 Sixth Floor Museum oral history, Coughlin

19. Walt Coughlin stated on video in 2014 for the Sixth Floor Museum oral history project that JFK was "very cooperative" with the Secret Service. In addition, Walt said the only time he ever heard that JFK ever ordered the agents off the limo was in Dallas. However, Walt was not in Dallas, so what he "heard" is what we all heard: second-hand stories via some of the agents. Also, Walt was on the Florida trip. It is telling that he didn't hear of any alleged orders there. As far as the notion of conspiracy in the JFK assassination, Walt, speaking for himself and his colleagues, said "a lot of us

said, "He was a wonderful man to work with. I loved the job ... But he would listen if you told him not to do something. He would, as long as you didn't 'cry wolf' all the time. If you said, you know, 'Don't do that', he assumed you had a good reason. He was good about that ... had an agent been allowed to stay on that right bumper, he would have blocked the shot ... And it's a terrible thing to say, but Kennedy really helped improve the Secret Service."

JFK Agent Toby Chandler said the following during his 11/20/10 Sixth Floor Museum Oral History: "They [Presidents] have all, in my experience, listened to us. Almost all of them, within reason, have made their point or, in the end, accepted our advice. I don't know of anybody who deliberately or blatantly over-ruled a Secret Service suggestion. Most of them observe our suggestions."

William Duncan, the advance agent for the Fort Worth stop, said during his 10/15/05 Sixth Floor Museum oral history that JFK was a "real fine gentleman with a magnetic personality" who was "very friendly" and "very concerned about the people around him – a real pleasure to work with" who was also "easy to work very hard for." Most importantly, the former agent stated that President Kennedy "let you do your job." Duncan went on to guard President Nixon. One of Duncan's colleagues, Mike Endicott, wrote in his book that, during the 1968 campaign, he told Nancy Reagan, wife of presidential candidate Ronald Reagan, that she and her family "must respond at once to what any agent told them."[20]

Agent J. Frank Yeager, who assisted in the advance work for both Tampa and Austin, stated in a letter dated 12/29/03: "I did not think that President Kennedy was particularly 'difficult' to protect. In fact, I thought that his personality made it easier than some because he was easy to get along with." In response to the author's question, "Did President Kennedy ever order the agents off the rear of his limousine?" Yeager wrote, "I know of no "order" directly from President Kennedy... I also do not know who actually made the final decision, but we did not have agents on the rear of the President's car in Dallas.

While Yeager was one of three agents in correspondence (O'Rourke and Ron Pontius were the other two) who seemed to indicate that this alleged order may have originated with Chief of Staff Kenny O'Donnell, I was granted permission to view the transcript of O'Donnell's interviews with author William Manchester – nothing whatsoever is mentioned

believe it was organized crime." Fellow agent Joe Paolella said the same thing.
20. *Walking With Presidents: Stories From Inside The Perimeter* (2008), page 48.

concerning any alleged presidential security-related orders of any kind. O'Donnell does not mention anything about telling agents to remove themselves from the limousine during his lengthy Warren Commission testimony, nor in his or his daughter's books. The same is true for the other two Presidential aides: Larry O'Brien and Dave Powers. In fact, as mentioned above, Powers refutes this whole idea. JFK's staff is not mentioned as a factor during any of the agents' Warren Commission testimony, nor in the five reports submitted in April 1964.[21] Agents Rowley, Behn, Boring, Godfrey and Kinney denounced the "staff/O'Donnell" notion (see chapter one of my first book *Survivor's Guilt*). It is interesting to note that, like JFK, O'Donnell was not blamed for any security deficiencies and the like until after his death in 1977, when he was thus unable to refute any allegations.

As for agent Ron Pontius' personal knowledge, on page 162 of *The Kennedy Detail* he stated, "I've never heard the president say anything about agents on the back of the car." Perhaps the coup de grace comes from Helen O'Donnell, daughter of JFK Chief of Staff Ken O'Donnell. In a message to the author, based on both her memory and her father's audio tapes, Helen wrote, "Suffice to say that you are correct; JFK did not order anybody off the car, he never interfered with my dad's direction on the Secret Service, and this is much backed up by my Dad's tapes. I think and know from the tapes Dallas always haunted him because of the might-have-beens – but they involved the motorcade route."

Agent and *Kennedy Detail* author Gerald Blaine, on the Florida trip (advance agent for Tampa, working with agent Yeager, above) and the Texas trip (among many others), told me on 2/7/04, years before he published his 2010 book, that President Kennedy was "very cooperative. He didn't interfere with our actions. President Kennedy was very likeable – he never had a harsh word for anyone. He never interfered with our actions." When I phoned Blaine on 6/10/05, he said the remark regarding "Ivy League charlatans," made infamous in both Manchester's book[22] and

21. 7 H 440-457. Manchester, page 666 (O'Donnell was interviewed 5/4/64, 6/4/64, 8/6/64 & 11/23/64). O'Donnell passed away 9/9/77. For what it's worth, neither Presidential Aide's Larry O'Brien [7 H 457-472] or Dave Powers [7 H 472-474] mentioned any JFK "desires," either (also, see Powers, above). In addition, nothing of the sort is mentioned in *Johnny, We Hardly Knew Ye* [see especially p. 20], nor in Kenny O'Donnell's daughter's book *A Common Good: The Friendship of Robert F. Kennedy and Kenneth P. O'Donnell*. She wrote: "Much of the material in this book has been gathered from the private tapes of my father, Kenneth P. O'Donnell."
22. Floyd Boring (and quite a few of his colleagues) categorically denied to me what William Manchester reports in his acclaimed massive best-seller, *The Death of a President*: "Kennedy grew weary of seeing bodyguards roosting behind him every time he turned around, and in Tampa on November 18, just four days before his death, he dryly asked Agent Floyd Boring to 'Keep those Ivy League charlatans off the back of the car'. Boring wasn't offended. There had been no animosity in the

his own book[23], came "from the guys ... I can't remember who [said it] ... I can't remember." Thus, Blaine confirms that he did not hear the remark from JFK. Blaine now denies that either himself or Floyd Boring were interviewed by William Manchester![24] And so it goes. The bottom line: the whole "Ivy League Charlatans" remark was made up – Boring and others told me *JFK did not say that!* As author and researcher John Onesti wrote on 11/10/13: "I highly doubt JFK would use the language "Ivy League Charlatans." Whoever made it up (Blaine?) obviously doesn't know much about east coast schools and that Harvard is in the Ivy League. JFK having graduated from Harvard cum laude would not have used such words having taken school serious. Now if he said "Get those Skull and Bones lackeys and freemasons off my car" that still would not sound like him but it would ring more true. For JFK to use those terms would be like me (a University of Illinois graduate) saying "get those Big Ten [expletives] off my car!" It makes no sense. It is just another example of liars like Hill, Blaine & Manchester not being able to play both sides of the chess board."

I wrote to former Florida Congressman Samuel Melville Gibbons on 1/7/04 and asked him if he had heard President Kennedy order the agents off the rear of the limousine. Gibbons rode in the rear seat with JFK and Senator George Smathers on the Tampa trip of 11/18/63. Here is Gibbons' response in full, dated 1/15/04: "I rode with Kennedy every time he rode. I heard no such order. As I remember it the agents rode on the rear bumper all the way. Kennedy was very happy during his visit to Tampa: Sam Gibbons."

Jacqueline Kennedy "played the events over and over in her mind ... She did not want to accept Jack's death as a freak accident, for that meant his life could have been spared – if only the driver in the front seat of the presidential limousine [Agent William R. Greer] had reacted more quickly and stepped on the gas ... if only the Secret Service had stationed agents on the rear bumper."[25]

Rocky Stone, Fort Worth (Texas) police department – in a newly discovered film from WBAP-TV (KXAS) NBC 11/22/63: Talking about the Kennedy Detail, President John F. Kennedy's Secret Service men: "They had nothing but praise for President Kennedy and his manner in which he felt about the Secret Service men. They said that by far he was

remark..." (Pages 37-38; see chapter one of *Survivor's Guilt*).
23. *The Kennedy Detail* by Gerald Blaine (2010), numerous, but see especially pages 148 and 286.
24. Blaine 11/19/10, Sixth Floor Museum Oral History (agent Clint Hill sat beside him during the interview).
25. *Just Jackie: Her Private Years*, pp. 58-59 & 374: based on an interview Klein had with Kitty Carlisle Hart re: Hart's conversation with Jackie.

more considerate of them and their feelings than any of the previous presidents they had been taking care of. *They said that he always went by their decisions to protect him.* That he was always considerate of their (sic) fact that he never tried to do anything that they thought was against the rules in which to protect him. They stated that President Kennedy referred to them as 'his boys' and that at times when there were large crowds of people that the president always looked around to see where 'his boys' was (sic) at so, at a moment's notice, they were able to be at his side and get him out of the crowds as he possibly could be in danger. In the moments after, they said the Secret Service was very, very short of money and that even some of the agents had to buy the two-way radios they used out of their own pocket and they did need more money to operate on to hire more men in order to be successful in protecting the president out of state [presumably Washington, D.C.]. "[26]

Eighty-seven year-old Dallas detective Elmer Boyd joins the chorus: "It was the Secret Service who made the primary decisions about the president's security. *Boyd was engaged in the security preparations leading up to the president's visit, but as it would be today, the Secret Service made the key decisions ...* Boyd pointed out that a Dallas newspaper ran an extensive article on the morning before the assassination about how the social issues of the era provoked some Texas tension for the president. *But Boyd said those concerns were not reflected in the Secret Service briefings in the days and hours before the shots were fired* at Kennedy around 12:30 in the afternoon on November 22, 1963."[27]

Judge John Tunheim, in charge of the federal board put together by Presidents George H.W. Bush and Bill Clinton to oversee the release of millions of pages of withheld documents, the Assassination Records Review Board (ARRB), said: "The lack of protection for the president in Dallas was appalling. It was unconscionable what happened that day. No one had checked the buildings that they went by," he said, noting that Kennedy's car slowed to a crawl as it turned corners. "It was just a horrible lack of security."[28]

President Clinton receives the ARRB Final Report from Judge John Tunheim (right), surrounded by the other members of the ARRB, at the White House.

26. http://www.nbcuniversalarchives.com/nbcuni/clip/51A02395_s01.do
27. http://wdtn.com/2015/07/24/dallas-detective-reflects-back-on-jfk-assassination-oswald-ruby/
28. http://www.startribune.com/local/east/223771331.html

Oswald-acted-alone author Vincent Bugliosi wrote me on 7/14/07: "I agree with you that they did not do a good job protecting the president (e.g. see p. 1443 of my book)." Former Warren Commission lawyer Howard Willens wrote on 7/23/13: "I definitely agree that the Secret Service could and should have done more to protect the President." Oswald-acted-alone author Gerald Posner[29] blamed the Secret Service – specifically, driver Bill Greer – for the success of the assassination on the November 1993 CBS program *JFK: The Final Chapter*.

Finally, President Nixon attempted to flex his muscle with the Secret Service to no avail. On 8/8/74, he was caught on video saying the following:

"Is there any Secret Service in the room?"

"Just one, Mr. President, answered [Stephen] Bull.

"Out!" Nixon snapped, waving his arm.

[SAIC Richard] Keiser stepped out from behind the TV camera in full view of the President.

"You don't have to stay, do you?" asked Nixon.

"Yes, sir," replied Keiser, firmly.

"You're required to?"

"Yes, sir."[30]

---

29. I have corresponded with Posner and have also had a fair share of social media contact with him.
30. *TV Guide*, 8/6/94.

CHAPTER THREE

AGENT WADE RODHAM, HILLARY RODHAM CLINTON'S UNCLE SHE HAS NEVER MENTIONED … AND NO ONE ELSE HAS, EITHER!

WADE RODHAM

Secret Service agent Wade J. Rodham was the Special Agent in Charge of the Kennedy residence in Middleburg (ATOKA), VA and was quite a prominent agent, to put it mildly, especially in comparison to the countless typical yet anonymous agents who have served 1865-2017 … yet Hillary Rodham Clinton, former First Lady, Senator, Secretary of State and presidential candidate has *never* mentioned (and neither has Bill) that Wade was her *Uncle* – no book, press release, video, or any other official or unofficial media mentions it in any way, shape or form. This connection only came about during interviews I conducted with former agents circa 2007-2011! Agent Don Cox, who served on the Clinton detail in the 1990's, wrote to me in an e-mail dated 9/21/2008:"Hillary's uncle (Rodham) was also an agent and riding in the [Vice President] Nixon vehicle that came under attack in Caracas." Ironically, Wade's niece would go on to try to bring President Nixon down as a 27-year-old staff attorney for the House Judiciary Committee during the Watergate investigation.

Hillary Rodham circa 1973:

Wade Rodham (without the Hillary connection, of course) is mentioned – with regard to pulling his gun out to protect Nixon – in Rufus Youngblood's book,[1] in *Six Crises* by Richard Nixon himself,[2] and *The Secret Service Story* by Michael Dorman.[3]

Wade Rodham received the Exceptional Civilian Service Award for protecting then-Vice President Nixon in Caracas, Venezuela (5/13/58). Rodham passed away in March 1983. A relative of Wade's, Maureen McKivigan Crawford, wrote to me on 3/27/16: "Wade is actually my Great Uncle Wade. We spent many Christmas days at his farm in Virginia. I was just a kid when we used to visit but my dad would spend hours holed up with Uncle Wade. Dad was a high school History teacher in DC so he loved Uncle Wade's stories. Honestly back in those days [the] Secret Service actually respected the people they protected so not much gossip. He was still friends with Jackie Kennedy and they would visit. He never mentioned his niece Hillary." John Pulawski wrote to me on 3/17/16: "Her Uncle was a Secret Service agent during the Kennedy Administration. I knew her brother when he ran for the Senate in Florida and learned what a complex background they had. Wade had an interesting influence on Hillary – I suspect her Janus methods especially. I have heard that in her seduction of poor innocent William Jefferson Clinton, she used talk of Uncle Wade to make a great impression upon him. In 1988 I was a

---

1   *20 Years in the Secret Service*, pages 70-71
2   Page 216.
3   Pages 143-145

key Dukakis campaign worker, and in the early 90's I had an environmental radio program in Miami, so I got involved, or tried to get involved, in numerous Democratic campaigns. Meeting with Hugh [Rodham, Hillary's brother], I was less than impressed. Like Hillary, he felt entitled to the Senate seat because of his importance related to whom he knows. I

had mentioned my having met JFK as an infant, and Bobby in the third Grade, and how hard I worked for Ted in the 1980 campaign, and he came back with how his Uncle was protecting JFK, but 11-22 was not his fault."

So, just think: at the very same time this photo was taken of future President Bill Clinton meeting President Kennedy, Clinton's future wife's uncle was protecting Kennedy's family. In addition to Nixon and (of course) JFK, Wade would also protect LBJ, Jackie, JFK Jr., and Ambassador to Japan when she was a little girl, Caroline Kennedy.

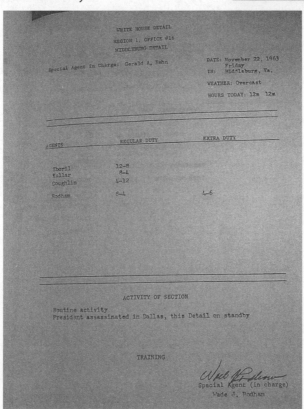

Rodham was at the Kennedy residence in Middleburg, Virginia when JFK was shot.

Wade Rodham (second from right) at fellow agent Thomas Kelley's going away party in the Washington field office in 1955 (Kelley, holding the pen holders here, was the last agent to interview Oswald before Jack Ruby shot him).

Hugh Simpson Rodham was Hillary Rodham Clinton's grandfather.4 Her grandfather's brother was Wade Rodham, Sr. Agent Wade Rodham, Jr., was Wade Senior's son.[5] Technically, this would make Wade Hillary's first cousin (once removed – same generation as her father, Hugh Ellsworth Rodham, born in 1911, the year before Wade, Jr.). However, many people understandably think of this connection as an uncle or great uncle (or "kinda uncle," to use the vernacular), thus the reason several people refer to Wade Jr. – like Wade Sr. – as her (great) uncle. Like Wade Junior and Senior, many of the Rodham's, from the great grandfather on down, came from Scranton (Lackawanna County), PA – including Hugh Rodham Senior (grandfather); Hugh Rodham II (father). [Hugh Rodham III, Hillary's brother, came from Chicago, although he did attend Penn State]; Hugh Senior's 11 siblings, including Wade Senior; and, of course, Wade Junior.

> Via the United States Census, 1930:
> Name: Wade J Rodham
> Event Type: Census
> Event Year: 1930
> Event Place: Scranton, Lackawanna, Pennsylvania, United States
> Gender: Male
> Age: 18 (born 3/21/12)
> Marital Status: Single
> Race: White
> Race (Original): White
> Relationship to Head of Household: Son

4. http://www.findagrave.com/cgi-bin/fg.cgi?page=gr&GRid=22300674
5. http://us-census.mooseroots.com/l/293502910/Wade-J-Rodham

Relationship to Head of Household (Original): Son
Birth Year (Estimated): 1912
Birthplace: Pennsylvania
 Father's Birthplace: Pennsylvania
Mother's Birthplace: Pennsylvania
Household Role Gender Age Birthplace
 Wade Rodham Head M 42 Pennsylvania
Laura Rodham Wife F 37 Pennsylvania
Wade J Rodham Son M 18 Pennsylvania
Robert Rodham Son M 15 Pennsylvania

Wade Rodham protecting the Kennedys in their very first official motorcade as President and First Lady.

7/24/63: Kennedy certainly knew who agent Rodham was. It is a very safe bet that they shook hands, as well…and the very same hands that shook Hillary's uncle's hand shook Bill Clinton's hand. Small world, indeed! Again, it is a real mystery why Hillary, Bill, nor any other media source has ever mentioned this fact.

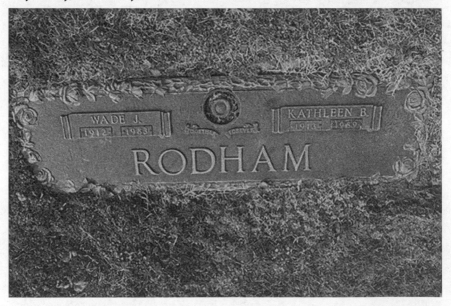

CHAPTER FOUR

1957-ERA SECURITY FOR
PRESIDENT EISENHOWER AND QUEEN ELIZABETH

If only JFK and Jackie would have received this kind of protection and coverage six years later in Dallas: Agents beside the partial bubbletop limousine, press photographers in flatbed trucks in front of limo, excellent police and motorcycle coverage (New York and Washington, D.C. motorcades):

Regarding President Eisenhower, former agent Floyd Boring commented: "I never really particularly cared for the guy until he got out [of the presidency]. When he got out, then I got fairly fond of him."[1] Ironically, this sentiment is one echoed by many agents concerning President Carter, who was rather cold and distant to the agents while he was president, yet, as an ex-president, was warm and gracious, even letting the agents fish on his property (although he appears to have been close to SAIC Jerry Parr, as he had Parr and his entire family with him up at Camp David).[2] Agent Rufus Youngblood shared his thoughts on Ike: "I thought of him as my commanding officer. I felt like we had won World War II together. He spent a lot of time in Augusta on the golf course, and since I was a Georgian familiar with the area, I would often accompany him on those trips. Eisenhower was really great for relying on a table of organization. You also have to remember that the country was a lot more peaceful during his administration. The problems we had during the Eisenhower administration and the Truman administration are almost nil when compared to the problems we are confronting today."[3]

Although President Eisenhower frequently rode in an open car, he was not adverse, as a former military man, to protocol and protection. His motorcades often had good motorcycle coverage, buildings guarded, and agents walking or jogging beside his limousine.[4]

1. Boring's Truman Library oral history, 9/21/88.
2. Photo section on the website of Jerry Parr's 2013 book *In The Secret Service*, as well as the book itself.
3. I spoke to Youngblood twice: once in 1992, the other time in 1994. Youngblood passed away 10/2/96.
4. A photo of agents Stout, Boring, Horn and Arvid Dahlguist surrounding Ike's limousine graces the cover of *Dar's Story: Memoirs of a Secret Service Agent* by Darwin Horn. Inside, there is also a picture of Horn, Kellerman, Behn, and Dale Grubb doing the same thing on another trip with Ike. See also the front cover and p. 30 of C.B. Colby's 1966 book, *Secret Service: History, Duties, and Equipment*.

However, not all was rosy in the lazy Eisenhower years, as I discovered in this rare article:

From *The Chicago American*, 11/23/63: "Hagerty Tells 2 Plots Against Ike New York" (AP)-James C. Hagerty, former press secretary to President Eisenhower and now an American Broadcasting company executive said there were two plots against Eisenhower's life during his term. Hagerty said both plots had been traced to the Nationalist party of Puerto Rico. That group was accused of the abortive attempt earlier on the life of President Truman. Hagerty explained that in the spring of 1958 secret service agents learned an attempt would be made to toss grenades into Eisenhower's car during a trip thru a Midwest city. He said two grenades were found in the mail sent from outside the country to a fictitious name in care of a post office in a southwest city. The cities were not named. The second plan to assassinate Eisenhower, he said, was reported to the secret service in the spring of 1959 on word that Puerto Rican nationalists had met and decided to kill the President. Security measures were tightened and the reported attempt failed. Hagerty said no one was arrested in either plot."

MEMBERS OF THE WHITE HOUSE DETAIL (AND RELATED) DURING THE EISENHOWER ADMINISTRATION[5]:

HOWARD S. ANDERSON, ERNEST I. ARAGON, Frank Bales, DANIEL BARTON (grandchildren detail), Chief U.E. BAUGHMAN, ASAIC GERALD A. BEHN, GERALD BLAINE, WALTER BLASCHAK (headquarters clerk), LILBURN "PAT" BOGGS, ATSAIC FLOYD M. BORING, DONALD BURKE (Mamie Eisenhower detail), JAMES BURKE,

---

Stout is depicted walking beside President Eisenhower's car, along with three other agents. Google searches yield similar results.
5. Not including numerous field office agents. Based on numerous sources, including the Dwight Eisenhower Presidential Library

ASAIC JOHN E. CAMPION, BILL CANTRELL, TOBY J. CHANDLER, GEORGE CHANEY, CARL CHAVERIN, ARVID J. DAHLQUIST, Assistant Chief RUSSELL "BUCK" DANIEL, LUBERT F. 'BERT' DE FREESE (Grandchildren detail), HERBERT C. DIXON (later SAIC of former President Eisenhower detail), PAUL B. DOSTER, ROBERT DOWLING, WILLIAM L. "BILL" DUNCAN, FRANK FARNSWORTH, DEETER B. "DICK" FLOHR, ROBERT W. FOSTER, JAMES K. "JACK" FOX, KENNETH S. GIANNOULES, MORGAN L. GIES, ARTHUR L. GODFREY, JOHN GOLDEN (protected VP Nixon in 1960), HOWARD D. "DALE" GRUBB (also on the grandchildren detail), ROBERT F. GRUBE (protected VP Nixon in 1960), FORREST GUTHRIE, DENNIS R. HALTERMAN, HARRY HASTINGS, HARVEY HENDERSON, CLINTON J. HILL, DARWIN HORN, JIM JEFFERIES, RICHARD E. JOHNSEN, JOHN PAUL JONES (Grandchildren detail), ROY KELLERMAN, FRANK J. KENNEY (Oregon), SAM KINNEY, H. STUART KNIGHT, PAUL E. LANDIS, JR., JOHN LARSON, ARNOLD LAU, WINSTON G. LAWSON, LEROY M. "ROY" LETTEER, ROBERT E. LILLEY, BOB MAMPEL, CHARLES J. MARASS, MAURICE G. MARTINEAU (temporary assignment), JAMES M. "MIKE" MASTROVITO, GERARD B. MCCANN, JOE MCCANN, JAMES E. MCCOWN (later ASAIC of former President Eisenhower detail), Richard McCully (Grandchildren detail), VINCENT P. MROZ, Assistant Chief HARRY NEAL, ROBERT NEWBRAND, ANDREW P. O'MALLEY, JACK PARKER, MAX D. PHILLIPS (Grandchildren detail), RONALD M. PONTIUS, JOHN POWERS, RICHARD QUINN, EMORY P. ROBERTS, WADE J. RODHAM, DICK ROTH, SAIC JAMES J. ROWLEY, PAUL S. RUNDLE, (Special Officer) HENRY J. "HANK" RYBKA, JOHN E. SCHLEY, JOHN T. "JACK" SHERWOOD (SAIC VP/Nixon Detail), WILLIAM F. SHIELDS, THOMAS B. SHIPMAN, LARRY SHORT, FRANK SLOCUM, FRANK G. STONER, STEWART G. STOUT (Mamie Eisenhower detail), SAMUEL E. SULLIMAN, CHARLES E. TAYLOR, JR [Washington Field Office; on Caracas trip with Nixon], JOHN TAYLOR, ROBERT H. TAYLOR, Chief Inspector MICHAEL TORINA, RONALD C. TOWNS, ED Z. TUCKER, WILLIAM WALTER, JOHN A. WALTERS (Secret Service linguist), JOHN W. "JACK" WARNER III, GEORGE WEISHEIT, THOMAS H. WELLS, THOMAS WHITE, KENNETH J. WIESMAN, Assistant Chief EDGAR A. WILDY, THOMAS K. WOOGE, RUFUS W. YOUNGBLOOD

CHAPTER FIVE

PRESIDENT TRUMAN WAS ADORED …
BY THE SECRET SERVICE

Above: future top JFK agents John Campion (running board next to driver), Floyd Boring (driver) and Roy Kellerman (directly behind Truman)

Above: the heroes of 11/1/50 – future JFK agents Vince Mroz, Stu Stout, and Floyd Boring

SAIC George Drescher with President Truman and a high military aide

While President Kennedy was popular with most of the agents of WHD, the White House Detail (the operative word being "most"), with Presidents Ford, Reagan and Bush 43 also being favorites among agents of PPD, the Presidential Protective Division, if there was one president who was unanimously adored by the agency, it was President Harry S. Truman. The agents enjoyed their morning walks with the president and the feeling was mutual, as Truman, the ultimate everyday man, would converse freely with the men, getting to know them, asking about their families, and occasionally giving them small tokens of appreciation. Former agent

Frank Stoner was an admirer of Truman for this kind of thoughtfulness. Stoner told me that Truman laid out a whole bunch of nice ties on his hotel bed and said for him to take any of them he wanted. Truman told future agent Lois Sims who was considering joining the Secret Service: "If the outfit can be that close to me and not get in my hair, that's a pretty good outfit."[1] Inspired, Sims promptly set out to join the agency.

From my many interviews with former Secret Service agents, the level of enthusiasm in their affection of Truman was nearly contagious. As I have enjoyed reading books on Truman (notably *Truman*, the best-selling Pulitzer Prize winning magnum opus by historian and author extraordinaire David McCullough), it was nice to hear positive feelings for the man from the border state. Gerald Behn told me "all the presidents were nice, but he [Truman] was my favorite" (Behn served from 1939-1967 and, thus, served under Presidents FDR-LBJ). [2] Floyd Boring, an agent who served from 1944-1967 (FDR-LBJ) and famously prevented the assassination of President Truman on 11/1/50, conveyed to me his high regard for Truman.[3]

Boring previously told former Chief U.E. Baughman: "I'll never forget the first time I was introduced to him by my chief on the Detail," Floyd said. "Truman could have been your uncle or your own father. I was to chauffeur him temporarily. He shook hands with me and said he was glad to meet me and I recall wondering whether he could possibly be a little shy. He seemed that way. Well, we were alone in the car and I drove him for several minutes. Then he said, as if he'd been saving the question up: 'What's you first name?' 'Floyd, sir', I answered. Five minutes more went by. Then he cleared his throat and spoke heartily, as if he'd just got his courage up, 'I wonder if you'd mind if I call you Floyd,' he said. It tore your heart out. You couldn't do enough for a man like that. Imagine, President of the United States and that humble and ordinary with his temporary chauffeur. That's greatness to me."[4]

During an interview with the author conducted on 2/7/04, former agent Vince Mroz – like Boring, one of the heroes from the 11/1/50 Truman assassination attempt – said that President Kennedy was "friendly, congenial – he was really easy to get along with ... just like Truman." Likewise, former agent Sam Kinney made the same analogy in an interview conducted on 3/5/94: "Harry S. Truman was a jewel just like John F. Kennedy was. 99% of the agents would agree." Likewise, former agent

1. 7/2/11 interview with Sims conducted by Zeke Campfield.
2. Interview with Gerald Behn 9/27/92.
3. Interviews with Floyd Boring 9/22/93 and 3/4/94.
4. *Secret Service Chief* by U.E. Baughman (1962), pages 68-69.

Robert Steuart waxed emotional about President Truman in an interview conducted on 10/22/92, adding that Truman was "a good Democrat." Former agent Jackson Krill had been in the Kansas City, MO office and was close to President Truman's brother, J.V. Truman, and always checked on the former President, as well as his mother and sister.[5] Former agent Rex Scouten, with whom I had the pleasure of corresponding, said: "He would treat us almost like sons."[6] Agent Charles Taylor said Truman was personable, called him by his first name, and asked about his family.[7] Agent Rufus Youngblood shared his thoughts on Truman: "He was an immaculate dresser, probably a carryover from his days when he was haberdasher. He was also one of the most brilliant historians I ever ran across. He did a lot of reading of history as a hobby. It was always quite interesting to listen to him."[8] Agent James Le Gette said "Truman was the best guy they ever had to work around as far as being friendly. The whole idea, cooperative, understanding, first name basis. And they liked his politics too for the most part. Truman is the standout president clear up until the last Bush."[9]

When it came to presidential protection, President Truman deferred to his agents, as they often rode on or near the rear of the presidential limousine, with good motorcycle coverage and building rooftops guarded during parades. President Truman himself said: "The Secret Service was the only boss that the President of the United States really had,"[10] remarks later repeated by both President Johnson and President Clinton.[11] FBI Director J. Edgar Hoover had been champing at the bit to take over presidential protection, at least since the Franklin Roosevelt era. In fact, President Harry Truman noted in a letter to his wife in 1947, "Edgar Hoover would give his right eye to take over …"[12]

While much has been written about the attempt on the life of President Truman on 11/1/50 at Blair House by two Puerto Rican Nationalists (a definitive book, *American Gunfight*, tells this story quite well), I was

5. Rowley Oral History, Truman Library, p. 31.
6. *American Gunfight* (2005), page 52.
7. http://www.insidenova.com/news/fairfax/secret-service-veteran-details-years-with-presidents/article_5a1b38ee-702f-11e5-ab5c-7fbb17dba160.html
8. I spoke to Youngblood in 1992 and 1994.
9. "Tales of the Secret Service," *ticklethewire*, 3/31/2009.
10. Chief James J. Rowley oral history, LBJ Library, January 22, 1969, p. 2. See also *Extreme Careers: Secret Service Agents: Life Protecting the President*, by David Seidman, p. 11. Rowley himself said, "Most Presidents have responded to our requests …."
11. Citation: William J. Clinton: "Remarks Dedicating the United States Secret Service Memorial Building," October 14, 1999. 11/23/63 President Johnson remarks to the Secret Service and presentation of an award to James J. Rowley: http://www.presidency.ucsb.edu/ws/?pid=29254
12. Melanson, *The Secret Service*, p. 51; see also pp. 42, 44-46, 85, and 210.

President Truman and USSS Agents (Roy Kellerman, Frank J. Kenney, Guy Spaman, and Howard Anderson) on the tarmac – circa 1945. [Archives of Special Agent in Charge Frank J. Kenney, with permission of Michael Wood].

able to glean further information based on my own personal interviews and correspondence with several former agents. Frank Stoner wrote to me on 2/15/04: ""SA Stewart "Stu" Stout was inside the Blair House when [the] shooting started. He grabbed a Thompson submachine gun and ran upstairs to where [the] President was taking a nap. The President was looking out of the window and SA Stout told him to get under his bed, and then he took up post at [the] top of [the] stairs. SA Stout was a much-decorated Army veteran who served in WW II, as were some of the other agents in the USSS at that time."

While Truman was sleeping in Blair House during the renovation of the White House, two Puerto Rican Nationalists launched their assassination attempt with guns ablaze. Agent Floyd Boring and his comrades fired some of the few shots ever fired "in anger" by Secret Service agents in their long history of protecting the nation's presidents.[13] One of the would-be assassins, Oscar Collazo, was wounded by Boring[14] who told the author, "Collazo

13. Author's interviews with Floyd Boring, 9/22/93 and 3/4/94. See also the 1995 Discovery Channel documentary *Inside The Secret Service* and the 1997 PBS documentary *Truman*, based on David McCullough's book of the same name (Rex Scouten also appeared on the latter program). On both programs, Boring's remarks were confined to Truman and Eisenhower.
14. See also Boring & Rowley Oral Histories, Truman Library. Later pardoned by President Jimmy

said the guy in the grey suit had hit him. Well, I was the only guy wearing a grey suit." Former agent Frank Stoner wrote to the author on 2/15/04: "I was on that shift that day, but was in advance of the President who was to visit the Arlington National Cemetery. Only a small crew was left at Blair House. Boring was there and played an important part of the defense."

As one can plainly see, the Secret Service greatly admired President Truman and the feeling was mutual...except for (maybe) these ten fellows:

10 of Truman Guard Called Into Service

WASHINGTON, June 11.—(P)— Ten Secret Service agents recently transferred from the White House presidential-guard detail have been called into active service in the Army, it was learned today.

The agents range in age from 29 to 39. Six are married men, five of them with children.

The ten were involved in a recent shake-up of the 25 or more agents assigned to the White House and had been members of the late President's personal guard since the war began.

Their status in relation to the draft was that of enlisted reserve men, placed on inactive army duty.

Their call to active service was confirmed at the Treasury, supervising Secret Service, but Chief of the Service, was not available immediately for comment.

Included in the ten is Michael Reilly, of Anaconda, Mont., chief of the White House detail, recently replaced by George Dresher.

Others called to active duty are Wilmer Deckard of Middletown, Pa.; Frank Wood, Pittsburgh; Rowland Savage, Everett, Mass.; Robert Hastings, New York City; James Griffith, Pittsburgh; Burrill Peterson, Iowa; Roger Williams, Long Beach, Calif.; John Marshall, Harrisburg, Pa., and Robert Lowery, Syracuse, N. Y.

A month after President Roosevelt died, they were shifted from the White House detail to the field

Carter, Collazo passed away in 1994.

MEMBERS OF THE WHITE HOUSE DETAIL (AND RELATED AGENTS) DURING THE TRUMAN ADMINISTRATION[15]:

WILLIAM B. ABERT, ASAIC HOWARD S. ANDERSON, FRANK M. BARRY, Chief U.E. BAUGHMAN, ASAIC GERALD A. BEHN, J. FRANK BLACKISTONE, LILBURN "PAT" BOGGS, FLOYD M. BORING, ARTHUR R. BREOR, JAMES T. BURKE, JOHN E. CAMPION, HARRY CHARNLEY, ARVID J. DAHLQUIST, ANDREW G. DAIGLE, WILMER DECKARD, JOHN H. DORSEY, PAUL B. DOSTER, SAIC GEORGE C. DRESCHER 4/12/45-5/3/46, ROBERT A. DUFFY, SAIC of PRS [after Hutchinson, before Bouck] JOSEPH J. ELLIS, JR., JAMES K. FOX, BARTLEY A. FUGLER, HARRY W. GEIGLEIN, MORGAN L. GIES, WILSON A. GILLIAM, ARTHUR L. GODFREY, WILLIAM R. GREER, JAMES H. GRIFFITH, DALE GRUBB, KENNETH B. HALE, RAY M. HARE, ROBERT HASTINGS, PAUL HENNE (VP Detail via Washington Field Office), JAMES M. HIRST, BOB HOLMES (VP/ Barkley detail), C.S. HONESS, SAIC PRS LEONARD P. HUTCHINSON, ROBERT JAMISON, RICHARD G. KAUFFMANN, ROY H. KELLERMAN, FRANK J. KENNEY (Oregon), H. STUART KNIGHT, ROBERT R. LAPHAM, WILLIAM LOWERY, Chief JAMES MALONEY, JOHN A. MARSHALL, GERARD B. McCANN, Assistant Chief-Telegraph, Code and Travel Service + Secret Service RALPH A. McMULLIN, ELMER W. MOORE, CARMINE MOTTO, ROBERT J. MOTTO, VINCENT P. MROZ, FRANK MURRAY, ASAIC HENRY J. NICHOLSON, ANDREW P. O'MALLEY, PAUL J. PATERNI, BURRILL PETERSON, CHARLES E. PEYTON, EMORY P. ROBERTS, SAIC JAMES J. ROWLEY 5/3/46-1/53 [August 1961], ROWLAND SAVAGE, REX SCOUTEN, JOHN T. "JACK" SHERWOOD, WILLIAM F. SHIELDS, BYRD B. SMITH, GUY H. SPAMAN, VERNON D. SPICER, FRANK G. STONER, STEWART G. STOUT, CHARLES TAYLOR, ROBERT H. TAYLOR, MICHAEL TORINA, WILLIAM J. URICK, PAUL T. USHER, JOHN A. WALTERS, EDWARD WATERS, ROGER WILLIAMS, Chief FRANK J. WILSON, FRANK WOOD, RUFUS W. YOUNGBLOOD

---

15. Not including numerous field office agents. Based on various sources, including numerous documents from the Truman Presidential Library.

CHAPTER SIX

BUILDING ROOFTOPS WERE REGULARLY GUARDED DURING THE FDR, TRUMAN, IKE, AND JFK ERAS … AND POLICE INTERMINGLED IN CROWDS, TOO

Newspaper headline in the summer of 1963

During the research for my first book *Survivor's Guilt: The Secret Service & the Failure to Protect President Kennedy*, I made a major discovery, based on both personal interviews with former agents and through newspaper archives and other somewhat obscure source material: not merely as a response to the JFK assassination were building rooftops guarded during motorcades … they were regularly guarded at least from the 1940's onward! I knew there had to be a reason (or reasons) that presidents survived before the Kennedy murder beyond just good old-fashioned luck. In short, this method of protection – along with the intermingling of police in the crowds themselves, often in plainclothes – was how the Secret Service "got around" the so-called lack of manpower they sometimes faced, as well as the need to not always look so obtrusive with security, not to mention being able to protect our presidents with confidence.

This was a major factor that eluded me for years, as well-meaning people would sometimes play devil's advocate with me, observing a still photo from some motorcade online or in a book that, on the surface, appeared to leave President Kennedy a sitting duck. Compared to today's very overt security, with notable exceptions, it is rather easy to find a photo from the Kennedy years that can appear to make JFK's security seem paltry, to put it mildly. What cannot be gauged in a still photo is the speed of the limousine, the presence of protective officers in the crowd, and, again, building rooftops (at least multi-story structures) guarded along the route of travel.

I cannot emphasize how important this discovery is – not only would a well-designed conspiracy have been foiled if these measures were employed in Dallas (which they were not), even the designs of a lone-nut killer would perhaps have stood an even greater chance of failure. Imagine if Dealey Plaza would have had some well-armed men, whose job it was to protect the president and vice president, standing tall and maintaining vigilance from above.

The evidence for this discovery is so important to history – and was perhaps covered a tad too briefly in my first book – that a detailed look at the evidence is in order here. While direct, verbatim quotes from news articles and the like are obviously crucial evidence, nothing replaces actually viewing this primary source information first hand (a picture is truly worth a thousand words, indeed). Thus, these rare and forgotten images are presented here, after years of unique research, for the first time anywhere.

The Pittsburgh Press - Oct 22, 1944

Ten thousand policemen—vacations and leaves had been canceled —were stationed along the motorcade's route. Rooftops were ordered cleared of spectators, and the Secret Service and probably the FBI were on the job.

The old Roosevelt smile was very much in evidence, and he acknowledged bursts of applause with a wave of his hat or by clasping his hands over his head. Mrs. Roosevelt, wearing a dark red fur-collared coat and a felt hat, smiled and nodded to crowds standing three-deep along the curb.

FDR era.

Truman era.

Truman Heavily Guarded By 300 Police Here

Some Perch on Hills and Buildings. Others Mingle in Crowd of 3,000 at PRR

By VINCE JOHNSON
Post-Gazette Staff Writer

Security precautions for President Truman's Pittsburgh stop were so thorough that one out of every 10 persons in Pennsylvania Station was a policeman.

The crowd gathered to greet the President was estimated at 3,000. Police of all types, ranging from a Secret Service detail from the White House to city officers totaled ...

Police, Detectives Along the Streets

THE streets over which the president travels to his hotel are guarded by hundreds of uniformed New York police, and detectives are scattered through the crowds.

Other officers guard his point of entrance into the hotel, the elevators, the fire escapes and every door he will pass. Fire escapes and rooftops of adjoining buildings are manned by picked officers. Occupants of the buildings adjoining are investigated.

When the president sits down to his meal he can see a secret service officer at a table to the front of him and one to the left and right at other tables on the floor, blending in with the guests.

At such end of the ...

Ike Guarded In Panama

(Continued from Page One)

order of the names of their countries. Panamanian troops armed with carbines or submachine guns stood guard on nearby balconies and rooftops.

Ike Seventh to Arrive

Mr. Eisenhower was the seventh to arrive, riding in a special "bubble-topped" Lincoln escorted by several carloads of Secret Service agents. Other U.S. agents stood guard around Arias' residence.

In 1959, when President Eisenhower visited Paris, I witnessed a security operation that left me stunned. First of all, the police did a sweep of all high-risk types and tucked them away someplace for a week. Then on the day of Ike's arrival every cop in France must have been on the scene: there was a rifleman on every rooftop covering the windows opposite, access roads were blocked, and every third person in the crowd wore a uniform. DeGaulle, himself the target of numerous attempts, mainly with explosives, took no chances.

Ike era.

And now, perhaps the most important era, as it has a direct bearing on the tragedy of November 22, 1963: the Kennedy era, in detail.

The next image is from a 1962 book written with the help of Chief Inspector Michael Torina, as well as Chief James Rowley and the Secret Service, in general. Torina, whom I corresponded with twice, confirmed the veracity of what is written. These important standard security procedures were not used in Dallas.

Chief Inspector Michael W. Torina told author William Manchester back in 1961 that wherever a Presidential motorcade must slow down for a turn, the entire intersection must be checked in advance.[1]

JFK Agent Lynn Meredith wrote the author, stating that one of the main reasons JFK was killed was the following: "Inadequate security along the entire ten-mile motorcade route from the airport to downtown Dallas that day, particularly in the buildings along the route of travel." As the former SAIC of the FDR detail, Mike Reilly, wrote in his book: "He [an agent] was derelict in his duty if he permitted the Chief Executive of the United States to get in any place or position where his life was endangered."[2]

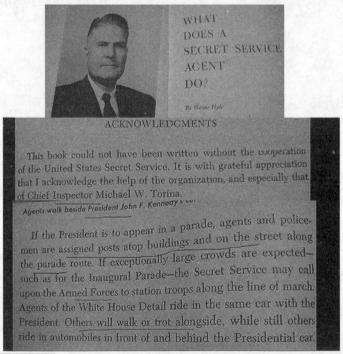

WHAT DOES A SECRET SERVICE AGENT DO?

By Wayne Hyde

ACKNOWLEDGMENTS

This book could not have been written without the cooperation of the United States Secret Service. It is with grateful appreciation that I acknowledge the help of the organization, and especially that of Chief Inspector Michael W. Torina.

Agents walk beside President John F. Kennedy's car.

If the President is to appear in a parade, agents and policemen are assigned posts atop buildings and on the street along the parade route. If exceptionally large crowds are expected—such as for the Inaugural Parade—the Secret Service may call upon the Armed Forces to station troops along the line of march. Agents of the White House Detail ride in the same car with the President. Others will walk or trot alongside, while still others ride in automobiles in front of and behind the Presidential car.

---

1. *The Death of a President* by William Manchester, page 32. An eyewitness to JFK's Alameda, CA motorcade wrote to me the following: "Motorcades are supposed to avoid hairpin turns! I saw a JFK motorcade in May of '62 in Alameda, CA. His limo was 4th or 5th in line, not in front as was the case in Dallas. There were motorcycles flanking his car. It sped by at a seeming 50+ MPH. It didn't crawl along as in Dallas."

2. *Reilly of the White House* (1947), page 96.

Security for JFK on foreign soil.

2   CORPUS CHRISTI TIMES, Friday, June 21, 1963

President Will Have Plenty Of Protection While Abroad

By DOUGLAS B. CORNELL.

WASHINGTON. (AP)—When President Kennedy visits Europe, he's going to be just about as safe as if he stayed home.

In fact, he would stay home if there were any question about his safety—the U.S. Secret Service would see to that.

The Secret Service, by law, is charged with protecting the President anywhere. And it does so in shifts around the clock, at a palace or embassy abroad as it does at the White House in Washington.

In this country, the Secret Service has the sole responsibility for safeguarding the Chief Executive, although it also calls on local and state police and occasionally the military for assistance. On trips to other countries, the foreign counterpart of the Secret Service is responsible technically for the security of the President. But actually it is the Secret Service that sets forth the security requirements, working in close cooperation with its opposite number abroad.

WHEN A president travels in other lands, the sharp-eyed, well-built young men constantly by his side draw exclamations from the crowds. Foreigners always figure they are FBI men or G-men. But the FBI has no specific authority for guarding the president.

Congress put this power in the hands of the Secret Service years ago. The Secret Service is an agency of the U.S. Treasury Department, and one of its other major duties is running down counterfeiters.

A Special Secret Service detail is assigned to the White House

under Gerald A. Behn, a young-looking, gum-chewing veteran who goes back to the days of the late President Franklin D. Roosevelt.

As on all presidential trips, the one to Europe which begins tomorrow night is being checked out carefully by an advance party which includes Secret Service agents. These agents and plenty of others—the White House doesn't wish to advertise the exact number—will accompany Kennedy when he starts his 10-day travels to West Germany, Ireland, Britain and Italy.

PROBABLY A flying freighter will take along a huge, specially built and equipped car for the Secret Service, as well as Kennedy's limousine with a removable metal or plastic top.

The Secret Service car has running boards and hand grips. In a motorcade, agents are hopping on and off constantly and racing ahead to run alongside Ken-

San Francisco To Be Site of U. S. World Trade Fair

SAN FRANCISCO. (AP) — San Francisco will host the seventh United States World Trade Fair Sept. 10-20 — the first time the event has been held outside New York City — Mayor George Christopher announced yesterday.

More than 60 nations in Europe, Asia, Africa, the Middle East, and Central and South America have exhibited at the international trade event in the past.

nedy's car. The two cars travel almost bumper to bumper.

Usually each is driven by an agent. Now and then there are exceptions, as when a turbaned, red-coated Indian was at the wheel of the president's car when former President Dwight D. Eisenhower visited New Delhi.

At the airports, along the roads and streets, at public buildings, and all other places the President will visit, Secret Service and local security agents will have combed over the entire route in advance.

They ask local authorities to put police on top of buildings and along the streets. Bridges get special attention. Servants, waiters and other employes in places the President visits will be checked. So will kitchens.

ALL THIS doesn't mean that crowds won't get a good look at the President or the photographers and reporters won't be able to cover his activities.

At ceremonies, representatives of the press probably will be no more than 20 feet away. And at times even closer. The general public may not be much farther away. In fact, some people are likely to see Kennedy close up. He is a gregarious kind of person who seldom passes up the chance to wander over to a crowd behind a fence or other barricade and walk along with a smile and outstretched hand, offering handclasps and sometimes yielding to requests for autographs.

Or he might get right into the crowd and mingle. This rather worries the Secret Service, because it never knows for sure what the President is going to do about joining the crowd. That's the kind of man he is.

Author Jim Bishop, of *The Day Kennedy Was Shot* fame, who interviewed Chief Rowley and William Greer, among others, wrote, "Every street the President planned to traverse in each city had to be 'sanitized' long in advance by agents.... Every building Mr. Kennedy might step into had to be screened and searched."[3] Inspector Thomas Kelley also noted the Secret Service's concern regarding warehouses, even those that were partially occupied.[4] Of course, the Texas School Book Depository was a partially occu-

3. *The Day Kennedy Was Shot*, Page 38.
4. 3 HSCA 335 See also 18 H 677.

pied warehouse. From former Chief U.E. Baughman's book, *Secret Service Chief*, written before the JFK assassination: "Here are a few of the security measures called for: Every manhole and sewer along the route ... had to be sealed ... every single building and all of its occupants along the parade route had to be checked. We had to have a dossier on each occupant sufficient to guarantee that he was 'safe'. Only then could we grant him the privilege of viewing the parade from his window or his rooftop."[5]

Aside from being constant shadows of the President and his family, the Secret Service men have other king-sized tasks to perform whenever Mr. Kennedy travels. An advance party checks ahead with local police authorities. Who will prepare the President's food? Have all known crackpots who have written threatening letters been rounded up? Will the sewers, manhole covers, balconies and rooftops along the Presidential route be guarded? Has the President's tem-	How can anyone plot to kill a man who isn't sure where he is going? President Kennedy attends mass at any one of three churches in the Washington area, and no one is sure which one until he gives directions to the driver. He works well with the Secret Service and won't go to a football game without giving advance warning to Jerry Behn, present chief of the White House detail. Mr. Behn and his men "sanitize" the stadium.

Right: An excerpt from the December 1962 issue of *Boy's Life* magazine, complete with various quotes from Chief Rowley. Left: 11/14/63 national article by Jim Bishop:

Death threats preceded JFK's 1963 Ireland visit:

"Police, newspaper received warnings months before president's killing.

"The documents indicated that 6,404 police officers were on duty throughout Ireland the night Kennedy arrived, of whom 2,690 lined the U.S. president's route from Dublin airport to the Phoenix Park mansion of Irish President Eamon de Valera.

"Costigan wrote that, although the death threats were considered likely to be hoaxes, his officers would use binoculars to monitor rooftops along the route of the presidential motorcade. He said some police would carry firearms, an exceptional measure in a country with a largely unarmed police force, to engage any would-be sniper.

"A rifle as well as Thompson guns and revolvers were carried for use against a possible sniper," Costigan wrote in a post-Kennedy visit memorandum released Friday."[6]

5. Pages 39-40.
6. http://www.nbcnews.com/id/16390691/

Agents rode on (the rear of) the limousine and the bubbletop was used, as well.

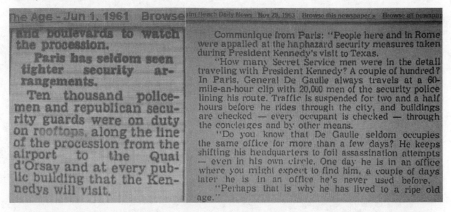

Right: JFK's trip to Paris, France 1961. Left: The Secret Service worked with the French Surete (security police) – they knew what to do:

JFK's inaugural security (quoting Chief Inspector Michael Torina again), including an un-published document provided to me by Secret Service agent Frank Stoner.

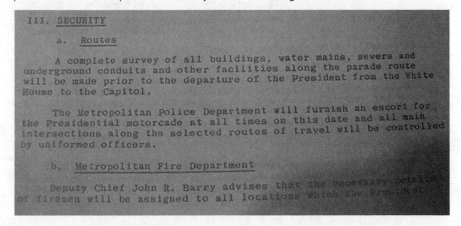

Above and next page: JFK's trip to Caracas, Venezuela December 1961 (note that "helicopters hovered over the official motorcade along the entire route," among other items of interest).

Guard Of 35,000 Lines Streets To Assure Safety Of President

CARACAS, Venezuela (UPI) — Venezuela put an estimated 35,000 troops and police on duty today to assure the safety of President Kennedy in his visit to the city where Vice President Richard M. Nixon was stoned and spat upon three years ago.

As the soldiers and police lined the streets to provide the strictest security measures ever provided for an American president, the crowds cheered, applauded, and waved American flags. There were no signs of hostility along the route taken by the welcoming motorcade from the airport into the city.

But in the light of scattered outbreaks of anti-American violence here earlier this week the government was taking no chances.

Green-clad soldiers lined the entire 27-mile length of the motorcade route, and in the Catia section where Nixon was attacked the troops were stationed every six feet. The concentration of troops and police also was heavy in El Silencio section where a number of Communists live. A double cordon of troops kept the crowd back at least 100 yards from the street in El Silencio.

At the airport where Kennedy was welcomed by President Romulo Betancourt about 3,000 soldiers were on guard duty.

As the motorcade traveled along the eight-lane highway into the city at a 25-mile-an-hour clip security officers were in evidence all the way. In the 21 cars following the President's White House bubble-top limousine all but the one carrying Mrs. Kennedy and Mrs. Betancourt were filled with security officers, who had tommy guns and pistols on the seats and floors of the cars.

Many of the soldiers standing guard along the way had bayonets fixed on their rifles.

Except in the El Silencio area the spectators were permitted to stand at the edge of the avenue but the troops with fixed bayonets and equipped with gas masks for use if needed stood facing them.

Helicopters hovered over the official motorcade along the entire route from the airport to the city, and in addition to the soldiers and police there were a number of civilians wearing arm bands who had been recruited to help maintain order.

As a special precaution groups of soldiers were stationed around the gasoline pumps at all service stations along the route. Officers carrying walkie talkies gave orders to the troops.

The security precautions went into effect some time before the presidential motorcade was due. Pedestrians were banned from crossing the street immediately preceding the arrival of the presidential car, and motorized patrols moved up and down the avenue. The route took Kennedy along the Avenida Sucre, the street where Nixon was encircled by jeering students on his South American tour.

The first troops appeared at their stations shortly after dawn, standing in the rain to await the President's arrival. Near the United States Embassy on Avenida Miranda helmeted soldiers were posted every 10 yards. Some others took up positions on first floor balconies.

JFK motorcade in D.C. 1961– Police on the roof of a building overlooking a JFK motorcade, while both police and military lined the streets, common security measures used before Dallas, yet only a small number of police lined the streets in Dallas, did not face the crowd, with no military lining the streets and no men guarding rooftops.

The Windsor Star - Apr 27, 1961   Browse this ne

icemen on the president is one of them.

Wherever President Kennedy drives or stays his car or his person will be surrounded by his bodyguards. Others will be circulating among the crowds. The R.C.M.P. will also be out but in larger numbers, some of the Mounties in plain clothes mingling with the spectators.

JFK's trip to Canada April 1961.

JFK's trip to Seattle, WA 11/16/61 – buildings were guarded; police mingled within crowds; military lined street; press photographers close by; agents by limo; SAIC Gerald Behn in front passenger seat.

71

...ng of Lee Harvey Oswald ...man believed to have ...President Kennedy's as... ...n Seattle police and dep... sheriffs talked about it ...rtheless.

...e questions: How do you ...ct a President or an in... ...us prisoner from fana-

...ere is no simple answer.

...SISTANT Police Chief ...les Rouse had sympathy ...ell as criticism for the ...s Police Department.

I think they were ...ped by the immensity ...the problem," Rouse I. "They apparently be... ...ed they had to operate ...ly but they should have ...a willing to be crafty to ...ect their prisoner.

This is one of the basic ...its of police work — ...t an officer is respon... ...e for the safety of his ...oner. Police officers ...e sacrificed their lives to ...tect prisoners during our ...ury."

...e breakdown in protection Oswald apparently came ...use one or more Dallas ...men recognized Jack ...y as the man whose ...

is being taken to trial a dep- uty sheriff is handcuffed to a prisoner with perhaps two or three other deputies preced- ing the pair through the mar- ble hallways.

Most prisoners are trans- ferred from the Seattle City Jail to the County Jail in the courthouse a c r o s s James Street on Third Avenue via a basement tunnel connecting the two buildings.

William J. Walsh, c h i e f criminal deputy for the sher- iff's office, yesterday recalled the meticulous detail indulged in by the U.S. Secret Service and local law enforcement agencies d u r i n g President Kennedy's visits to this area.

WHEN President Kennedy touched down at the Seattle- Tacoma International Airport September 27 Walsh had men stationed on the roofs of the buildings, in the crowd, and on the field.

"Somebody had left a suitcase on the f i e l d," Walsh recalled. "The Se- cret Service got it out of there in a hurry—it was

for the President's protection that is established by the Se- cret Service plus any extra precautions approved by the Secret Service.

"When President Kennedy traveled to the University of Washington from downtown Seattle Nov. 16, 1961, there were 300 Seattle policemen di- rectly involved in protecting the President plus the Secret Service detail. The President on that occasion spoke at a special University convoca- tion honoring the University's 100th anniversary.

THAT NIGHT as the Presi- dent slept on the ninth floor of the Olympic Hotel—rather than in the Presidential Suite on the 10th floor—Seattle po- licemen patrolled the roof of the hotel and guarded every exit and entrance to the top two floors. Even at that two college students made it to the 10th floor and were quickly hustled away.

Before his 1961 visit here the Secret Service had re- ceived two threats against the President. Secret S e r v i c e

JFK's trip to Seattle, WA 11/16/61.

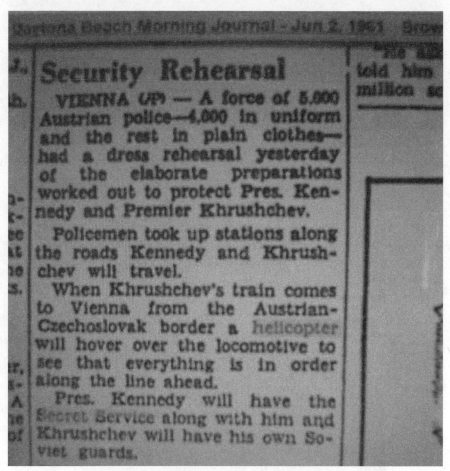

Daytona Beach Morning Journal - Jun 2, 1961   Brow

Security Rehearsal

VIENNA (UP) — A force of 5,900 Austrian police—4,000 in uniform and the rest in plain clothes—had a dress rehearsal yesterday of the elaborate preparations worked out to protect Pres. Kennedy and Premier Khrushchev.

Policemen took up stations along the roads Kennedy and Khrushchev will travel.

When Khrushchev's train comes to Vienna from the Austrian-Czechoslovak border a helicopter will hover over the locomotive to see that everything is in order along the line ahead.

Pres. Kennedy will have the Secret Service along with him and Khrushchev will have his own Soviet guards.

told him million s

JFK's trip to Vienna 1961.

JFK's trip to Chicago 3/23/63:

Col. George J. McNally, White House Signal Corps and former Secret Service agent, wrote in his book: "But during the Chicago visit [3/23/63], the motorcade was slowed to the pace of a mounted Black Horse Troop, and the police got a warning of Puerto Rican snipers. Helicopters searched the roofs along the way, and no incidents occurred."[7] Agent Don Lawton rode on the rear of the limousine and six motorcycles bracketed the vehicle.[8]

JFK's motorcade/ trip to Nashville, TN 5/18/63:

SAIC of the Nashville office (and former JFK WHD agent) Paul Doster told the *Nashville Banner* on 5/18/63 that "a complete check of the entire

---

7. *A Million Miles of Presidents*, p. 204.
8. Secret Service Final Survey Report for 3/23/63 Chicago trip

motorcade route" was done for JFK's trip to Nashville. In addition, Doster stated, "Other [police] officers were assigned atop the municipal terminal and other buildings along the route. These men took their posts at 8 a.m. and remained at their rooftop stations until the president and his party passed."

A helicopter was used on the route, as well.

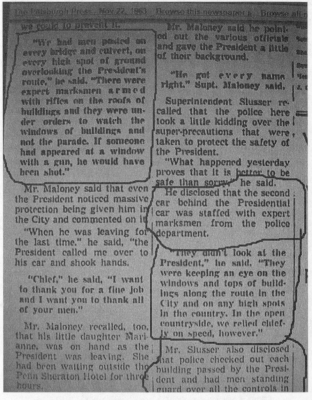

JFK's trip to Pittsburgh, PA October 1962.

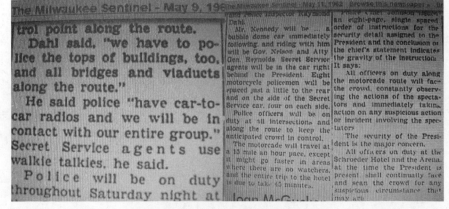

JFK's trip to Milwaukee, WI May 196.:

JFK's trip to Milwaukee, WI May 1962.

JFK's trip to Pueblo, CO 8/17/62.

JFK's trip to New York, NY 9/20/63.

The limousine's bubbletop in nice weather, including a helicopter overhead. Some gentleman named "Daniel W." sent me this photo, claiming to be a then-17 year old photographer. He said the weather was perfect and the helicopter pictured buzzed overhead. In addition, the limo was going pretty fast.

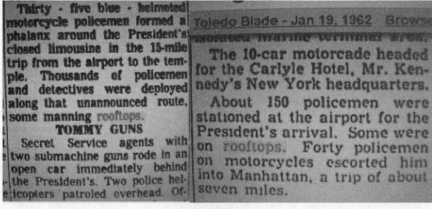

Thirty - five blue - helmeted motorcycle policemen formed a phalanx around the President's closed limousine in the 15-mile trip from the airport to the temple. Thousands of policemen and detectives were deployed along that unannounced route, some manning rooftops.

TOMMY GUNS

Secret Service agents with two submachine guns rode in an open car immediately behind the President's. Two police helicopters patroled overhead. Of-

Toledo Blade - Jan 19, 1962   Browse

The 10-car motorcade headed for the Carlyle Hotel, Mr. Kennedy's New York headquarters.

About 150 policemen were stationed at the airport for the President's arrival. Some were on rooftops. Forty policemen on motorcycles escorted him into Manhattan, a trip of about seven miles.

Other NY trips.

JFK's trip to Duluth, MN 9/24/63:

The following appeared on p. 6 in the October 31, 1963 issue of *The Wanderer*, which catered predominantly to right-wingers. The Taylor Caldwell that wrote the following letter is the well-known author and

John Bircher. Caldwell is replying to Sheldon Emry's letter dated Oct. 17 commenting on the extensive protection that JFK had around him on his trip to Duluth in early October 1963. "President Kennedy in Danger?" By Taylor Caldwell: "I was deeply interested in Sheldon Emrey's [sic] account [*Wanderer Forum*, October 17th] of *Air Force men, soldiers with rifles at the ready, Highway Patrol officers, helicopters, guards, etc., being out in full force day and night when President Kennedy visited Duluth.* This account is most extraordinary – but even more alarming, and not for the reasons Mr. Emery [sic] gives: *"Mr. Kennedy is now showing a visible power in the soldiers that he had not openly displayed before"…* It is possible that Mr. Kennedy is in personal jeopardy from them, a matter which is not being mentioned in the newspapers. Indeed, it is very probable. Presidents have been murdered before in our history, and in less dreadful times…The very fact that Mr. Kennedy is apparently now being so closely guarded should alarm all of us very deeply, whether or not we agree with the President on political matters. The mere thought of Mr. Kennedy being assassinated should make all of us shudder for the repercussions in America would be most terrible and disorder would result at the very least [emphasis added]." The bubbletop was used on this trip, as well.

Researcher Chad Carlson wrote to me regarding this very same trip: "I am friends with a man here who was in charge of JFK's trip to Duluth, MN here in September of 1963. I ask him a lot about JFK. He got to talk one-on-one with the President for 30 minutes before he made his rounds and speeches. His name is *Larry Yetka, former Minnesota Supreme Court justice. Larry said that he wondered what [Mafia boss] Sam Giancana of Chicago was up to on 11-22-63.* I told him that I had been watching the motorcade in Dallas on 11-22-63 and told him it looked very "lax." *He said, "Yes it was." So I asked him how was security in Duluth in Sept.1963? He said, "Tight as hell-men were on the rooftops even."* So that's the answers I got out of him on that. Vince, that Larry Yetka guy is quite the man. He had met President's Truman, Kennedy, and LBJ. He was close friends with former Vice-President Hubert Humphrey of Minnesota. He also met former Vice-President Walter Mondale of Minnesota. Larry went to the 1956 and 1964 Democratic National Conventions…at one of them he exchanged unpleasant words with Texas Gov. John Connolly. I'd have to ask him again what happened with that. He was invited to the White House rose garden ceremony under LBJ. The man was a lawyer, and a Minnesota Supreme Court Justice. I think he's around 86 so the time to ask questions is now." [9]

9. Larry Yetka's bona fides: https://en.wikipedia.org/wiki/Lawrence_R._Yetka

Police were on rooftops in Billings, MT–September 1963:

This was confirmed by researcher Deb Galentine's assistant police chief father who worked on the security for this trip, as conveyed to the author on 2/17/14. Deb further wrote: "Weeks before JFK's arrival, my father, who would be in charge of the local police protection, met with Billings' leaders and some of President Kennedy's advance people. JFK's planners wanted the fastest, safest routes possible. They desired routes with no tall buildings and hoped to avoid Billings' Rimrocks as well. The Rimrocks, a natural sandstone formation riddled with caves, paths, and ledges and dotted with pine trees and shrubs, unevenly jut about 500 feet above the city of Billings. Avoiding them would be impossible since Billings' airport lies perched atop them. Three separate routes were available from the airport to the President's venue, and the planners decided to use the one that provided the safest and fastest passage away from the Rimrocks."

Ed Martin (Galentine's father) with JFK 9/25/63.

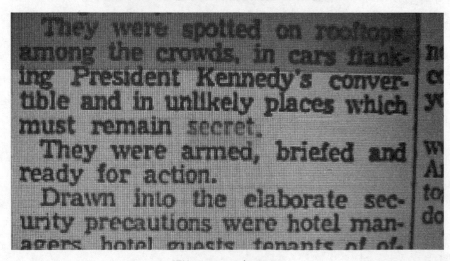

They were spotted on rooftops among the crowds, in cars flanking President Kennedy's convertible and in unlikely places which must remain secret.

They were armed, briefed and ready for action.

Drawn into the elaborate security precautions were hotel managers, hotel guests, tenants of of...

JFK motorcade 1961.

While the stage was set for a meeting of President Kennedy and Alabama's segregationist Gov. George C. Wallace in north Alabama, police here ordered tighter security measures.

Kennedy and Wallace were expected to meet at a Tennessee Valley Authority anniversary observance at Muscle Shoals, where the President is scheduled to speak.

While rumors forecast an uneasy weekend, police chief Jamie Moore said: "We are taking precautions which we consider necessary."

Although he declined to elaborate, armed guards were posted at some buildings which could possibly be targets of bombers. Highway patrolmen guarded the streets, as they have since last weekend's violence.

Anonymous telephone threats have been received by Negro leaders, some white businessmen and various places of business.

In other developments:

—Atty. Gen. Robert F. Kennedy

The south was a dangerous place.

Kennedy is due to spend Sunday through Wednesday in Germany. Around Cologne and Bonn, where he will be most of the time, officials say 4,000 policemen will be on the job.

They will have to cover a 10-mile drive from the airport to Cologne, his brief stay in Cologne, the 20 miles of highway between Cologne and Bonn, and his day and a half in this West German capital. In Berlin, 13,000 police will be on guard.

The most conspicuous part of his escort will be 17 police motorcyclists. The Germans call them "white mice" because of their white helmets and jackets.

Less obvious will be thousands of plainclothesmen and West German police in their light green uniforms—and of course a detachment of the President's own Secret Service.

De Gaulle's car. Ambulances parked in the side streets. Doctors with supplies of blood of De Gaulle's type were stationed along the road.

Although authorities were refusing to give out details, it seemed unlikely that the precautions for Kennedy would be anything like as elaborate.

After he leaves Bonn, Kennedy will be spending half a day inspecting U.S. troops at Hanau, where he will have all the protection the American Army can give him. At his next stop, in Frankfurt and Wiesbaden, the big security job will again be in West German hands.

His last German appearance will be in West Berlin. To get there, he has to fly over nearly 200 miles of Communist territory. This is something De Gaulle did not do.

President Kennedy's motorcade in Berlin in June 1963 was the longest motorcade he ever had, foreign or domestic. Agents rode on the rear of the limousine and the security measures shown at left were also invoked.

JFK's motorcade in Berlin, Germany, June, 1963 – helicopters check the route [indicated by two dashes], agents on limo, tremendous motorcycle formation, press photographers in front of limo.

JFK's trip to Miami 11/18/63:

Bob Hoelscher worked for the Miami-Dade Police Department for 50 years and was a counter-sniper and observer on the terrace deck of the airport hotel on November 18, 1963, the day Kennedy arrived in Miami. He guarded almost every VIP that came through Dade County from Kennedy to Clinton and started the tactical special weapons team, later known as SWAT, in 1970. Documents reveal a bomb threat against JFK in Miami just days before his death. Hoelscher told CBSMiami.com that he knew of potential threats to the president ahead of his November visit.

"I was told that information had been developed that the Cubans might start a protest at an unknown location and they might make an attempt on the life of the President if there was sufficient distraction," Hoelscher said. "I was told to keep this information to myself, watch the periphery and look for anything unusual."

While Hoelscher and some others in the police department knew, it was strictly on a "need to know" basis.

"The information about the death threat was not shared with the rank and file out of fear that the media would find out," Hoelscher said.[10]

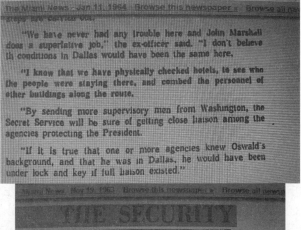

More on Miami trips by JFK.

10. http://miami.cbslocal.com/2013/11/21/exclusive-jfk-death-threat-note-in-nov-1963-in-miami-revealed-for-1st-time/#.VpFxbxKn8Es.facebook

White House Detail   Washington, D. C.

                                      December 4, 1963

                                      FINAL SURVEY REPORT

                              Re: Visit of the President to Tampa, Florida,
                                      on November 18, 1963, where He Partici-
                                      pated in Ceremonies for Strike Command,
                                      Florida Chamber of Commerce, and United
                                      Steel Workers.

        Mr. James J. Rowley
        Chief, U. S. Secret Service
        Washington, D. C.

        Sir:

        INTRODUCTION

        This survey was conducted by SAs Gerald S. Blaine and J. Frank Yeager, White
        House Detail, SAIC Rudolph M. McDavid, Jacksonville, and RA Arnold K. Pep-
        pers, Tampa, in and around Tampa, Florida, from November 11 through November
        18, 1963.

        A parade motorcade with motorcycle escort was used on all movements in
        Tampa, with a pilot car used in advance of the motorcade. All intersections
        ――――――――――――――

        along the route were controlled by uniformed police officers and these
        men were reinforced by motorcycle escort intersection control. The
        sheriff's office secured the roofs of major buildings in the downtown
        and suburban areas.

        All underpasses were controlled by police and military units. The police
        department secured all rail traffic during the visit as the motorcade
        passed over rail arteries enroute.

Kennedy's 11/18/63 Tampa, Florida motorcade was the longest domestic motorcade he ever had, far longer than Dallas and many other trips (second only
to the above-mentioned Berlin trip for length). Here is an excerpt from the official Secret Service survey report written by *Kennedy Detail* author Gerald Blaine:

Russell Groover, a Tampa police motorcycle officer during Kennedy's 11/18/63 motorcade, confirms my research. On 8/27/13, he wrote:
"Vince, yes, every building along the route [in Tampa, FL on 11/18/63]
was manned on every floor and roof with either law enforcement or military. All armed. We traveled only about 25 mph in the sparsely populated area just before we got to Mac Dill Air Force Base. The highest speed
could have gotten up to 35 mph. The only reason we have photos at all is
they didn't think to confiscate Tony Zappone's[11] because he was only a 16
year old kid. Remember history changes and memories fail." In fact, on
the *JFK in Tampa 50th Anniversary special aired on PBS in Tampa, Florida,
the program went into great detail about how there was an officer on every
building and officers and agents in the streets to control the crowds*.

On 8/29/13, Groover further clarified the matter:

"Vince, *in the residential to light business areas Secret Service did not
ride on his car.* They did in the business district and congested areas.

11. Now a friend and author who I have spoken to and corresponded with many times.

We went to Mac Dill AFB where another ceremony was held and the president spoke to the airmen and their family. He then shook the policemen's hands (34) thanking each one of us personally for our dedication. He took his time and made it personal. He then boarded Air Force One and we left. *The area just before the air force base is mostly residential and no one rode on his car*. The security was in the buildings taller than one story but not in residents." [Emphasis added]

On 8/30/13, seeking even further clarification, Groover wrote:

"I would say the fastest we ever ran was between 25 and 35 in the sparsely populated area just before Mac Dill AFB close to the *end of his trip*."

Also, photographer Tony Zappone, then a 16-year-old witness to the motorcade in Tampa (one of whose photos from this motorcade was ironically used in *The Kennedy Detail* book!), told me that the agents were "definitely on the back of the car for most of the day until they started back for MacDill AFB *at the end of the day*." (Emphasis added)

Mr Groover knew nothing about any alleged orders from JFK. The agents rode on the rear of the limo for the majority of the trip (including walking beside the car) and only chose not to ride on the rear of the car in "light" and one-story/residential areas. The motorcade was also going much faster than in Dallas, as confirmed by the aforementioned witness Tony Zappone, who also told me the agents were definitely on the rear of the car until they headed back to the AFB at the end of the day. Mr Groover and Mr Zappone thus explain the logical, *real* reason the agents weren't there at that time: the fast speed of car and the light/residential (one story) area. Case closed … or so one would believe.

Postscript from two best-selling authors – a former agent and a prominent television commentator:

In Larry Sabato's best-selling book *The Kennedy Half Century*, he begins a decent discussion of the protection afforded President Kennedy on page 225. This discussion is appreciated and, while some good points are made, Sabato's mistake is relying on Gerald Blaine's book *The Kennedy Detail* as a primary source, even contacting the author directly. The old warhorses of "manpower" and "overworked agents" rears its ugly head again, obviously overlooking the use of *local* field office agents, local police, and the military. In addition, these agents had one primary job and one primary job only: to protect the president. That was what they took an oath to do and that was the mission. Staying out late and drinking the night before works against this mission, but I digress for the time being and the specific discussion at hand.

To be fair to Sabato, he does offer an above-average, better-than-most criticism and appraisal of the Secret Service failure on 11/22/63. However, it is a classic case of "garbage in, garbage out" (using a computer phrase): by relying on Secret Service propaganda (post-assassination CYA documents and statements [Page 512]) and 47-year-old memoirs (Blaine's statements), Sabato falls for a few common misperceptions along the way.

On page 227, it is duly noted that the Secret Service circa 1963 used pretty modern and proper security procedures in guarding buildings for special events in Washington, D.C. Sabato correctly notes that these procedures were also used in Tampa, Florida on 11/18/63 and wonders – as I do in my first book and in much more detail for this one – why these procedures were not used in Dallas only a few days later. These procedures were, in fact, used countless times *before* Dallas (FDR-JFK and beyond).

On page 512, the notes for pages 226-228, a 1/9/13 e-mail from Gerald Blaine is referenced, in which the former agent wrongly merges and misrepresents certain items and facts – perhaps a sign of old age, who knows. In any event, Blaine claims he released the Tampa Final Survey Report because conspiracy theorists wrongly claimed there was a three-man hit team in Tampa and JFK knew about it. First of all, Blaine doesn't get it and never will – as authors Lamar Waldron and Thom Hartmann also wrongly thought (in their various books – see especially *Ultimate Sacrifice*), *the Tampa Florida survey report was already released by the government in the late 1990's, over 10 years before Blaine "donated" his copy to the National Archives!* I have the survey report. Blaine did this because he was angry at the fact that the ARRB (and "conspiracy theorists") *correctly* stated that the Secret Service knowingly destroyed survey reports and related documents for several of JFK's trips in the fall of 1963. The ones that did survive the Secret Service shredder, including the Tampa documents, were released in the late 1990's and are duly noted in an online article I have had up since 1998.[12]

Needless to say, the surviving documents – and much more – are also dealt with in my first book.

---

12. http://mcadams.posc.mu.edu/palamara/ssrosters.html

In any event, Blaine also errs when he mentions the "three-man hit team" – *no one* has claimed that but him. He obviously has morphed or merged the allegations of a *four*-man hit team in Chicago, IL on 11/2/63 with the fictional, only-in-Blaine's-head three-man team "in" Tampa, FL on 11/18/63. While Blaine rightly notes the threats from individuals named Wayne Gainey and John Warrington, he conveniently makes no mention of the many other threats to JFK apart from those two seeming "lone nuts" – in Tampa, in Miami, and elsewhere (see chapter 2 of my first book for much more). Blaine also thinks Agent Robert Jamison's statements to the HSCA regarding "a mobile, unidentified rifleman shooting from a window of a tall building with a high-powered rifle fitted with a scope" may be a reference to the Joseph Milteer threat. Maybe, maybe not. Nevertheless, this in no way diminishes or negates the importance of Jamison's comment or the Milteer threat itself, known to the agents *before* both the Florida and Texas trips.

On pages 512-513, Sabato quotes from a recent article about JFK's 3/23/63 Chicago, IL trip and claims it appears Kennedy took risks on this trip that complicated his security. However, as I demonstrate in my first book (Chapter 17 and the photo section) and in this chapter (above), this trip actually entailed heavy protection, as the Secret Service were tipped off to threats to Kennedy. In this case, I trust my research (contemporary documents and statements) more than the 50-year-old ruminations in a remembrance article. And, once again, this proves the fallacy in observing a still photo as "proof" that JFK's security appeared light, as a still photo does not take into account the actual speed of the car, police intermingled in crowds, helicopters hovering overhead, good preventive intelligence, and building rooftops guarded.

To his credit, on pages 227-228 and page 513, Sabato references my online blog and my dissent to Blaine's blaming-the-victim mantra, although one can obviously tell a bias toward wishing to give Blaine and company the benefit of the doubt (being in direct personal touch with Blaine no doubt contributed to this bias). That said, Blaine commits a knowing error in his penchant to rewrite history to suit his ends, claiming on page 228 that "In Dallas they...did not have enough resources to man all of the roof tops" [ellipsis in text]. Who is "they"? The Secret Service? The police? The not-used military?

Bottom line: on many previous motorcade routes before 11/22/63, including one that was *the second longest motorcade in the history of the Kennedy years* (Tampa, FL, 11/18/63), agents and/ or police and/ or military guarded building rooftops in the downtown and suburban areas – multi-story buildings and major buildings, as one story "common" buildings (such as homes) could be safely guarded via police and/ or military lining the street and facing the crowd, not to mention the FASTER speed of the motorcade thru these smaller building districts, as was the case in Tampa, to name but one example (see chapter 6 of my first book for much more). Former Secret Service Officer John Norris, referring to Dealey Plaza and security failures, said, "That plaza's the Bermuda Triangle of Dallas... Anyone trained in security could take one look at it and know it was an ideal place to get Kennedy. There definitely should have been coverage from the buildings that overlook the plaza, or, at the very least, there should have been a helicopter hovering over the area to scout the buildings and rooftops"[13]

So, let me get this straight – the Secret Service, in conjunction with their police and military counter-parts, *had* the resources to man equal or *much longer* motorcades right before Dallas, yet they allegedly did not have those resources in Dallas? Total bunk and he knows better.

And now you do, as well.

Things that happened on 11/18/63 in Tampa that did not happen on 11/22/63 in Dallas[14]:

– agents on the rear of the limo (other than Clint Hill, briefly, 4 times before they got to Dealey Plaza);

– military aide in front seat between driver and agent in charge (McHugh was asked, for the first time in Dallas, not to ride there!);

– press photographers flatbed truck in front of limo (canceled at last minute at Love Field);

– fast speed of cars (slow in Dallas);

– ASAIC Boring on trip (SAIC Behn and Boring always accompanied JFK in motorcades. A third-stringer, Kellerman, goes in their place);

– multi story rooftops guarded (officially, no buildings were guarded in Dallas. Eyewitnesses Arnold and Barbara Rowland *did* see a man with a rifle in the Texas School Book Depository building before the motorcade reached the eventual site of the assassination and, tellingly, thought the man was a Secret Service agent.[15] Rowland later testified to the Warren Commission on his thought process at the time: "I must honestly say my opinion was based on movies I have seen, on the attempted assassination of Theo-

---

13. *Survivor's Guilt,* page 147.
14. See my first book *Survivor's Guilt*.
15. Arnold Rowland's and Barbara Rowland's (separate) statements to the Sheriff's office 11/22/63 (as also dramatized in the 1991 movie *JFK* and mentioned in many JFK assassination books).

dore Roosevelt where they had Secret Service men up in the building such as that with rifles watching the crowds, and another one concerned with attempted assassination of the other one, Franklin Roosevelt, and both of these had Secret Service men up in windows or on top of buildings with rifles, and this is how my opinion was based and why it didn't alarm me."[16]);

• multiple motorcycles running next to JFK in a wedge formation (they repeated this coverage 11/18-11/22/63 [morning in Fort Worth]...until Dallas, when the Secret Service reduced the coverage and had the few motorcycles that were remaining drop back from the rear wheels of JFK's limo, rendering them ineffective or, as the HSCA stated, "uniquely insecure");

• White House Press Photographer Cecil Stoughton riding in follow-up car taking photos (he did 11/18-11/21/63...until they got to Dallas. No satisfactory answer has ever been given as to why Stoughton was not there on 11/22/63);

• Pierre Salinger on trip (Assistant Malcolm Kilduff makes his first trip on his own to Texas; Salinger said he missed only "one or two trips" with JFK...Texas was one of them!);

• Dr Burkley close to JFK (Burkley protested being placed far away from JFK in Dallas, for this was the only time, save in Rome, this ever happened to him);

Former JFK Secret Service Chief U.E. Baughman came clean right after the JFK assassination:

16. 2 H 165 onward. Barbara Rowland: 6 H 177 onward.

In a 11/23/63 UPI article "Secret Service Men Wary of Motorcade," based in part on "private conversations" with former agents, Baughman is further corroborated: "Buildings frequently are checked, along with records of occupants to make sure there are no known President-haters on the premises." Remember what Chief Inspector Michael Torina conveyed above: ""If the President is to appear in a parade, agents and policemen are assigned posts atop buildings and on the street along the parade route." Author Jim Bishop, who interviewed Chief Rowley and William Greer, among others, wrote, "Every street the President planned to traverse in each city had to be 'sanitized' long in advance by agents... Every building Mr. Kennedy might step into had to be screened and searched."[17]

JFK's motorcade in San Antonio, TX, 11/21/63:

Forty members of the military police from Ft. Sam Houston, Texas were used for traffic control, motorcade route security, and intersection control.[18] In addition, there were many flanking motorcycles and, as the following two photos depict (from a motion picture included for the first time ever in a television production I was credited in[19]), a police helicopter was utilized along the route.

JFK motorcade in Fort Worth, TX 11/21-11/22/63:
Building rooftops (including the Hotel Texas) were guarded.[20]

17. *The Day Kennedy Was Shot* by Jim Bishop, page 38.
18. *RIF# 154-10002-10424-Secret Service survey report.* See also: http://mcadams.posc.mu.edu/palamara/ssrosters.html
19. *JFK: THE FINAL HOURS* DVD (2013).
20. *The Death of a President*, page 88; *November Patriots* by Larry Hancock, page 423.

Rome News-Tribune - Dec 22, 1963

During President Kennedy's administration, it was argued by some of the television cameramen that they could not get a good view of the President in a parade if he was too closely surrounded by Secret Service men. In the Dallas motorcade, the Secret Service men were not placed around the President as closely as they have been on other occasions.

Newsmen noticed the differences

One thought comes to mind when reading the following newspaper excerpt.

Why weren't they concerned a few short months later?

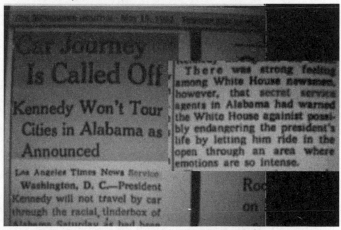

Car Journey Is Called Off

Kennedy Won't Tour Cities in Alabama as Announced

Los Angeles Times News Service
Washington, D. C.—President Kennedy will not travel by car through the racial tinderbox of Alabama Saturday as had been

There was strong feeling among White House newsmen, however, that secret service agents in Alabama had warned the White House against possibly endangering the president's life by letting him ride in the open through an area where emotions are so intense.

Finally – an amazing find (*The Daily Reporter*, Dover, OH, 11/25/63):

Doverites' Son-In-Law Was With JFK

Glen Bennett, husband of Mrs. Glenna Kline Bennett, former society editor of The Daily Reporter, was a member of the presidential Secret Service detail assigned to guard John F. Kennedy during his Dallas visit.

Bennett was in the agents' car immediately behind the presidential limousine when the fatal shooting occurred. He also accompanied Mr. Kennedy's body back to Washington.

Normally on the White House detail, Agent Bennett recently was assigned to the tour detail and was with Mr. Kennedy when

he spoke in New York, Florida and in the West.

Mrs. Bennett's parents are Mr. and Mrs. George Aebersold of 340 Main St., Dover. They got

TV glimpses of their son-in-law on Mr. Kennedy's arrival in Dallas, when his body was placed aboard the plane and again when it arrived in Washington.

The Doctor Writes:

Stature May Be Inherited

Discovered in early 2014, after publication of my first book, PRS (Intelligence Division) agent Glen Bennett admits being on the NY, FL, and TX trips. As revealed in chapter two from my first book, he lied under oath to the HSCA and stated that he was *not* on the Florida trip – he was on every single stop (Cape Canaveral, Palm Beach, Miami, and Tampa, often riding in the follow-up car)-and did not volunteer that he was also on the NY trip. Bennett's presence on all these trips was only confirmed via document releases in the late 1990's by myself.[21] Bennett was a PRS agent – an administrative agent who monitored threats to the president and stayed back in D.C. His presence on these trips (and later denials) confirms my suspicions that he was a covert monitor of mortal threats to JFK's life in-progress and that this was covered up afterwards for fear of reprisals from Congress and the public, as many people would cry out "wait – you knew there were mortal threats and plots to kill JFK and even had a special agent on these trips just for that purpose, yet Kennedy died?" Bennett rode in the follow-up car in Tampa and Dallas, as well.

After the assassination, the Secret Service received a lot more money, equipment, and personnel, greatly remedying not only the situation the agency faced pre-Dallas, but also a situation that most do not realize was in existence since at least the year before.

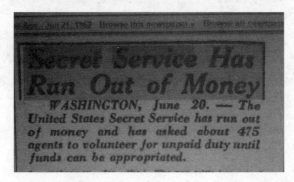

Secret Service Has Run Out of Money

WASHINGTON, June 20. — The United States Secret Service has run out of money and has asked about 475 agents to volunteer for unpaid duty until funds can be appropriated.

---

21   See chapter 2 of my book *Survivor's Guilt*.

CHAPTER SEVEN

FDR – TRAINING GROUND FOR THE TRUMAN, IKE, AND KENNEDY BODYGUARDS (INCLUDING AN ASSASSINATION ATTEMPT IN AN OPEN CAR)

President Franklin Roosevelt with members of the White House detail – (Front row, left to right) James Rowley, Mike Reilly, FDR, Charlie Fredericks and Neal Shannon. (Back row, left to right) Howard Anderson, Jim Griffith, Guy Spaman, Jim Beary, Roy Kellerman, Wilbur Deckard, and Bob Hastings.

U.S. Secret Service agents, clockwise from center, behind Roosevelt: James "Jim" Rowley, Wilmer Deckard, John Marshall, Elmer Hipsley, Charles "Charlie" Fredericks, Guy Spaman, and Jack Willard.

Future SAIC of the JFK and LBJ detail Gerald Behn with the Roosevelts[1]:

A typical, heavily-secured FDR motorcade:

---

1. Unpublished photo graciously provided by a relative of Behn's.

While all the members of FDR's White House Detail are long dead, I was blessed to speak to and correspond with several of them: Gerald Behn, Floyd Boring, and James Rowley, as well as several surviving family members, such as the widow of Roy Kellerman. However, what they had to tell me was of primary importance to my JFK assassination writing, so here are a few more family member anecdotes:

Elizabeth Madeline Foeckler Blair, the niece of the late former agent Dan Moriarty, 7/28/15-

> Dan told us he was one of the federal agents that shot John Dillinger. Also, Dan told us that when he was "in residence" at the White House, he always had some hard candy to keep him from wanting a drink. FDR's little Scotty dog Fala would seek Dan out for a treat. Once when FDR was being wheeled out to his private little library, Fala fell behind, looking for Dan and some candy. FDR told the attendant pushing him "That damned Moriarty is around here somewhere," and sure enough, there Dan was trying to shoo Fala back to FDR."

Martha Bowden, the niece of the late former agent John Campion, 5/5/15:

> My uncle was John Campion, who was a secret service agent for Roosevelt, Truman, Eisenhower, Kennedy and Johnson (in an administrative role for Johnson). His widow, my aunt, is currently 100. He was one of the good guys. He never told us much about what he did--he honored the confidence that was placed in him and was later upset when several agents wrote books or gave interviews that he felt were inappropriate. He was asked many times for interviews or to write a biography but would have none of that. Visiting his widow recently, I asked if she would write his biography and she said no, she would honor John's wishes not to tell stories. John died on July 4, 1983 in Southern Pines, North Carolina--a heart attack while playing golf. He was an avid golfer and played golf with Eisenhower, and played poker with Truman--Truman would sign the dollar bills when he lost. He was also in Warm Springs when Roosevelt died and carried the coffin to the train. He had moved out of the White House detail in 1962 to an administrative role as a step to become the Director of the Secret Service--his widow had it confirmed from several sources after Kennedy was assassinated. He never got that job but she did tell me that he had to replace sev-

eral of the White House detail under Johnson because the agents disliked LBJ so much John never spoke of the assassination. But he did tell me that he had been asked personally by Bobby Kennedy to head up his security detail when Bobby decided to run for President. He said he told him no, because he knew that Bobby would never follow John's instructions on security.

Larry Fox, the son-in-law of the late former agent Rudolph Marion "Pete" McDavid, 11/12/11:

Pete, who did the advance and the security for the Cape Canaveral visit for JFK 11/18/63, had been told by the head of the Dallas office [Forrest V. Sorrels] (they served on the WHD together in 1939-1940[2]) he would be needed in Dallas, but the day before the early Florida departure he was told he was no longer needed.

Elizabeth Willard Wilson, the granddaughter of the late former agent Jack Willard, 1/20/09:

Jack Willard was an agent for FDR in the 1940's. Thank you – I did not know he was mentioned in former Chief Frank Wilson's book!"

Mike Wood, whose ancestor was the late former agent Frank Kenney, 3/7/16:

He was active in the WH Detail for FDR. He was in the Service from 1941 to 1966. I have several photos of Frank on duty with FDR (Potsdam, where he was personally requested by Churchill), Truman, Nixon (when he was VP), Kennedy, and Johnson. Frank was part of the protective detail for FDR at Tehran Conference in November 1943. As you know, a Nazi assignation plot against FDR/Churchill was foiled during this conference by the KGB. Frank Kenney met Churchill during his visit to Washington in late December 1941. Churchill asked for Agent Kenney whenever he came to the USA. Agent Frank Kenney also carried the U.N. Charter handcuffed to his wrist on the plane from S.F. to N.Y. in June 1945.

A close relative of former SAIC Mike Reilly contacted me looking for more information, as well.

I suppose it pays to be a Secret Service expert.

---

2. Unless it was a temporary assignment that he failed to mention during his Warren Commission and HSCA testimony, there is no evidence that Sorrels, the SAIC of the Dallas field office, was a member of FDR's White House Detail. Sorrels did work on FDR's 1936 trip to Dallas.

SECRET SERVICE DRINKING DURING THE FDR ERA

"At 9:20 A.M., on January 21, dressed in a felt hat and gray suit, [FDR] set off in an olive-drab Daimler limousine escorted by motorcycles, reconnaissance cars, and a pair of jeeps bristling with Secret Service agents.... To distract curious onlookers from the Daimler, Secret Service agents stood in their jeeps and pointed at the sky or pretended to tumble halfway out of the vehicles. Outside Rabat, agents erected a privacy screen and lifted Roosevelt from the car into the front seat of a jeep. "Patton, immaculate in jodhpurs and gloves, greeted him with a salute and a crinkled grin. Though he hid it well, the strain of guaranteeing security for SYMBOL [the Casablanca Conference] had exhausted him. At three one morning Patton barged into the Secret Service command post at Anfa. 'The Heinies know the president is here and they're coming to get him!' he warned. The Agents calmed him down and sent him packing – 'They are a bunch of cheap detectives always smelling of drink,' Patton fumed. The demands of this inspection trip further inflamed him. First, [Gen. Mark] Clark had ordered him to find some 'Negro troops who had participated in our landings' to show the president, who was considered partial to Negroes. Then the Secret Service insisted that all 20,000 troops under review be disarmed and kept 300 feet from the road; soldiers could keep their rifles but no bullets. Now as the motorcade rolled through the 2nd Armored Division, a dozen agents kept their submachine guns trained on the docile troops standing at attention. Patton was furious....

"Cold rain drenched the Secret Service agents in their jeeps on the return to Casablanca. The sight pleased Patton, who was riding in the Daimler with the president...."[3]

The Secret Service was fond of the paternal, elderly FDR and the feeling seemed to be mutual. During long motorcades in the cold and rain, the Secret Service would engineer predetermined pit stops in order for the president to rest, dry off, and have a glass of brandy before returning to the motorcade for the vast amount of spectators to cheer him on. One time, agent James Griffith leaped over the rear seat and onto President Roosevelt as a foreign object came hurtling into the car during a long motorcade in the Bronx. When they became untangled and the president discovered it was merely a bagel, FDR shared a hearty laugh about it![4] The SAIC of FDR's detail, Mike Reilly, wrote this about President Frank-

---

3. *An Army at Dawn* by Rick Atkinson (2007), p. 290-291.
4. *The Secret Service* (History Channel, 1995).

lin Roosevelt: "First of all, he was a nice guy…He never was "one of the boys," although he frequently made a good try. It was such a good try that it never quite came off…When you did something for him that he felt was either a favor or a task well done he told you about it. On the other hand, if you erred he let you know he was displeased. Quietly, but thoroughly. He relaxed among his friends with something approximating gusto. He laughed easily and hard. He contributed a great deal to the hilarity of his gatherings of friends, yet, in fairness, I must say I always suspected the roars of appreciative laughter that greeted his sallies stemmed as often from reverence as they did from his humor. The President was very moderate in everything he did. He ate substantially, but not to excess, although he was inordinately fond of game and fish. His weight was always a serious problem, not only on purely aesthetic grounds, but because every pound made his braces more painful…His drinking was moderate, too. He did like a cocktail or two before dinner, and because he drank them in the privacy of his home he could see no reason including votes why he should not drink them at public banquets. So he did. He liked martinis and bourbon old-fashioneds. His after-dinner drink, which he rarely took, was scotch and soda. But he invariably made quite a ceremony of the pre-dinner cocktail, mixing it himself with great enthusiasm and a running commentary for his friends. Whenever he was in a gathering where there was prolonged drinking he would ask for a "horse's neck," a drink made of ginger ale, lemon peel, and no alcohol. "[5]

SECRET SERVICE AGENT PAUL PATERNI – THE MAN, THE ENIGMA

---

5. *Reilly of the White House*, pages 56-58.

Deputy Chief Paul J. Paterni was a member of the OSS, the predecessor of the CIA, during WWII and served in Milan, Italy with fellow OSS men James Jesus Angleton, and Ray Rocca, later liaison to the Warren Commission.[6] Chief Inspector Michael Torina wrote to me, stating the following: "Specifically, Paul Paterni (my very good friend) served [in the Secret Service] from the late 1930's through the mid-1960's,"[7] which means that Paterni was a member of the OSS at the same time he was a member of the Secret Service. PRS Agent Frank Stoner also wrote to me: "Paul Paterni was a great agent and I did know about [his service in the] OSS."[8] When I asked former agent Walt Coughlin, "Did you know about Deputy Chief Paul Paterni's OSS background in WWII?" he responded, "Had heard that."[9] Paterni then went on to replace Russell "Buck" Daniels as Assistant Chief on 1/31/61 at the start of the Kennedy administration.[10]

In fact, according to press reports, Paterni was a leading candidate to become the Chief:

Secret Service chief resigns

WASHINGTON (UPI) — U. E. Baughman, chief of the U.S. Secret Service since 1948, submitted his resignation today effective Aug. 31.

Treasury Secretary Douglas Dillon accepted "with genuine regret" Baughman's decision to retire after 33 years service.

The Secret Service is responsible for guarding the life of the President and his family. Its major assignment is to stamp out counterfeiting of U.S. currency and coins.

There was no announcement of Baughman's successor. But Treasury sources said the job may go to Paul J. Paterni, deputy chief who was transferred to Washington less than a year ago. He previously headed the agency's Chicago office.

---

6. Julius Mader, *Who's Who in the CIA* (Berlin: Julius Mader, 1968); *Cloak and Gown*, p. 363; Burton Hersh, *The Old Boys: The American Elite and the Origins of the CIA* (New York: Scribner's, 1992), p. 182.

7. Letter to author 12/5/97.

8. E-mail to author dated 1/19/04.

9. E-mail to author dated 2/29/04.

10. *Washington Post*, 1/27/61.

As anyone who has read my first book would know, Paterni played a huge yet largely under-reported role in the JFK assassination aftermath that made him a central figure into both the investigation of the evidence against Oswald and the actual evidence itself, especially in regard to the critical chain of possession of that evidence. Yet, so little about him is known or reported that he truly is an enigma. Thus, his importance to the not-so-Secret-Service story.

A Montana law enforcement officer who adamantly requested that I not reveal his identity wrote me the following (after I confirmed his bona fides):

> I am a Sr. Deputy Sheriff in Missoula, Montana. This is where Paul Paterni retired to at the end of his career. I however never met Mr. Paterni but, through a chain of events, I met his wife in the mid 1990's. She had called 911 thinking someone had shot a hole in her home. I then had the chance to sit down and talk for almost 2 hours to one of the most interesting ladies I have ever met! I am writing for a few reasons to you. I remember her name being Rosellini Paterni. I ask you to correct me if my memory has failed. She also told me of her work in the underground in Italy during WWII with her family. I would love to research more about her also, do you know her maiden name? During my talk with her about Presidents she ever met, when I spoke of JFK, she even began to cry as she talked of him. She showed me so many items and told so many stories... I wish I had more time then to talk with her. When I returned to check on her, the house was empty. I do not know where she went. I heard she had a son in Billings, Montana but am not sure. I expect at the time I write this, she has passed on. During my visit, she gave me a folder that she told me President Johnson gave to Paul as a Christmas Present. The folder was made by JFK and is etchings printed from the plates used to print money and other stocks etc. The Presidential Seal is on the cover. She stated JFK only had about 100 to 200 copies of this folder of Presidential Etchings made. I have attempted to research this item even calling the US Treasury. I was even told after many calls that they have never seen one since the 1960's, not even thinking any existed anymore. I had an appraisal on it but I don't think the appraiser knew anything about it. Do you know anything about it? Paul was with the Secret Service and OSS. President Roosevelt called his mother upon Paul's arrival in North Africa. After the war ended he returned to the Secret Service. Paterni was Deputy Chief of the Secret Service under President Kennedy and was very much involved in the investigations after the President was shot."

Incredibly, Paterni was on the game show *What's My Line* on 1/28/62[11], as was Gerald Behn (on 12/27/59)[12] and Chief U.E. Baughman (on 11/27/55[13]; Baughman was also on the game show *To Tell The Truth* on 4/9/57[14]).

The law enforcement officer wrote back with this photograph and information, presumably from a Paterni relative or friend:

Mrs. Paul Paterni

"Rossana Paterni was so regal, so elegant and yet such a homebody, too, that it's hard to image the daring and extraordinarily dangerous feats she performed as a young woman.

Paterni, who was born in Florence, Italy, and died April 2011 in Missoula at the age of 89, was a young woman when Nazi troops occupied Florence during World War II.

Italian partisans waged guerrilla warfare against them, their efforts aided by Rossana and her sister, Lea.

The women rode their bikes through the Tuscan hills and boarded trains packed with German soldiers, carrying messages back and forth among partisan groups. "They just jumped right in," said her son, Mike Paterni, of Missoula.

11. https://www.youtube.com/watch?v=5GydR4aQMXc
12. https://www.youtube.com/watch?v=sso3PL-sLbk
13 https://en.wikipedia.org/wiki/U._E._Baughman
14 https://www.youtube.com/watch?v=5Ek41o3aahk

The risk was immeasurable and Rossana's awareness of it was deeply personal. All four of her brothers were partisans and her younger brother, Dante Valobra, was one of 30 men shot by German soldiers as retaliation for a partisan action, Mike Paterni said.

"If someone had found her out, it wouldn't have ended well," he said.

Her life continued to be adventurous after the war, when she went to work as a secretary in a British military intelligence office in Florence. Rossana Valobra spoke no English. But she often talked with Paul Paterni, an American in the Office of Strategic Services (the U.S. agency that preceded the CIA), who was stationed in the British unit and was fluent in Italian.

Theirs was an old-fashioned courtship, Mike Paterni said, strictly supervised by her parents, Benvenuto Vaolobra and Aurelia Taglietti. The two married in Italy, but moved soon afterward to the United States, first to Michigan, where Paul Paterni had roots that were foreign in ways that went beyond life in a different country.

"Her parents had been successful business people" living in a cosmopolitan city, Mike Paterni said. Paul Paterni's family emigrated from Italy to Michigan's Upper Peninsula, where the men worked in copper mines.

"You can imagine the contrast," her son said. "But they just loved her."

The couple stayed just long enough in Detroit, where Paul Paterni worked for the Secret Service, for her to fall in love with his family, too, then began decades of moving around the country as her husband rose through the ranks of the Secret Service, retiring from the agency as deputy chief. The couple retired to Missoula in 1973, Rossana Paterni finally accepting the fact that they'd never return to Italy.

While she'd had been an athletic young woman, cycling and hiking in Tuscany and northern Italy, she largely focused on her home in her later years.

"She mostly liked to be at home. She didn't like too much to go out," said her friend, Giuseppina "Pina" Fellin, of Missoula.

Home, after all, was where her family was. Rossana Paterni maintained her Italian traditions when she moved to this country. She spoke Italian with friends such as Fellin, she cooked wonderfully and in quantity for whomever walked through her door, but more than anything, her family was the center of her world.

"She was just tremendously devoted to family," said Mike Paterni, and her concept of family was all-encompassing. It wasn't unusual, when he was in college, to drop in unannounced "with a horde of hungry friends" who'd within moments find themselves at the table.

"She was as devoted to her sons" – Mike Paterni's brother, Mark, and his family live in Baltimore – "as only an Italian mother can be," said Susan Wright, Rossana Paterni's neighbor in the Rattlesnake, where she lived in her final years. That devotion went both ways, Wright said.

"This is the most incredible son on earth," Wright said of Mike Paterni. "He was over here at least once a day, every day."

Paul Paterni died in 1984[15], leaving "a tremendous hole in my mom's heart," Mike Paterni said. Fortunately, Mike and Kathy Paterni's daughter Jin came along a year later.

"From the moment Rossana laid eyes on that baby and that baby laid eyes on her, it was incredible," Wright said.

Mike Paterni said that when Jin was older, she acquired a big black Lab, Oscar, who quickly came to occupy a similar place in his mother's heart. "The dog would crawl up on the couch with my mother," he said.

This, in a home that Rossana Paterni kept immaculate, surrounding herself with fine things.

"She had nice paintings and a few sculptures. ... She had very, very good taste," Fellin said. "Rosanna, she was very simple and she dressed really simple, but really elegant. She knew what nice things were."

But the tiny, lovely woman also had another stereotypically Italian characteristic.

"Ooooh, that temper!" Wright said. "She would just get…" Wright clenched her fist and shook it.

When other homes were being built in the neighborhood, the noise and dirt bothered Paterni something fierce, Wright said.

She'd go out and let the workmen know in no uncertain terms, Wright said. "And then she'd start laughing and make them coffee. They all called her Grandma Rossana."

When Paterni died, her son found a copy of "Italian Boys at Fort Missoula, Montana, 1941-1943," longtime Missoula resident Umberto Benedetti's account of the Italians interned there during World War II.

Paterni was friends with Benedetti and Alfredo Cipolato, who like Benedetti was detained at Fort Missoula, and with others in Missoula's small but close-knit Italian community.

Benedetti died in 2009, Cipolato a year earlier. Now, Paterni.

"She had a long life," her son Mike said, "and we got to share it with her."

---

15. Paul Paterni died 2/5/84: *Washington Post*, 2/15/84.

From a 1/11/09 follow-up e-mail from the law enforcement officer:

I do know that Rosellini had her house almost a shrine of Paul's career. She had on her mantle a crystal award Paul was given for being, as I remember her calling it, "Secret Service Agent of the year" or something to this effect. I remember it being something of a crystal pyramid shape. She had about every magazine or book on Kennedy and the assassination. I asked her through her marriage with Paul if she had the chance to meet the different presidents and if so, which ones did she like. As she spoke of Kennedy, she actually cried. The other president she said she met that she thought much of was Nixon. She said behind the scenes, he was a very caring man toward his staff and the agents.

Rosellini told me she was upset because her kids never took an interest in their dad's work or her past history in Italy. At the time I spoke with her, one son worked as a law enforcement officer in the city of Billings, Montana. I am going to contact the department to see if he still works there and if he will talk to me. I would like to even know his mother's maiden name.

Rosellini told me as we sat, that she and her family were a significant part of the Italian underground during WWII. She told me how her and her siblings helped smuggle people through the country. I admit I questioned in my mind all she told me about her and her sibling's big role in WWII in Italy…. that was until she brought out an ACTUAL signed letter threatening her and her family's lives. The letter was signed my Mussolini himself! NO KIDDING! She had saved it from the time period. As a HUGE history buff as I am, I asked her if I could come back off-duty to talk to her and learn more. She was thrilled that somebody cared about history. I came back two weeks later and the house was empty. I have no idea what happened. I saw no obituaries in the paper so I assume a family member came and took her [indeed, his message was sent long before she passed away].

As for the folder I sent the pictures of, one appraiser told me it was worth $3000 as it sits. If I was to frame each lithograph professionally and sell them, I could get as much as $5000. I would NEVER split the set. The appraiser was astonished that one of these folders still existed as all were thought to have disappeared or been destroyed during the Johnson administration.

Agents Jim Rowley, Jerry Behn and others on FDR's Al Capone armored vehicle.

IT SEEMS ROOSEVELT'S BACKUP CAR WAS AL CAPONE'S LINCOLN

From a *Washington Post* article dated 9/13/1976:

> Morgan L. Gies, a veteran Secret Service agent who drove for President Franklin D. Roosevelt, was recalling how a 1937 armored Lincoln that originally had been owned by gangster Al Capone had ended up as Roosevelt's back-up limousine when he suddenly stopped. "I don't think that's come out yet," he snapped. "Don't print that."

Actually, it already was a matter of record and in print. In former SAIC of the FDR detail Mike Reilly's book, he wrote: "Mr. President, I've taken the liberty of getting a new car. It's armored, I'm afraid it's a little uncomfortable, and I know it has a dubious reputation." "Dubious reputation?"

"Yes, sir. It belonged to Al Capone. The Treasury Department had a little trouble with Al, you know, and they got it from him in the subsequent legal complications. I got it from Treasury."

The Boss looked at it a moment and said, "This is very interesting. I hope Mr. Capone doesn't mind."[16]

During the FDR administrations (1933-1945), agents rode on or near the rear of the limousine frequently, many motorcycles surrounded Roosevelt's car, and building rooftops were guarded. Former agent Frank Stoner sent the author several great photos of himself and his colleagues during the FDR, Truman, and JFK days. Included was a particularly compelling picture of Kellerman walking beside FDR's limousine in

16. *Reilly of the White House*, page 28.

Fort Worth, Texas, while fellow future ASAIC John Campion, the man Kellerman replaced, walks on the opposite side of the car. In yet another photo he sent, future JFK SAIC Gerald Behn rides the fender of FDR's car. FDR knew of the risks firsthand: he faced an assassination attempt on 2/15/33 in Miami, Florida by gunman Giuseppe Zangara. As Roosevelt appeared in his open car, Zangara fired five shots, killing Chicago Mayor Anton Cermak and wounding Secret Service agent Robert Clark and several others. As with the later attempt on Ford on 9/22/75, it was a civilian, perhaps two,-who thwarted the assassin by grabbing his arm.[17]

Regarding the death of FDR on 4/12/45 at Warm Springs, GA, agent Floyd Boring said: "I'll tell you why I remember [the death of FDR]; there was a move on foot for [Chief] Frank J. Wilson to remove all the agents from the White House Detail. I had been on the White House Detail, and that was kind of worrisome to me. But I found out that I wasn't one of the people they were shooting for, so I stayed there."[18]

17. *Looking Back and Seeing The Future, pages 29-30; The Secret Service Story* by Michael Dorman, pages 57-58; *The Secret Service* 1995 History Channel.
18. Boring's Truman Library oral history, 9/21/88.

MEMBERS OF THE WHITE HOUSE DETAIL (AND RELATED AGENTS) DURING THE FDR ERA, 1933-1945 [WHD IN 1939: 16+2 SUPERVISORS; WHD START OF WWII: 37][19]:

HOWARD S. ANDERSON, JULIAN T. BABER, JIM M. BEARY, GERALD A. BEHN, J. FRANK BLACKISTONE, GEORGE F. BOOS, FLOYD BORING, ROBERT BOUCK, JOHN E. CAMPION, WILLIAM D. CAWLEY, FREDERICK M. CLARK, ROBERT CLARK, ANDREW G. DAIGLE, WILBUR DECKARD, JOHN H. DORSEY, GEORGE C. DRESCHER, JOHN FALLON, JOHN FITZGERALD (PRS), CHARLIE FREDERICKS, JAMES J. GARVEY, AUGUST "GUS" GENNERICH[20], MORGAN L. GIES, ROWLAND GODDARD, SAMUEL T. GOLDMAN, JOHNNY T. GORHAM, JOHN L. GRENNAN, JIM H. GRIFFITH, WALTER HAMAN, TOM H. HANSON, PAUL M. HART, BOB R. HASTINGS, JAMES HEALY, ELMER R. HIPSLEY, JAMES M. HIRST, ROBERT E. HOLMES, LEONARD P. HUTCHINSON (PRS), DICK JERVIS, WILLIAM KARP, ROY KELLERMAN, FRANK J. KENNEY (Oregon), WILLIAM F. LOWERY, CHARLES F. "KEITH" LUMMIS, FRANK A. LYONS, Assistant Chief JAMES MALONEY, White House Police Captain HERBERT L. MARCEY, JOHN MARSHALL, MAURICE G. MARTINEAU, FRANK MASI, GERARD B. MCCANN, RUDOLPH "PETE" MCDAVID, GERALD J. MCGINNISS, LT. COL. GEORGE J. MCNALLY, LEE MONTGOMERY, CHIEF WILLIAM H. MORAN (1917-1936); DAN L. MORIARTY, Assistant Chief JOSEPH E. MURPHY, FRANK MURRAY, Assistant Chief HARRY NEAL, VAL NOLAN, JR., DANIEL J. O'DRISCOLL, JOHN E. OSBORN, PAUL J. PATERNI, GEORGE W. PEARS, ALBERT L. PECK, BURRILL A. PETERSON, JAMES R. PRATHER, THOMAS J. QUALTERS (ASAIC 1943), C.R. RAUM, MIKE F. REILLY (ASAIC, 1941-1943; SAIC, 1943-1945), JAMES J. ROWLEY, ROLAND M. SAVAGE, GEORGE A. SCHNELBACH, ARTHUR SECKLER, NEAL SHANNON, WILLIAM D. SIMMONS, JIM SLOAN, FORREST V. SORRELS, ASAIC GUY SPAMAN, VERNON D. SPICER, COL. EDMUND W. STARLING, FRANK G. STONER, STEWART G. STOUT, JR., HENRY C. TAGGART, JOHN S. TUCKER, EDMUND J. WATERS, DALE B. WHITESIDE, JACK L. WILLARD, ROGER WILLIAMS, FRANK J. WILSON – Chief (1936-1946), FRANK B. WOOD

---

19. Based on numerous reports in the FDR presidential library (travel logs).
20. FDR's favorite Secret Service agent, according to SAIC Mike Reilly: *Reilly of the White House*, page 110.

CHAPTER EIGHT

THE AGENT WHO WAS TOO CLOSE TO LBJ

Emory P. Roberts

Agent Emory Roberts was the President's receptionist during the Johnson administration while still a member of the Secret Service, effectively replacing loyal JFK aide Dave Powers. This is an unprecedented, disturbing and unique position that Roberts held, as the agents are supposed to be apolitical and certainly not to be holding a parallel position in the administration. Roberts is an agent already under deep suspicion for not moving to President Kennedy's aide during the assassination, ordering the agents not to move during the shooting, and even recalling two agents at Love Field during the very start of the motorcade.[1]

What's more, there are alarming parallels between what LBJ thought of Roberts and what he thought of Bobby Baker, a man he referred to as his son (Baker was his longtime aide who was later embroiled in scandal, serving time in jail): "Bobby is my strong right arm. He is the last person I see at night and the first person I see in the morning." LBJ said this of Roberts on 11/23/68: "He greets me every morning and tells me good-bye every night."

1. See chapters one and ten in *Survivor's Guilt: The Secret Service and the Failure to Protect President Kennedy* (2013).

Since publication of my first book, *Survivor's Guilt,* I found out that ole LBJ went even further to help Roberts' career, nominating him for the highly prestigious, influential and high-paying U.S. Parole Board, perhaps with a nod to bail him or his cronies out in case they were in immediate legal peril, as the following two obscure and long-forgotten news article excerpts confirm:

A White House Receptionist Nominated for Parole Board

WASHINGTON, Oct. 1 (AP) — President Johnson announced today that he would nominate a Secret Service agent, Emory P. Roberts, who has been a White House receptionist since 1965, to be a member of the United States Board of Parole.

Hold Up 155 Nominated For Jobs By Johnson

By FRANCES LEWINE

WASHINGTON (AP) — President Nixon has withdrawn 155 nominations—including two ambassadors, five judges and dozens of postmasters—submitted to the Senate by Lyndon Johnson in the last days of his administration.

Press Secretary Ronald L. Ziegler said Nixon wants a chance to review them all case-by-case "without prejudice." "There is a possibility," Ziegler

Also involved was Emory P. Roberts of Maryland, a veteran Secret Service agent who had been appointed to the Federal Parole Board. Roberts is still on duty in his post as a receptionist in the West Lobby of the White House, where visitors come through to see the President.

Youngstown Firm Bids Low on Park Dam Job

'RECEPTIONIST'

President Johnson's White House staff, still undergoing a shakedown, has acquired a Secret Service agent to serve as a "receptionist."

Emory Roberts, 50, who has been with the service for 21 years, sat down Wednesday at the big reception desk in the lobby of the west wing which official greeter David Powers has occupied since 1961.

New Receptionist

One change — not connected with the inaugural — has been the placing of a Secret Service agent in the job of White House receptionist.

Emory Roberts, a 20-year veteran of the service and longtime member of the White House detail, replaced David Powers, a Kennedy crony and Boston politician who was given the post by the late president.

Roberts is the first receptionist to be an active Secret Service agent as well. His assignment to a job that had been traditionally filled by a political appointment was a clear indication that security had become the overriding consideration.

Herald-Journal - Jan 15, 1965 Browse this

Secrecy-Lid Clamped On LBJ Staff Changes

WASHINGTON (AP) — The White House Wednesday clamped a secrecy lid for the time being on changes in President Johnson's staff, expanding an earlier bar to the disclosure of staff salaries.

The question of the current composition of Johnson's official family came up after a veteran Secret Service agent, Emory Roberts, was seen performing the receptionist chores formerly carried out by David F. Powers, who was a close friend of the late President John F. Kennedy.

Asked about Roberts' day-long appearance at the receptionist's desk in the White House lobby, Press Secretary George E. Reedy said the presidential body guard was carrying out his regular assignment as a Secret Service agent. Reedy referred vaguely to Roberts' checking the passes of people passing through the lobby. Reporters observed no pass-checking by Roberts, but did see him greeting Japanese Prime Minister Eisaku Sato, and other visitors.

Reedy was asked whether Powers, a Kennedy appointee, had resigned.

"I've not seen any resignation from him," Reedy replied.

The press secretary said that he would say nothing about the status of the White House staff until he could give "a complete picture at one time."

Several weeks ago, Reedy said he would not discuss the salaries of the staff until he could similarly cite all salaries at one time.

MRS. JESSIE MAXWELL

Services for Mrs. Jessie W. Maxwell, formerly of Spartanburg County who died Monday at New York, 2 Saturday Hopewell Baptist Church, the Rev. S. E. Kay. Burial Mayfield Chapel Cemetery.

J. W. Woodward Funeral Home.

GREER DRIVE-IN
GREER, S. C.   TONITE
1st RUN   In Color

Emory Roberts listening to President Johnson.

Roberts had Johnson's ear and vice versa.

Less than 24 hours after an actual umbrella man was at the site of the JFK assassination with Roberts, Agent Roberts holds an open umbrella over the new president's head while fellow agent Jerry Kivett, also in the Dallas motorcade, looks on in disgust.

From a memo President Johnson read to Agent Youngblood shortly after the murder: "Morale in the Secret Service is at an all-time low. A number of agents of the White House Detail have been asking for transfers. This is a great body of men. These men feel they are being prevented from doing their job properly. They do not want favors; they just want to be accepted. We need them badly ..." LBJ further told Youngblood that " ... somebody in your outfit has been bellyaching to [one of Kennedy's top people] ... There's enough truth in it to see that somebody talked ... you know I can't have disloyalty and I can't talk in front of your people and have them repeat it. I told Chief Rowley that, to call 'em in and take the resignations of anybody who wanted out, and I'll be glad to have his, yours or anybody else's. If they don't want to handle it we can get the FBI to do it ... I'll get Hoover to send me over a couple of twenty-one-year-old accountants and they'll probably do as good a job!" Youngblood responded, "We'll stick with you sir."[2] We now know how LBJ felt about agent Roy Kellerman: "This fellow Kellerman ... he was about as loyal a man as you could find. But he was about as dumb as an ox."[3]Conversely,

2. *20 Years in the Secret Service*, pp. 147-149; This phone conversation was also aired on *The Secret White House Tapes*, A&E Network, 3/97.

3. *Reaching For Glory: Lyndon Johnson's Secret White House Tapes, 1964-1965* by Michael R. Beschloss

LBJ called agent Rufus Youngblood "the dearest of all."[4] Perhaps this is why Youngblood seems to be the only former agent with kind things to say about LBJ: "Of all the presidents, he was probably the most professional politician. Politics was his hobby. He was also the most down-to-earth human being who was in the White House during my time there. Little things bothered the hell out of him. He said to me once that the big decisions didn't bother him, but some of the little bitty things.... He would tell you how to turn a screw clockwise or counterclockwise."[5]

President Kennedy picked Gerald Behn to be the SAIC of the White House Detail. Johnson replaced him with Rufus Youngblood:

WASHINGTON (UPI) — President Kennedy today picked Gerald Behn to head the White House Secret Service detail charged with guarding his life.

N.Y. Herald Tribune Service

WASHINGTON—In an unexpected administrative shake up announced late Friday evening, President Johnson named Rufus W. Youngblood, his longtime personal bodyguard, as head of the Secret Service White House detail.

Former agent Frank Yeager wrote me: "In my opinion, President Johnson did pose more "problems" than President Kennedy because he was much more difficult to deal with on a personal level. He did not try to please anyone that I saw, unless it was his wife, and I am not sure about that." Former agent Walt Coughlin wrote to me his feelings about LBJ: "Didn't like anyone and could be very surly. Hard to protect – did not like to take advice."

It seems LBJ was not generally liked by the agency. As agent Dennis McCarthy wrote, "Johnson had not been very well liked by any of the agents on the detail. He treated us as if we were the hired help on his ranch, cursed at us regularly, and was generally a royal pain to deal with."[6] Agent Sam Kinney told me: "I had my run-ins with LBJ. About the only one

(New York: Simon & Schuster, 2002), p. 703.
4. *20 years in the Secret Service* by Rufus Youngblood, page 230.
5. I spoke to Youngblood in 1992 and 1994.
6. *Protecting the President*, p. 25.

who could tame him was agent Paul Rundle."[7] Regarding the transition from JFK to LBJ, Coughlin wrote, "Transition was very difficult – firstly we were all very despondent and we really liked JFK and it was mutual. LBJ was anything but friendly and he did not want anything to do with us. Also – the culture shock was significant: from Hyannis Port, Palm Beach and Palm Springs to the dirty ranch and cattle guards of south Texas was a real setback."[8] Coughlin later wrote, "LBJ was a first class prick."[9]

That is not to say that everyone from the Secret Service held President Johnson in contempt.

For : Floyd M. Boring
With best regards.

Members of the White House Detail (and Related Agents) During the Jfk & Lbj Administrations[10]:

Howard S. Anderson (SAIC of Personnel), William J. Bacherman, D. Baldelli, Rick Barbuto (VP Humphrey detail), Chief (1961) Urbanus U.E. Baughman, VP LBJ Detail Ger-

---

7. Interview with Kinney 3/5/94. I also corresponded with Rundle once.
8. E-mail to author 2/26/04.
9. E-mail to author 4/27/05.
10. Not including numerous field office agents. Based on numerous sources, including countless interviews with former agents, Secret Service shift reports and other documents, and many books cited in the introduction.

ALD W. BECHTLE, TOM BEHL (guarded JFK in Hyannisport),
SAIC of WHD (Aug 1961-Jan 1965) GERALD A. BEHN, VP LBJ
Detail DONALD BENDICKSON, PRS Agent GLEN A. BENNETT,
ANDREW E. BERGER, WES BISHOP (Training Division), GERALD
S. BLAINE, ARTHUR W. BLAKE (guarded JFK in Hyannisport),
WHS Clerk WALTER BLASCHAK, ABRAHAM W. BOLDEN, SR.
(1961; Chicago office), ASAIC FLOYD M. BORING, SAIC of PRS
ROBERT I. BOUCK, DONALD F. BRETT (guarded JFK in Hyan-
nisport), PERCY HAMILTON "HAM" BROWN, WARNER BROWN,
ROBERT R. BURKE, PAUL A. BURNS, ASAIC JOHN E. CAMPI-
ON (later, Aide to the Assistant Chief for Security), JAMES R.
CANTRELL (guarded JFK in Hyannisport), A. CHALFANT, TOBY
J. CHANDLER, GEORGE CHANEY, JOHN CHIPPS (LBJ era), J. WAL-
TER COUGHLIN, ROGER COUNTS (VP Humphrey detail), Depu-
ty Chief (until 1/31/61) RUSSELL "BUCK" DANIELS, WILLIAM
C. DAVIS, EARL E. DECIMA (member of Transportation Section,
LBJ era), LUBERT F. "BURT" DE FREESE, WHD secretary EVE B.
DEMPSHER, ROBERT DEPROSPERO (LBJ Era), JERRY DOLAN,
PAUL B. DOSTER, Bouck's secretary EDITH E. DUNCAN (had
been Baughman's secretary), WILLIAM L. DUNCAN, ROBERT R.
FAISON, FRANK FARNSWORTH (guarded JFK in Hyannisport),
PRS agent (formerly Ike's driver) DEETER B. "DICK" FLOHR,
ROBERT W. FOSTER, PRS photographer JAMES K. "JACK" FOX,
TOM FRIDLEY, Special Officer STANLEY B. GALUP, STEVE GAR-
MON, BOB GAUGH (guarded JFK in Hyannisport), WILLIAM C.
GEASA, KENNETH S. GIANNOULES, HORACE J. "HARRY" GIBBS,
MORGAN L. GIES, WINSTON GINTZ (guarded JFK in Hyannis-
port), JIM GIOVENETTI (guarded JFK in Hyannisport), Kennedy
children detail JOHN J. GIUFFRE, JACK GLEASON (guarded JFK
in Hyannisport), ATSAIC ARTHUR L. GODFREY, JOHN GOLD-
EN (member of Transportation Section, LBJ era), VP LBJ Detail
JAMES R. GOODENOUGH (also guarded JFK in Hyannisport), DA-
VID B. GRANT (Hill's brother in law), WILLIAM R. GREER, FOR-
REST GUTHRIE, DENNIS R. HALTERMAN, NED HALL II, JAMES M.
HARDIN, COIN HAUK (member of Transportation Section, LBJ
era), HARVEY HENDERSON, BOB HEYN (LBJ era), GEORGE W.
HICKEY, JR., SAIC of Jackie Detail CLINTON J. HILL (later, SAIC
LBJ Detail), GUS HOLMES (member of Transportation Section,
LBJ era), VP LBJ Detail JOHN C. "JACK" HOLTZHAUER, DAR-
WIN HORN, JAMES F. "MIKE" HOWARD (guarded JFK in Hyan-
nisport; LBJ WHD), JOHN JOE HOWLETT, DAN HURLEY (LBJ
era), ANDREW M. HUTCH, KENNETH D. IACOVONI, ROBERT

JAMISON (guarded JFK in Hyannisport), SAIC Jackie Detail (replaced by Hill) JIM JEFFERIES, JFK & ASAIC VP LBJ Detail agent THOMAS L. "LEM" JOHNS (later, SAIC LBJ Detail and Assistant Director), RICHARD E. JOHNSEN, JAMES B. "JIMMY" JOHNSON, VP LBJ Detail JOHN PAUL JONES, RADFORD W. JONES, KENT D. JORDAN, Assistant Director for Administration PHIL JORDAN, DALE E. KEANER, BROOKS T. KELLER, ASAIC ROY H. KELLERMAN, Inspector THOMAS J. KELLEY, FRANK J. KENNEY (Oregon), WILLIAM J. KIERAN, SAMUEL A. KINNEY, VP LBJ Detail JERRY D. KIVETT, SAIC LBJ Ranch CLARENCE KNETSCH, JFK agent & SAIC of VP LBJ Detail H. STUART "STU" KNIGHT, ROBERT L. KOLLAR, Chief Inspector JACKSON N. KRILL, CHARLIE KUNKEL, First Lady Detail PAUL E. LANDIS, JR., ARNOLD LAU (Assistant Director of Training), PRS ELMER C. LAWRENCE, WINSTON G. LAWSON, DONALD J. LAWTON, JAMES E. LE GETTE, SAIC Forgery Division J. LEROY LEWIS, ROBERT E. LILLEY, WILSON "BILL" LIVINGOOD, ROBERT LUTZ, ROGER MANTHE, JAMES M. "MIKE" MASTROVITO, ROBERT MELCHIORI, Kennedy Children Detail LYNN S. MEREDITH, RICHARD METZINGER, Inspector GERARD B. MCCANN, DENNIS V.N. MCCARTHY (LBJ era), JOHN J. MCCARTHY, WILLIAM T. "TIM" MCINTYRE, JERRY MCKINNEY (guarded Lady Bird), BILL MCLARIN (Assistant Director of Training), ASAIC of PRS CHESTER J. MILLER, JIMMY L.C. MILLER, JIM MITCHELL (member of Transportation Section, LBJ era), EARL MOORE, EDWARD MOREY, ED MOUGIN, VINCENT P. MROZ (part-time, JFK era; LBJ), LARRY NEWMAN, ED NOLAND, JOSEPH E. NOONAN, JR., PRS technician HOWARD K. NORTON, ROY "GENE" NUNN, JOHN J. "MUGGSY" O'LEARY, ERNEST E. OLSSON, JR., GERALD W. O'ROURKE, JOSEPH PAOLELLA, JACK PARKER, JERRY PARR, Deputy Chief (replacing Daniels) PAUL J. PATERNI, WILLIAM B. PAYNE, Inspector BURRILL A. PETERSON, PRS MAX D. PHILLIPS, PRS ROBERT PINE (Baughman's brother in law), RONALD M. PONTIUS, HOWELL "HAL" PURVIS, JOHN D. "JACK" READY, EMORY P. ROBERTS, CHUCK ROCHNER, WADE J. RODHAM, RICHARD ROTH, SAIC of WHD (1946-Aug 1961) and Chief (Sept 1961-1973) James J. Rowley, JFK & ATSAIC VP LBJ Detail PAUL S. RUNDLE, HENRY J. "HANK" RYBKA, GARY SEALE (guarded JFK in Hyannisport), VP LBJ Detail MICHAEL J. SHANNON, D. SHAW, BILL SHERLOCK (guarded JFK in Hyannisport), ANTHONY SHERMAN, JR., THOMAS B. SHIPMAN, JOHN SIMPSON, LOIS B. SIMS (30-day temp), BILL SKILES, WILL SLADE (member of Transportation Section, LBJ era), LEON SPENCER (photographer, Visual Intelligence Branch), PRS FRANK G. STONER, AT-SAIC STEWART G. "STU" STOUT, JR., WILLIAM R. STRAUGHN, PHILIP STROTHER, SAMUEL E. SULLIMAN, MAC SWEAZEY, PRS CECIL TAYLOR, VP LBJ Detail CHARLES E. TAYLOR, JR., JIMMY TAYLOR, SAIC LBJ-Nixon (1968-1973) ROBERT H. TAYLOR, VP LBJ Detail WARREN "WOODY" TAYLOR, JERRY TERRY, Head Inspector of PRS ELLIOT C. THACKER, HAL THOMAS (VP Humphrey detail), PAUL THOMPSON, BOB TILL (guarded JFK in Hyannisport), Chief Inspector MICHAEL W. TORINA, RONALD C. TOWNS (SAIC, Intelligence), SCOTT TRUNDLE, EDWARD Z. TUCKER (also helped protect Kennedy children), EDWARD P. WALSH, VP LBJ Detail JOHN F. "JACK" WALSH, DOC WALTERS (guarded JFK in Hyannisport), JOHN W. "JACK" WARNER, JR. III, ROGER WARNER (VP Humphrey detail), GLENN WEAVER, Kennedy children Detail THOMAS H. WELLS, PRS THOMAS WHITE, KENNETH J. WIESMAN, Deputy Chief EDGAR A. WILDY, MILT WILHITE, secretary CARROLL A. WINSLOW, GENE F. WOFFORD, THOMAS WOOGE, A. DALE WUNDERLICH, JOHN F. "FRANK" YEAGER, PRS WALTER H. YOUNG, JFK & ASAIC VP LBJ agent RUFUS W. YOUNGBLOOD (later, SAIC LBJ detail and Assistant Director), CHARLES T. "CHUCK" ZBORIL

LBJ with his Secret Service detail in 1968:

CHAPTER NINE

DEBUNKING AGENT GERALD BLAINE'S THE KENNEDY DETAIL[1]

SA Gerald Blaine (far left), author of *The Kennedy Detail*, and Harvey Henderson (speaking to Blaine, middle), with JFK in 1961 – Henderson was a very racist person who greatly bothered fellow agent Abraham Bolden, while Blaine claims to have been on Abe's temporary shift on the White House Detail in 1961, a matter in some dispute. Abe's book *The Echo From Dealey Plaza* is far superior to Blaine's propaganda[2]

I n his book *The Kennedy Detail*, co-authored by Lisa McCubbin, Blaine writes in the third person, giving the impression that someone else wrote it. Try writing about yourself in that manner. I can't do it myself. It feels like scratching on a blackboard. Why he chose to go this route is beyond me, unless it was done with the goal of clouding who was the author of a partic-

1. This chapter augments and provides additional information to be found in my first book *Survivor's Guilt: The Secret Service & The Failure to Protect President Kennedy* (2013), as well as my popular online review of Blaine's book which can be found on the CTKA website here: http://www.ctka. net/reviews/kennedydetailreview.html. See also: http://ctka.net/reviews/slick_propaganda.html and http://www.ctka.net/reviews/MrsKennedy_Hill_Review_Palamara.html and http://www.ctka. net/2016/book-review-five-presidents/five-presidents-by-clint-hill-with-lisa-mccubbin-a-review. html
2. See chapter 17 of my book *Survivor's Guilt,* re: Bolden, as well as Abraham Bolden's book *The Echo From Dealey Plaza*

ular alleged fact and giving the impression that he was speaking for all the other agents.

Blaine's book has no footnotes, endnotes, links, references, documented quotes or any confirmations that what he writes is true. It's obvious that Blaine is not presenting his book as a scholarly work, but as a biography of sorts. This is actually a great shame. Blaine obviously had a great number of inside contacts, people close to the action who would have felt more comfortable talking with Blaine than with a stranger. To not have all those discussions and interviews documented or recorded for the general public is a great loss. Then again, it serves the purpose of clouding exactly who can be attributable for any and all alleged facts and suppositions.

Instead of providing insight into the assassination, the book drones on about (1) agent's complaining about not getting to eat meals, being away from their families, being overworked, not getting sleep, etc. (2) how fantastic every agent on the detail was, (3) how they couldn't have done anything more than they did to protect the president (4) how thorough the Warren Commission report was, (5) how emotionally affected each agent was after the assassination and (6) how mean people were suggesting that there was a conspiracy. The book was much more concerned with shaping a fictitious image of the Secret Service (or, CYA) and supporting the government fabrication about the tragedy in Dallas than shedding any light on the truth. Many of Blaine's comments are in direct contradiction to facts that even government agencies have indicated were true while other comments just gloss over anything that might interfere with his "reality".[3]

Just a handful of questions the book raises:

> Many of the agents in Dallas were out partying into the early morning hours of November 22. Even if, as he states, they were off duty and not inebriated, the question left unanswered is why weren't they back at the hotel sleeping since throughout the book they complain about not getting enough rest. He talks about how stressful they expected the day to be and how important "mental alertness" was for them being able to do their job. And yet, somehow, he doesn't see the inherent contradiction.

---

3. Former Secret Service agent Gerald Blaine claimed in 2010 that actress Marilyn Monroe was in President Kennedy's company only twice, and briefly. In his memoir, he wrote that "These were the only … times that I or any of the agents I have discussed this with remember Marilyn Monroe being in proximity to the president." That same year, Ronald Kessler's book, *In the President's Secret Service: Behind the Scenes with Agents in the Line of Fire and the Presidents They Protect* hit the bookstores. "According to Secret Service agents, Kennedy had sex with Marilyn Monroe at New York hotels and in a loft above the Justice Department office of then Attorney General Robert F. Kennedy, the president's brother," wrote Kessler.

Why was Johnson's detail already covering LBJ, who wasn't even a target, while Kennedy's detail still hadn't even reacted because "they weren't sure if what they heard was gunfire?"

In what fantasy world does anyone actually believe that Ruby killed Oswald because of how much he cared about the Kennedy family?

Why does agent Paul Landis, who at the time, says he thought at least one of the shots came from the grassy knoll and saw someone running in that direction after the fact, realize "when he thought back with a rational mind" years later that he was wrong? What pressure was applied to give him a clearer memory?

Why does Blaine see no validity in any assassination conspiracy theory yet when he couldn't sell the Secret Service IBM equipment, he placed blame on a conspiracy to pay him back for leaving the Service?

Blaine says Chief Rowley told agents to lie whenever asked if the president ordered them to stay off the back of his car in an effort to "protect the president." *What other lies might have been told in order to "protect" each other?*[4]

That being said, certain major points are easily refuted:

The book claims that the agents "Break Their Silence" in that they have not spoken since 1963, as if the Warren Commission, Manchester's best-seller, the HSCA, various interviews, and several other books, including my own[5], never happened in the intervening years.

Mr. Blaine states that President Eisenhower almost always rode in a closed car.

WRONG: the exact opposite is true. In point of fact, Ike often rode in an open limo , and ironically, Blaine's friend, Clint Hill, corroborated this point in his 2016 book *Five Presidents.*

Mr. Blaine states that JFK hardly ever rode in the limousine with the bubble top on the car.

WRONG: again, just by doing a Google image search, I found at least twenty five different times – in good weather – that President

---

4. A researcher in Florida wrote me: "Vince, I watched JFK in Tampa 50th Anniversary on PBS in Tampa last night. Guess who 2 of the main narrators were? Agents Blaine and Zboril spreading their usual bullshit about how JFK ordered them off the back of the car in Tampa because he wanted to be seen and how shocked they were. And yet every film, both private and professional in this documentary showed the agents riding on the back of the limo or running alongside. I guess we should believe them and not our lying eyes! It went into great detail about how there was an officer on every building and officers and agents in the streets to control the crowds. One film that really stuck out was a clip that showed 4 agents on the sides of the Queen Mary, 2 on the back of the limo and 2 running on the sides. Then you get Blaine smirking about what fun that trip was not knowing what lay ahead later that week."
5. My first book was available in some shape or form as a self-published entity since 1993.

Kennedy rode under the top (New York, Boston, Caracas, Paris, Ireland, England, etc.).

Mr. Blaine, during an earlier interview with myself, thought SAIC Gerald Behn was on the Tampa trip–

WRONG: It was actually ASAIC Floyd Boring. Mr. Behn was on vacation.[6] This seemingly innocent error is highly disturbing because Blaine speaks so authoritatively about what transpired on the Tampa trip, even using unsourced direct quotes from memory. How can Blaine write so authoritatively that he heard Boring over the radio relaying JFK's alleged instruction to remove Zboril and Lawton from the rear of the limousine in his book when, several years before, he told me it was *another* completely different agent on the trip? Likewise, his good friend, former agent and *Kennedy Detail* contributor Chuck Zboril, also on the Tampa trip (riding on the rear of JFK's limo, no less), erroneously thought Roy Kellerman was in charge of the Tampa trip and riding in the front seat of the presidential limo! Again, this is disturbing for the very same reasons, as Zboril vigorously defends Blaine's views in media appearances.[7] How can Zboril support Blaine's later-day Boring story when he thought it was yet *another* agent on the trip?[8] How can both Blaine and Zboril, with a straight face, endorse the story they attribute to Boring in Blaine's book when both

---

6. "Blaine even erroneously thought [SAIC Gerald] Behn was on the Florida trip, a testament to the frequency of his [Behn's] trips with the president." *Survivor's Guilt*, page 121 [author's interview with Blaine 2/7/04].

7. "Zboril was sure that Kellerman, who wasn't even on the Florida trip, was present in Tampa: "I thought it was Roy Kellerman, not Boring, in the car on the Tampa trip…that's my recollection." *Survivor's Guilt*, page 294 [author's interview with Chuck Zboril 11/15/95]. Interestingly, a 6/1/77 photo of Zboril with President Jimmy Carter and Vice President Walter Mondale comes with the caption stating that "Zboril was a young agent scheduled to be on the back of President John F. Kennedy's limousine on the day he was assassinated in Dallas, Texas" [Alamy.com; Ken Hawkins Pictures].

8. Postscript: it is a total non-issue about Boring telling the agents to not ride on the rear of the limousine right before the Texas trip. I BELIEVE this indeed happened (page 43 of my first book) and I also have no doubt that, if I was given the chance to speak to many of Blaine's colleagues circa late 1963-1965 (or perhaps even later), those gentlemen would have "rained on my parade" in droves and told me the fib that JFK ordered the agents off his limo (bottom of page 52 of my first book). The point is the *credibility* of this action by Boring, NOT that Boring performed this action of telling the agents not to ride there (albeit disobeyed by Agent Clint Hill – 4 times – on Main Street in Dallas!). By credibility, I mean that I do NOT believe JFK had anything to do with this – this was a decision made by Floyd Boring for reasons that appear sinister yet, at the same time, seem hard to fathom (according to what Tampa motorcycle officer Russell Groover told me, the point is a moot one: agents did not ride on the rear of the limo during the FINAL LEG of the long journey because the limo was going at a fast rate of speed in a residential area. In any event, both Groover and Congressman Sam Gibbons both told me that they heard no order from JFK. Even believing Boring's 1996 "story" to the ARRB, what JFK allegedly conveyed to him was hardly an order of any kind… and it was one that Hill ignored in any case). It was only with the advent of time, the release of films, photos, records, the ARRB, the internet, etc., as well as contacting White House aides/ non-Secret Service agents like Dave Powers with no horse in the race (no reason to lie and cover-up) that the truth came out. Take your pick: were the agents lying in 1963-1965 or were they lying to me?.

thought it was another person substituting on the trip? I think this is perhaps the biggest clue – the smoking gun – as to the lack of credibility in Blaine's book.

Interestingly, yet another agent I spoke to, Lynn Meredith, admittedly not on the Tampa trip and relying on the stories told by "good friends who were there," also believed Roy Kellerman, not Boring, was on the Tampa trip.[9] Finally, Zboril takes me to task (in his review of my first book on Amazon, of all places) for naming Agent David Grant (Clint Hill's brother-in-law) as an advance agent for the Tampa trip, yet the Warren Report itself confirms Grant's role[10]:

> work. Consequently, Agent Lawson did the advance work alone from November 13 to November 18, when he was joined by Agent David B. Grant, who had just completed advance work on the President's trip to Tampa.

Ironically, Zboril told me: "If you read it in there [the Warren Report], it happened." If that weren't enough, lead advance agent Win Lawson, who actually worked with Grant, told me that Grant *"had been on advance in Florida."*[11]

Mr. Blaine blames Kennedy for the top not being on the car in Dallas –

WRONG: agent Sam Kinney was adamant to me that he (Kinney) was solely responsible for the top's removal.

Mr. Blaine, in an online video, said that fellow agent Art Godfrey "gave his blessings" to his book-

WRONG: by his own admission, Mr. Blaine did not even begin his book until over three years *after* Mr. Godfrey passed away![12]

Mr. Blaine states in an online video that he "has never spoken to an author of a book"[13]-

WRONG: He spoke to both William Manchester and myself. Manchester's book references a 5/12/65 interview. What's more, Mr. Blaine is thanked by Mr. Manchester in his other JFK book *One Brief Shining Moment*. Thus, Mr. Blaine is 2 for 2: he is in both Manchester JFK books. In addition, Mr. Blaine spoke to myself in both 2004 and 2005, as well as corresponding via e-mail during this time. And, incidentally, Blaine *told* me he spoke to Manchester.

---

9. *Survivor's Guilt*, page 32.
10. Warren Report, page 445.
11. *Survivor's Guilt*, page 268.
12. https://www.youtube.com/watch?v=U_YqC5NJASA
13. https://www.youtube.com/watch?v=IbD1shPmla8

Mr. Blaine states, in yet another online video, that he specifically never spoke to Mr. Manchester.[14]

WRONG: (see above).

Mr. Blaine writes on page 201 of his book that the presidential limo "just didn't gather speed as quickly as he [Agent Greer] would like."

WRONG: Agent Kellerman told the Warren Commission under oath "we literally jumped out of the God-damned road" and many films depict the limousine traveling at a very high rate of speed (Agent Lilley told me that the limo reached speeds of over 50 mph – with both him and Agent Kellerman on the rear of the car – during one motorcade).

Mr. Blaine, on pages 221-222 of his book, referring to the president's physician, Admiral George Burkley, writes: "Normally the admiral rode in a staff car in the motorcade, or in the rear seat of the follow-up car, but he and the president's secretary, Evelyn Lincoln, had misjudged the timing of the motorcade's departure from Love Field and wound up scurrying to the VIP bus. He was furious for not having been in his normal seat but had nobody to blame but himself."

WRONG: Burkley protested that the Secret Service placed him further away from JFK than he normally rode (on 11/18/63 he rode in the lead car) – see Burkley's JFK Library oral history, among other sources.

Mr. Blaine writes, on page 74 of his book: "... the only way to have a chance at protecting the president against a shooter from a tall building would be to have agents posted on the back of the car."-

WRONG/NOT COMPLETE: as he himself wrote in his final survey report for the Tampa trip, the *other* way to guard against a shooter is to have the building rooftops guarded (as they were in Tampa and many other cities).[15]

14. https://www.youtube.com/watch?v=LxZVgPlt05o
15. Experienced agents would have helped, as well: At the time of the assassination, the White House Detail was in a weakened condition due to recent resignations and transfers. Nearly one-third of the 34 agents on the White House Detail assigned to protect JFK, including a number of experienced agents, had recently resigned or been transferred. "In the past two months alone, eleven of the most experienced agents on the Kennedy Detail had been replaced. It had been a purely personal choice by the agents—they'd requested, and had been granted, transfers to field offices... [N]early a third of the agents had decided they just couldn't do it anymore. Too many missed birthdays and anniversaries, too many holidays away from home." (This means that despite several known plots to assassinate the president, the Secret Service nonetheless was permitting numbers of its experienced agents to leave the Detail. Shouldn't it have been obvious under the circumstances that allowing so many experienced agents to depart was unwise?). Based on years of intensive research, here are the experienced veteran agents who left in 1963: Tom Fridley, Bill Skiles, Scott Trundle, Milt Wilhite, Tom Behl, Charlie Kunkel (Summer 1963), Jimmy Johnson (Aug 1963), Ed Z. Tucker (Summer 1963), Jerry Dolan (Fall 1963), Bob Lilley (Fall 1963), Larry Newman (Oct 1963), Anthony Sherman, Jr. (Oct 1963), Thomas B. Shipman (DIED 10/14/63), and Ken Wiesman (10/23/63). The new agents were Robert L. Kollar, Robert R. Burke (Summer 1963), Radford Jones (Summer 1963), George W. Hickey (July 1963), Robert R. Faison (Sept 1963), William T. McIn-

The Kennedy Detail repeats the legend that Clint Hill came within a split second of saving JFK and taking the fatal bullet. But he's not even in the Moorman photo (taken at the moment of the fatal head shot) and in the Muchmore film he's only climbing down from the follow up car *after* the head shot. Also, in the Altgens photo (which was taken *after* the second shot), Hill is still on the running board and staring at JFK but not running towards him.

(SOCIAL) MEDIA APPEARANCES, BOOKS AND CONTRADICTIONS

For her part, Lisa McCubbin, co-author (for Blaine and Hill) of *The Kennedy Detail, Mrs Kennedy & Me, Five Days in November,* and *Five Presidents,*[16] posted the following on 11/24/10 on the official Facebook edition of *The Kennedy Detail*: "Contrary to Vince Palamara's claims, the book was absolutely NOT written to counteract his letter to Clint Hill. *Mr. Hill never read Palamara's letter–it went straight into the trash.* Gerald Blaine wrote this book on his volition, and Mr. Hill contributed after much deliberation (emphasis added)." For his part, Hill told Brian Lamb on C-SPAN four days later: "I recall receiving a letter *which I sent back to him.* I didn't bother with it…he called me and I said "Hello" but that was about it. But he alleges that because he sent me a letter 22 pages in length apparently, and that I discussed that with Jerry. I forgot that I ever got a 22-page letter from this particular individual until I heard him say it on TV and *I never discussed it with Jerry or anybody else* because it wasn't important to me (emphasis added)." Yet, in the biggest contradiction of all, Blaine quoted from my letter to Hill when I spoke to him on 6/10/05 and mentioned his deep friendship with Hill, as well, extending back to the late 1950's! For the record, I received Hill's signed receipt for the letter and it was never returned to me, either. What's more, Hill conceded to author William Law: "Maybe he's (me, Vince) right, because I apparently turned him down or something, I don't know."[17]

During yet another 6th Floor Museum appearance (with Hill and Blaine, hosted by Gary Mack), co-author Lisa McCubbin mentions that, during the writing of the book, she would find things that contradicted

---

tyre (Fall 1963), Chuck Zboril (Fall 1963), Henry J. Rybka (Fall 1963), William Straughn (10/17/63), Bill Bacherman (11/10/63), Dick Metzinger (11/10/63), John J. McCarthy (11/10/63), Roy "Gene" Nunn (11/11/63), Gerald W. O'Rourke (11/11/63), Kent D. Jordan (11/15/63), Andrew M. Hutch (11/18/63), Ed Morey (11/20/63), Dale Keaner (11/23/63), Ken Thompson (11/23/63), Glenn Weaver (11/23/63) and Bill Livingood (11/23/63). Regarding Metzinger: His daughter Julie wrote to me on 6/19/16 and said: "My dad got sent home unexpectedly from the detail the day before Kennedy was shot" Also, PRS agent Glen Bennett was made a temporary agent of the WHD on 11/10/63 – see chapter 2 of my first book.
16. Interestingly, a *John McCubbin* was Captain of the White House police force in 1922 and hailed from the same area Lisa did – the MD/VA part of the country: http://ghostsofdc.org/2012/10/26/white-house-policeman-mccubbin/
17. The 2015 edition of *In The Eye of History* by William Law, page 39.

what Blaine was telling her. Ultimately, she copped out, stating "he was there"... no, he wasn't there on 11/22/63 in Dallas and what about all his colleagues who refute him? Geez. McCubbin strikes me as a good investigative reporter. One wonders if her closeness to Blaine (she grew up with him, dated his son, and now dates his best friend Hill) along with the allure of big money, swayed her to "look away," so to speak, at all the conflicting and contradictory evidence.

On page 124 from his book *Five Days In November*, Hill writes: "It strikes me that perhaps we should keep an agent with President Kennedy's body---out of respect for both President and Mrs. Kennedy, and in light of the questions that were raised at Parkland Hospital about taking the body back to Washington for the autopsy. This way, if there is ever any doubt about whether Dr. Burkley stayed with the body until the autopsy, *or suspicions about tampering*, there will be a Secret Service agent who also remained with the casket and *can vouch for the integrity of the body*. Agent Dick Johnsen is selected for the post because he is an agent who was with President Kennedy from the beginning and is familiar to Mrs. Kennedy, O'Donnell, and Powers [emphasis added]."

Beyond the absurdity of picking an *agent* as somehow relieving any person's suspicion that something could possibly be amiss ("oh, an agent was there? Alright, no suspicion there"), the agent chosen was none other than the official keeper of CE399, aka the magic bullet. What's more, Lifton's best-selling book did not appear until the early 1980's and the issue of body tampering/ alteration was not on anyone's minds until the early-mid 1970's at the earliest ... *why* would Hill write these comments? And, from the excerpt above as written, are we to somehow infer that it was HILL (not Kellerman, for example) who made the decision to have an agent stay with the body and decide that the specific person should be the magic bullet holder? Hmmm...

On pages 138-139 from his book *Five Days In November*, Hill writes: "The doctor points to a wound in the throat and explains that this is where the emergency tracheotomy was done at Parkland Hospital, which covered up the area *where a bullet had exited*. He rolls the president slightly onto his left side and points to a small wound just below the neckline, slightly to the right of the spinal column in the upper back. *This, he says, is where the bullet entered, and then came out the front of the neck*. The bullet that caused these wounds hit nothing but soft tissue. Those wounds, I knew without a doubt, *came from the first shot*. It corroborates what I saw---the president suddenly grabbing his throat *immediately after the first explosive noise.* The doctor points to a wound on the right rear of the head. This, he says, was the fatal wound. He lifts up a piece of the scalp, with skin and hair still attached, which reveals a hole in the skull, and an area in which a good portion of the brain matter is gone[emphasis added]."

To his "credit," as he also recently demonstrated on television, Hill repeats what he has said since 11/22/63 (and in all his other Lisa Mc-Cubbin co-authored books) that the right rear of JFK's head was missing (page 107), but what gives with the above?

Amazingly, Hill is now on record in his 2016 book *Five Presidents* denouncing the Warren Commission's single bullet theory, the entire keystone to their Oswald-acted-alone scenario, as is his colleague Paul Landis, according to an interview Landis did with the *Cleveland Plain Dealer* on 11/22/2016.

5/27/12 C-SPAN: Clint Hill addresses Vince Palamara

HILL: Well my wife and I are not together and haven't been for some time.

LAMB: *She's still alive?*

HILL: Yes.

LAMB: Did you – did you keep notes?

HILL: I did, but I destroyed them a few years ago which really made it more difficult.

LAMB: Why did you destroy them?

HILL: I promised that I would never write a book. I vowed that I would never do so, never contribute to a book, never talk to anybody about it and so just to kind of make sure I would never get myself involved, I burned everything. There are few mementos I kept, but for the most part, I burned all my notes. And now, when the opportunity presents itself and I decided to do it, I had to go back and talk to other agents who I worked with, who did have – still have some notes. And to check everything through newspaper archives for dates and times and places to make sure I was accurate and so it was very tedious to go through this and write the book.

LAMB: Do you remember the year you burned your notes?

HILL: It is 2012 [now] – it was [long pause] maybe 2005, something like that [Note: 2005 was the year I contacted Hill for the first time with my 22-page letter referenced above, so, needless to say, I find the specific timing of his note burning suspicious, to put it mildly].

LAMB: As an aside by the way, the fellow we talked about in the last interview, Vince Palamara.

HILL: Yes.

LAMB: You've seen his letter about your book?

HILL: I have not read it, no.

LAMB: I'm sure you probably know that he said that "Mrs. Kennedy and Me" is highly recommended to everyone for its honesty and rich body of truth." He actually fully endorsed your book[18] even though he's been critical of (pause) … are you worried that he's not being …? (Cutting Lamb off)

HILL: Maybe he has some secret agenda, I don't know. But I accept his praise, thank you."

11/10/10 C-SPAN: GERALD BLAINE AND CLINT HILL ADDRESS VINCE PALAMARA

LAMB: Now, we got some video from YouTube – one of the things you say in your book that made you want to write this book was all the conspiracy theories and you talked about the movie from Oliver Stone. This is a man named Vince Palamara. Do you know him?

BLAINE: I am familiar with him, I don't know him.

LAMB: He says that – and I guess we'll talk about this, that he sent you a 22 page letter?

HILL: I recall receiving a letter which I sent back to him. I didn't bother with it.

LAMB: You didn't talk to him ever?

HILL: He called me and I said "Hello" but that was about it.

LAMB: And over the years, have you both been called about this assassination on many occasions.

HILL: I had been called numerous times.

LAMB: What has been your attitude, how have you approached the people…

HILL: For the most part, I just said I have no comment, I just have nothing to say.

LAMB: And why is that?

---

18. Well, not entirely, although I like most of it: http://www.ctka.net/reviews/MrsKennedy_Hill_Review_Palamara.html

HILL: Well, most of it is from people who are writing conspiracy theory books that don't make any sense to me so if they are not going to deal in facts, then I don't want anything to do with it.

LAMB: And how about you?

BLAINE: I have never talked to any author of a book and that – I just felt we had it on our commission books: "worthy of trust of confidence" – and I felt those were issues that you should never talk to anybody on the outside about. And it was – I had to weigh and evaluate when I wrote this book because I felt I wasn't talking about the Secret Service, I wasn't talking about the Kennedy Family, but I was talking about the agents that I work with and the incidents that occurred and those were my friends. So that's when I decided to write.

LAMB: Did you have to get permission to do this from the secret service?

HILL: No.

LAMB: So this wasn't cleared by the Secret Services?

HILL: No.

BLAINE: No, but we had lunch today with the director of the Secret Service who thanked us very much for our contribution.

LAMB: Here is this video, it's not very long and this man's name is Vince Palamara, he is a citizen who has taken it on his own to become an expert. He is from Pennsylvania and I don't know him, I haven't talked to him and I have just seen it on the web and he is – I believe he is a graduate of Duquesne University so let us watch this and I'll get your reaction.

BLAINE: OK. [START OF VIDEO].

VINCE PALAMARA: Hi, this is Vince Palamara, the self-described Secret Service expert that Jerry Blaine accuses me of without naming me, OK? Back with my obsession about *The Kennedy Detail*. I have to read this, this is rich. Page 287 [of Blaine's book] is where Blaine is claiming what Rowley said. [Quoting from the book] "Rowley turned to Jerry Blaine. "And Jerry, since you were in the lead car, did you ever hear this over your radio as well?" "Yes, sir. I did. I heard exactly what Floyd just told you."

The thing about this-this is the whole 'Ivy League charlatans' crap. Jerry Blaine told me that the 'Ivy League charlatans' thing "came from the guys. I can't remember – I can't remember who said it." (Said sarcastically)Boy, his memory got real good five years later because now, he is claiming he heard it over the radio from Floyd Boring. It's unbelievable, and it's just amazing to me – you know, there never would have been a book if I didn't send a 22 page letter to Clint Hill that pissed him off so much that his very good friend, Jerry Blaine, came out with his book as a counter. OK? These are some good things in it. I recommend everyone to buy it, no censorship, it's my First Amendment rights, OK? There are some nice pictures and there are even some good assassination related things in here, but it's very odd. Other people have picked up on this, that's why there are some really bad reviews on Amazon right now, mine is the best-mine at three stars too. It's very obvious that it's a thinly veiled attempt to rewrite history and blame President Kennedy – without trying to blame him – for his own assassination. [END OF VIDEO].

LAMB: First of all, his is not the best of the reviews, there are seven with five stars just for the record that I saw today when I looked on Amazon. What's your reaction, could you hear?

BLAINE: Well, he wrote an assessment of the book about the – first time about five weeks before it was released. The second time on Amazon.com, he and four of his friends or four of his aliases put a statement on assessing the book a one, a two, and a three (stars). My assessment of Mr. Palamara is that he called probably all of the agents, and what agent who answers a phone is going to answer a question "was President Kennedy easy to protect?" Well, probably he was too easy to protect because he was assassinated. But the fact is that the agents aren't going to tell him anything and he alludes to the fact that when I wrote the book, most of these people were dead. Well, I worked with these people, I knew them like brothers and I knew exactly what was going on and always respected Jim Rowley because he stood up to the issue and said "Look, we can't say the President invited himself to be killed so let's squash this." So that was the word throughout the Secret Service and he – Mr. Palamara is – there are a number of things that had happened (sic) that he has no credibility. He is a self-described expert in his area which I don't know what it is, he was born after the assassination and he keeps creating solutions to the assassination until they are proven wrong. So he is… (Cutting Blaine off)

LAMB: A lot about –

HILL: *But he alleges that because he sent me a letter 22 pages in length apparently, and that I discussed that with Jerry. I forgot that I ever got a 22-page letter from this particular individual until I heard him say it on*

TV and I never discussed it with Jerry or anybody else because it wasn't important to me. And so far as him being an expert, I don't know where the expert part came from. I spent a long time in the Secret Service in protection and I'm not an expert, but apparently he became an expert somewhere up in Pennsylvania, I don't know where."

But Blaine wasn't finished with me just yet: "The Zapruder film, when the Zapruder film was run at normal speed, another theme that Palamara throws out is that Bill Greer stopped the car, when it's run at its normal speed, you will notice the car absolutely does not stop at all. This happened in less than six seconds after the President was hit in the throat and moving along." Oh, so you agree with my "solutions" that JFK was shot in the neck from the FRONT, do you, Mr. Blaine? And there were close to 60 witnesses to the limousine slowing or stopping, including 7 Secret Service agents and Jacqueline Kennedy – not my "theme" or theory, just the facts. Returning directly to *The Kennedy Detail* documentary, Agent Ron Pontius specifically refers to one of my articles (also a part of a chapter in my book) without naming me. As the narrator, Martin Sheen, notes: "The most painful theories point fingers at the agents themselves."

Who needs theories when we have facts: former agent Chuck Zboril served in the Marines with Lee Harvey Oswald! QUA Company, 1st Battalion, 2nd Infantry Training Regiment, Marine Corps Base, Camp Pendleton, California between 20th January 1957 and 26th February 1957: Oswald and Zboril. I only discovered this in October 2016 – no one ever reported this before.

3/22/06 CNN: HILL AND HIS WIFE

KING: What are you doing Clint?

HILL: I am completely retired. *I'm a homebody, my wife and I and our kids and grandkids*

KING: Clint, I thank you very much. I salute you for your service.

HILL: Thank you, Larry.

KING: And I thank you for coming here tonight on this special occasion for Mike Wallace.

HILL: Thank you very much. Good luck Mike.

WALLACE: Same to you

Clint. HILL: *My wife says hello.*

11/10/13 IRISH PRESS: HILL AND HIS CO-AUTHOR

"Hill, who lives in Virginia, is "happier than I have ever been" with Lisa McCubbin, the journalist he co-wrote the memoir with. "The calendar says I'm 81 and she's 48, but I feel 52." In his book he credits McCubbin "...for bringing me out of my dungeon, where I languished for years in my emotional prison ... you helped me find a reason to live, not just exist.""I was there for [Jackie Kennedy's] children, but I wasn't there for the birth of either of my sons [Chris and Corey, now 56 and 51 respectively]. They grew up without a father. My wife Gwen raised them herself." (They separated, "emotionally," years ago, but have not divorced.)[19]

FROM PAGE 241 OF HILL AND MCCUBBIN'S 2013 BOOK *FIVE DAYS IN NOVEMBER*:

Lisa says of Hill: "For some reason, we were brought together at the right time in both our lives, and I am so grateful we were. You are extraordinary."

Apparently, there was some bad blood-perhaps caused by the aforementioned relationship – between fellow agent David Grant, Clint Hill's brother-in-law, and Clint Hill (Perhaps including Gerald Blaine, as well. This relationship was mentioned in a passing comment from Gerald Blaine to myself in June 2005 and also later mentioned in Blaine's 2010 book). Grant, who passed away 12/28/13, turned down the producers of *The Kennedy Detail* movie-including Clint Hill-because he felt the Hollywood lawyers "were trying to buy his memories," yet he gladly agreed to appear on a BBC television program about Kennedy's trip to England.[20] I was amazed that Hill failed to mention his relationship to Grant in his two books and in his many media appearances in print, on the radio, and on television. In fact, both agents-Hill and Grant-appear, albeit separately, on *The Kennedy Detail* 2010 television documentary and, again, nothing was mentioned concerning this startling connection. What really did it for me was the fact that *Clint Hill is omitted from the obituary of David Grant, while Hill's wife Gwen is not; very telling, indeed.[21]In any event, I am delighted to learn that Blaine's Hollywood movie was scrapped. I wrote to the director and demonstrated the errors and omissions of Blaine's book. This move on my part led to petty harassment from a few of Blaine's friends, but it was worth it.*

19. http://www.irishexaminer.com/lifestyle/features/why-i-blame-myself-for-jfks-death-248893.html
20. http://www.bbc.co.uk/ariel/24944881
21. http://www.fairfaxmemorialfuneralhome.com/obituary/David-B.-Grant/Springfield-VA/1326770

DRINKS THE NIGHT BEFORE AND MORNING OF 11/22/63

Texas guitarist and songwriter Arvel Stricklin, who was playing that night at the Cellar Bar where many Secret Service agents were present, said: "I know I saw a lot of guys in suits. And the party went on until 6 a.m."[22]

Agent Clint Hill, the one who leaped on the trunk of the presidential limousine, told the Warren Commission that he stayed at the Cellar until 2:45 a.m. Speaking last year to *Vanity Fair*, he shaved about an hour off that statement, saying he left before 2 a.m., returned to the Hotel Texas and put in a breakfast order for 6 a.m.[23]

Agent Paul Landis, who, like Hill, rode on the running board of the Secret Service car behind the Kennedys, said he didn't leave the Cellar until 5 a.m.

One of those present at the club was a *Star-Telegram* reporter named Bob Schieffer, who went on to anchor the *CBS Evening News*. In his book, *This Just In*, Schieffer wrote about his visit to the Cellar in the earliest hours of Nov. 22, 1963: "It seemed a good idea at the time and must have been quite an evening. I remember that we stayed long enough for some of the Easterners to see their first Fort Worth sunrise."

It was a problem of hunger that led the Secret Service into the Texas night. Arriving in Fort Worth late from Houston, the president and first lady settled into their suite at the Hotel Texas. Of the 28 agents on the presidential detail, nine left the hotel after midnight in search of food.

The Fort Worth Press Club had stayed open late to feed visiting reporters covering the president, but by the time the Secret Service got there well after midnight, the food was gone. They stayed for Scotch and beer.

As Schieffer recently told *Vanity Fair*, "The Cellar was an all-night, San Francisco-style coffeehouse down the street, and some of the visiting reporters had heard about it and wanted to see it. So we all went over there, and some of the agents came along. The place didn't have a liquor license, but they did serve liquor to friends – usually grain alcohol and Kool-Aid."[24]

Six Secret Service agents stayed until around 3 a.m.

Abraham Bolden, a member of Kennedy's detail, was not with the team in Texas, but in a 2008 book, he wrote about the partying atmosphere among Kennedy's agents.

Last year, he told *Vanity Fair*: "The biggest problem I ran into with the Secret Service when I was an agent was their constant drinking. When we

22. http://www.dallasnews.com/entertainment/columnists/alan-peppard/20150210-secret-services-1963-night-in-fort-worths-cellar-recalled.ece
23. From the Oct 2014 *Vanity Fair* article that quotes from my book *Survivor's Guilt* (later to also be referenced in author Susan Cheever's 2015 book *Drinking In America*): http://www.vanityfair.com/news/politics/2014/10/secret-service-jfk-assassination
24. Ibid.

would get to a place, one of the first things they would do was stock up with liquor. They would drink and then we would go to work."

During the assassination in Dallas, Bolden says, "their reflexes were definitely affected by, number one, the loss of sleep and, number two, the fact that [some may have] consumed that amount of alcohol."[25]

Blaine's book makes numerous references to JFK being a great person to work and be around. But it seems Blaine includes such anecdotes to balance out his claims about JFK being reckless. Blaine takes direct aim at JFK in a way that contradicts most other accounts of his personality: "All that was left was a sense of futility. You could do only so much. But the one thing you couldn't do was protect the president from his own ego."[26]

His own ego?

Blaine compares JFK to his predecessor, Eisenhower, whom Blaine appears to have seen as a president with fewer personal faults:

"President Eisenhower did not have a narcissistic bone in his body… he did not necessarily like crowds and did not feel like he had to run over and shake every person's hand…he understood unnecessary exposure."[27]

Is it just me or did I read that last paragraph as a not-so-subtle suggestion that JFK was narcissistic, felt a need to shake everyone's hand, was "warm and fuzzy," but in an un-presidential way, and did not have confidence in the Secret Service's ability and no understanding of unnecessary risk?

Former agent Bill Carter said: *"I believe it was [JFK's] destiny to die that day in Dallas."*[28] *Besides being a disturbing sentiment to hold as a Secret Service agent who guarded President Kennedy shortly before Dallas, Carter is dead wrong – if the Secret Service would have done their normal, professional job, Kennedy would have survived Dallas.*[29]

THE *FINAL* NAIL IN THE COFFIN FOR *THE KENNEDY DETAIL*

*T*he ONLY time JFK and LBJ ever rode in an open-car motorcade together was when JFK was not yet the President (the Secret Service did not protect candidates back then [Nixon was already the V.P.] in Dallas 9/11/60-9/13/60… and Dallas on 11/22/63 (No other time as president did JFK

---

25. Ibid.
26. *The Kennedy Detail*, page 332.
27. Ibid page 398.
28. *Get Carter* by Bill Carter (2006), page 46.
29. This isn't the first time Kennedy era agents expressed controversial feelings. One of the Bethesda Navy autopsy technicians overheard two Secret Service agents who were standing in the hallway outside the Bethesda morgue during the Kennedy autopsy say "Well, from now on we won't have to feel like pimps." *In The Eye of History* by William Law (2015 edition), page 136

and LBJ ride together in a motorcade[30]). So, let me get this straight: JFK was running for President in 1960 and he did not mind motorcycles, police men, guards, and sundry other people surrounding his car, yet, the next time he ran for president in the same town, with LBJ once again a part of the motorcade, he now was bothered by it? Yeah, right.

Postscript

SECRET SERVICE DESTROYS JFK ASSASSINATION RELATED DOCUMENTS: WHAT WAS DESTROYED AND WHAT GERALD BLAINE "DONATED"[31]

Gerald Blaine turned over to the National Archives documents already made available – the Final Survey Report for the Tampa, FL trip of 11/18/63. Blaine mistakenly thought these were the documents "conspiracy theorists" thought were destroyed...as usual, he is wrong.

These were the *only* records released by the Secret Service, all in the late 1990's. I have them all, as any citizen with the money can order copies via the collection at the National Archives:

THE NOVEMBER 1963 SECRET SERVICE SHIFT REPORTS;

RIF #154-10002-10417:
Final Survey Report Philadelphia, PA trip 10/30/63;

RIF#154-10002-10418:
Final Survey Report Elkton, MD trip 11/14/63;

RIF#154-10002-10419:
Final Survey Report SECOND New York City trip 11/14-11/15/63;

RIF#154-10002-10420:
Final Survey Report Palm Beach, FL trip 11/18/63;

RIF#154-10002-10421:
Final Survey Report Cape Canaveral, FL 11/18/63;

---

30. As even Blaine conceded: "It was very rare for both the president and the vice president to be together at the same time in the same place" (*The Kennedy Detail*, page 224).
31. Special thanks to Bill Kelly and the ARRB's Doug Horne for their tremendous help in synthesizing this information, in conjunction with my own work.

RIF#154-10002-10423:
Final Survey Report Tampa, FL 11/18/63;

RIF#154-10002-10422:
Final Survey Report Miami, FL 11/18/63;

RIF#154-10002-10424:
Final Survey report San Antonio, TX, 11/21/63;

Here is what was destroyed, Gerald:

A SUMMARY OF THE RECORDS DESTROYED BY THE SECRET SERVICE IN JANUARY OF 1995.

The Protective Survey Reports destroyed by the Secret Service in January 1995 were part of a group of records transferred by the Secret Service to the General Services Administration's Washington National Records Center in Suitland, Maryland on August 7, 1974 under accession number 87-75-4. The instructions on the SF-135 ("Records Transmittal and Receipt" form) were: "Retain permanently for eventual transfer to the National Archives or a Presidential Library." There were six boxes transferred under the accession number, and the two that were destroyed in January of 1995 contained the following files:

Box 1 Protection of the President (John F. Kennedy)

Andrews Air Force Base 1961 (Arrivals and Departures)
Andrews Air Force Base 1962 (Arrivals and Departures)
Andrews Air Force Base 1963 (Arrivals and Departures)
 Arlington National Cemetery
Camp David
The Capitol
Churches
D.C. National Guard Armory
D.C. Stadium
Departures from South Grounds
Dulles International Airport
Embassies
Executive Office Building
Golf Clubs
Griffith Stadium
Homes of Friends
International Inn
Mayflower Hotel (three folders, for 1961-63)

National Press Club
Other Places Folders (#s 1-4, from January 1961-December of 1962)

Box 6 Protective Survey Reports for the following trips:

Duluth, Minnesota (9-24-63)
Ashland, Wisconsin (9-24-63)
Billings, Montana (9-25-63)
Grand Teton National Park, Wyoming (9-25-63)
Cheyenne, Wyoming (9-25-63)
Grand Forks, North Dakota (9-25-63)
Laramie, Wyoming (9-25-63)
Salt Lake City, Utah (9-26-63)
Great Falls, Montana (9-26-63)
Hanford, Washington (9-26-63)
Tongue Point, Oregon (9-27-63)
Redding, California (9-27-63)
Tacoma, Washington (9-27-63)
Palm Springs, California (9-28-63)
Las Vegas, Nevada (9-28-63)
Heber Springs, Arkansas (10-3-63)
Little Rock, Arkansas (10-3-63)
University of Maine (10-19-63)
Boston, Massachusetts (10-26-63)
Amherst, Massachusetts (10-26-63)
Philadelphia, Pennsylvania (10-30-63)
Chicago, Illinois (11-2-63): Three Folders [TRIP CANCELLED]
New York City (11-8-63)

In addition, one folder of vital records was missing from Box 2 in this accession, titled: "Other Places Folder #6" (for the period July-November 1963).

Clearly, withholding these two boxes of materials from any investigator would have kept that investigator from learning about normal protective procedures and concerns related to everyday activities throughout the Kennedy Presidency, and would furthermore have denied the investigator comparative knowledge regarding how JFK was protected in numerous venues just prior to the trip to Texas. Perhaps the reader can better understand now why Jeremy Gunn and David Marwell were so upset with the Secret Service. The records were destroyed in the fourth month following the establishment of the ARRB, and furthermore had originally been tagged: "Retain permanently for eventual transfer to the National Archives or a Presidential Library." Their destruction occurred long after the Secret Service was initially briefed on the requirements of the JFK Records Act in December of 1992 by the NARA staff, and required willful action by officials within that agency; it was hardly an accident. The Secret Service clearly didn't want the ARRB poking into its past procedures and practices; the agency had been the recipient of severe criticism in the HSCA's 1979 Report, and apparently did not wish to repeat that experience, or to have its sealed records released to the Archives for placement in the JFK Records Collection, for all JFK researchers to peruse in the future.

Chronology of Letters Exchanged Between the ARRB and the U.S. Secret Service over the Destruction of Protective Survey Reports:

On July 25, 1995 Review Board Chairman John R. Tunheim sent a powerfully worded letter to the Director of the Secret Service registering the Review Board's displeasure about its recent discovery that the two boxes in question had been destroyed over a half a year previously. A letter from Board Chair Jack Tunheim (rather than David Marwell or Jeremy Gunn) addressed directly to the Head of the Secret Service (instead of to the administrative officials with whom the ARRB staff had been dealing) was a powerful signal that the Review Board was immensely displeased and took the matter very seriously. Some key passages in Jack Tunheim's letter are quoted below:

> In January of this year, Dr. Jeremy Gunn of the Review Board staff requested of John Machado and Ann Parker of the Secret Service that the six boxes in the accession be made available for his review to evaluate the importance of the material for the JFK Collection in the Archives. Although four of the boxes were made available, we were not provided with boxes (1) and (6), the two most important boxes. On February 7, 1995 – and several times thereafter – Mr. Machado and Ms. Parker informed us that the Federal Records Center "could not locate" the two missing boxes....Although we repeatedly were told that special requests for these records had been made at the Federal Records Center, Ms. Ann Parker of the Secret Service finally informed Dr. Joan Zimmerman of the Review Board staff, on July 19, 1995 – six months after we had first requested the boxes – that the records had in fact been destroyed in January of this year at approximately the same time that we had requested them.

Tunheim's letter requested full accounting of what had happened to the two boxes; a listing of all other Secret Service records pertaining to

President Kennedy that had ever been destroyed; and instructed the Secret Service not to destroy any records of any kind relating to President Kennedy or his assassination without first allowing the Review Board and its staff to review them for relevance. For added emphasis a copy of the letter was sent to the Chief Counsel of the U.S. Secret Service, as well as to John Machado, the apparent culprit who presumably gave the orders to destroy the records.

The Secret Service made an immediate attempt to de-escalate the matter by assigning an official named W. Ralph Basham, its Administrative Director of Administration (later the Director), to reply. Basham's reply, dated July 31, 1995, was a five-and-one-half page single-spaced attempt at obfuscation, the administrative equivalent of a Senate filibuster. In addition to saying, in some many words, 'Hey, we didn't do anything wrong, we were following routine destruction procedures established years ago,' the Secret Service attempted to wiggle out of its predicament by simultaneously suggesting that perhaps the destruction was really the Review Board's fault because it was not in receipt of the ARRB's expanded definition of what constituted an "assassination record" until February 1995, after the records were destroyed. Perhaps most disturbing of all was the narrow definition that the Secret Service had used commencing in December 1992 (following its NARA briefing on the JFK Records Act) to define what constituted an assassination record: namely, White House detail shift reports only for the period November 18, 1963 to November 24, 1963. Mr. Basham also tried to downplay the significance of the missing Chicago protective survey reports for the cancelled November 2, 1963 trip (during which conspirators had planned to assassinate President Kennedy) by writing:

The folder concerning the canceled trip to Chicago would only have contained a preliminary survey report, if any document at all, since final reports are not conducted when a trip is cancelled. This report, if in fact it was even in the prepared folder, would have been of limited scope.

[Author's comments: there were 3 folders on the cancelled Chicago trip, not one, and this attempt to portray the Chicago file as one folder was duplicitous; furthermore, how did Basham presume to know that any reports written about the cancellation of the Chicago trip would have been "of limited scope?" It is easy to make such claim after evidence is destroyed, because there is no way you can be challenged.]

The ARRB's response to this "in your face" piece of administrative obfuscation was signed out by Executive Director David G. Marwell on August 7, 1995, and showed no mercy. Rather than simply allow the matter to "go away" or "die," as the Secret Service had hoped, Marwell's letter (co-drafted by him and Gunn) resurrected the seriousness of the matter in no uncertain terms. I quote below, in part:

> Although you concluded your letter by stating that you "trust this explanation will clarify any misunderstandings that may have arisen," I regret to say that not only does your letter not allay our concerns, it compounds them.

The President John F. Kennedy Assassination Records Collection (JFK Act) forbids the destruction of any documents "created *or made available for use by, obtained by, or [that] otherwise came into the possession of …. The Select Committee on Assassinations… of the House of Representatives." It is our understanding that the records in Accession 87-75-0004 that the Secret Service destroyed were examined by the House Select Committee on Assassinations and thus were "assassination records" under the JFK Act and they apparently were destroyed in violation of law.* [Emphasis in original, which is most unusual in official government correspondence – it is the equivalent of shouting at someone during a conversation]

We see the destruction of these assassination records as particularly ominous in light of the fact that the Secret Service revised its destruction schedule *after* passage of the JFK Act and that it targeted for destruction records that, at the time the law was passed, were slated to be held "permanently." [Emphasis in the original]

Rather than referring to and applying the standards of the JFK Act, your letter suggests that the responsibilities of the Secret Service extend no further than complying with standard records disposal schedules. After acknowledging that the Secret Service in fact destroyed records in 1995 from Accession 87-75-0004 (related to the protection of President Kennedy), you state that they were "processed in accordance with National Archives and Records (NARA) procedures, and in full compliance with approved records disposition schedules." The JFK Act, it should be clear, supersedes any law or any disposition schedule related to "assassination records."

This was a "right back in your face" response that told masters of obfuscation at the Secret Service that the ARRB wasn't going to be rolled, and wasn't going to go away. Marwell's letter then upped the ante by requesting a ton of information which any Federal agency would have had a difficult time finding the resources to accomplish. Marwell's letter ended with these words:

... we specifically request that you assure us that no Secret Service records related to Presidential protection between 1958 and 1969 or to the assassination of President Kennedy be destroyed *until* the Review Board has received prior written notice and has had an opportunity to inspect the records [emphasis in original]

Sensing that the ARRB was flexing its muscles and was about to "go nuclear" [which was true – public hearings were being considered], Mr. Basham replied on August 15, 1995 with a calming one-page letter and requesting a meeting to discuss the "additional issues" which he said were raised by Marwell's letter. That meeting was held the very next day (August 16, 1995) on ARRB turf, in the offices at 600 E Street, in Northwest Washington D.C.

Following the meeting, which lasted several hours, Jeremy Gunn (our General Counsel and Head of Research and Analysis) signed out a letter on August 21, 1995 to Mr. Basham and Mr. Personnette (Deputy Chief Counsel) of the Secret Service. Gunn recognized for the record that the Secret Service now had a much better understanding of what constituted an assassination record – the ARRB set the definition for this, not the agencies holding records, who all wished to minimize their work – and noted for the record that the Secret Service had agreed that no records related to Presidential protection for years 1958-1969 would be destroyed until after the ARRB had a chance to review them to verify that no assassination records were included. Gunn also recorded the agreement reached on August 16, 1995, that Dr. Joan Zimmerman of our staff would henceforth have full access to all Secret Service records upon demand, not just partial and limited access, as previously. The ARRB threw a face-saving bone to the Secret Service in Gunn's letter, as well:

As acknowledged in the meeting, we fully understand and accept your interest in ensuring that no documents are released that would compromise Presidential protection. As we have mentioned before, our professional staff is in possession of current security clearances and we will take all appropriate measures to safeguard the records and ensure full compliance with the law.

On the same date, August 21, 1995, Gunn signed out a letter to the miscreant John Machado (who had ordered the two boxes destroyed), which was much less friendly in tone and which bored in on him with a number of questions about dubious statements previously made by Machado, and made additional requests for information and records

The crisis had abated, and the Secret Service had avoided embarrassing public hearings which would have exposed their perfidy. The public was not to learn of this business until that one cryptic paragraph was published in the ARRB Final Report in late September of 1998, three years later. Unlike poor JFK, whom corrupt individuals in the Secret Service had helped set up in Dallas in 1963, the Secret Service in 1995, had 'dodged a bullet.'

Professor Jim Fetzer summed up the situation nicely with his comments in the documentary "The Smoking Guns," which aired on the History Channel in 2003:

> The Secret Service…deliberately destroyed…records that would have revealed that the motorcade in Dallas was a travesty, a violation of at least 15 different Secret Service policies for Presidential protection. This behavior on their part raises the most serious and deserving questions about their complicity in the entire affair… which of course, is the reason why the Secret Service destroyed the records of its own motorcades when they were asked for them by the Assassination Records Review Board.

* * * * *

Doug Horne, the chief analyst for military records of the Assassination Records Review Board (ARRB) wrote more extensively about the deliberate destruction of Secret Service records in his book, "Inside the ARRB" (2009, Volume V, p. 1451)

> HORNE: *The destruction of key documents by the Secret Service in 1995 suggested that the secret service cover-up of its own malfeasance continued, more than 30 years after the assassination.*
>
> In 1995, the Review Board Staff became aware that the U.S. Secret Service had destroyed protective survey reports related to John F. Kennedy's Presidency, and that they had done so well after the passage of the JFK Records Act, and well after having been briefed by the National Archives (NARA) on the Act's requirements to preserve all Assassination Records from destruction until the ARRB had made a determination that any such proposed destruction was acceptable
>
> I reported to work at the ARRB on August 7, 1995, and I still distinctly recall that this controversy was raging full force during the first two weeks I was on the job. I recall both General Counsel

Jeremy Gunn and Executive Director David Marwell being particularly upset; they were seriously considering holding public hearings in which the Secret Service officials responsible for said destruction would be called to account and castigated, in an open forum, with the media present. The thinking at the time was that doing so would: (a) cause the Secret Service to take the Review Board and the JFK Act seriously; and (b) send a warning to other government agencies, such as the FBI and CIA, to also take the Review Board and the JFK Act seriously, lest they, too be dragged into public hearings that would cause great discomfiture and professional embarrassment.

Eventually – and unfortunately – tempers cooled and no public hearings were held. I suspect that Board Chair Jack Tunheim played a major role in finessing the matter; presumably, the Board Members believed that since the ARRB was still in its first year of its three-year effort to locate and review assassination records, that we would get more out of the Secret Service in the future with honey, than with vinegar. Stern official letters levying charges and counter-charges were exchanged; a face-to-face meeting between high-level officials of the ARRB and Secret Service was held; tempers cooled; and no public hearings were ever held. Relations with the Secret Service remained testy throughout the remainder of the ARRB's lifespan. It was my impression, during my ongoing discussions with my fellow analysts on the Secret Service Records team for the next three years (from September 1995 to September 1998), that the Secret Service never "loosened up" and reached a comfortable working accommodation with the ARRB like the FBI, the CIA, and the Pentagon (or, at least the Joint Staff Secretariat) did. The Secret Service and the ARRB remained wary adversaries for four years.

The Review Board itself consciously soft-pedaled the dispute in its Final Report, devoting only one paragraph (and virtually no details whatsoever) to the incident, on page 149:

Congress passed the JFK Act in 1992. One month later, the Secret Service began its compliance efforts. However, in January 1995, the Secret Service destroyed Presidential protection survey reports for some of President Kennedy's trips in the fall of 1963. The Review Board learned of the destruction approximately one week after the Secret Service destroyed them, when the Board was drafting its request for additional information. The Board believed that the Secret Service files on the President's travel in the weeks preceding this murder would be relevant.

And that was it – that was the only mention of the entire imbroglio in the Final Report of the Assassinations Records Review Board. My intention here is to give the reader as much additional and relevant, information as I can at this writing, 14 years later. I was never "on the inside" of this problem, but I do have a correspondence file of letters exchanged, and will quote from them liberally to give the reader a sense of what it feels and sounds like when two bureaucracies go to war inside the Beltway. This is of more than mere academic interest, since the evidence presented in this chapter has shown that several Secret Service officials on the White House Detail were complicit in both the President's death – due to willful actions that greatly lessened the physical security around President Kennedy during the Dallas motorcade – and in the cover up of the damage to the limousine, which if left in its original damaged condition, would have proved JFK was caught in a crossfire, and therefore killed by a conspiracy.

GERALD BLAINE'S HANDWRITTEN "NOTES"

The Gerald Blaine documents consist of 28 pages – mostly duty assignments and travel vouchers, but there are two survey reports – one for Tampa and the one for a post assassination State Department reception between foreign dignitaries and LBJ. There is also a brief statement, a denial of having consumed any alcoholic beverages at the Press Club or the Cellar in Ft. Worth.

There are also three pages of handwritten notes, two pages written over a schedule dated from Nov. 8 to November 30 that I transcribe below:

Gerald Blaine's handwritten notes (*undated*):

> Frank Yeager and myself have the advance in Tampa, Fla. Everything goes well and I feel real good. Never a thought of the tragedy that is due to occur on the 22nd. *Kennedy makes the first of fateful steps that seem to lead toward the tragedy. He states that he wants no agents riding on the rear of his car as we did in Europe. If one was there the assassination might not have occurred. An agent's life is a frustrating one. You can set all of the security in the world, but it's only as good as the President lets it be.* The day will come when the only way the public will be able to see the president is by television. The country seems to be loaded with eccentrics and potentials.
>
> I don't think I have ever been filled so low emotionally by anything like the president's assassination. *There wasn't a thing anyone could have done to stop it and the Secret Service did everything it could do [can I puke now? VMP].* My shift worked midnight in Ft. Worth on the 22nd. We took them to the airport – They flew to Dallas, went to Austin to sleep for the next nights duty. I had been asleep about ten minutes in the

Commodore Perry Hotel. Art Godfrey came in the room and almost broke the door down. 'The boss was hit in Dallas.' I was groggy but the sickening truth seemed to sink through and I couldn't do anything but swing my legs over the bed and when the shock hit me I couldn't find the strength to stand and I was hit with a sudden wave of chills. Then I tried to fight off the despair and asked Art if he was sure. He said he knew that Kennedy was shot, but didn't know if it was fatal. We turned on the radio and finally got through on the security phone to hear the horrible truth. We just withdrew in our own thoughts.

We flew back in a SAC Bomber, myself, Art Godfrey, Bob Faison, Jerry O'Rourke, Paul Burns and John Bailey (National Democratic Chairman). We arrived back after Kennedy's body and set up security at the Johnson residence. (What a disgusting settlement – Kennedy replaced by Johnson – like a pro-ball player going from the Yankees to the bottom of the league.)"

They say that not many single things have an influence on history, but I am sure this one will."

"Even though we could have done nothing to prevent it, nor was there anything anyone could have done except use a bulletproof automobile, we are all suffering from guilt and failure in our one task. *The ordeal we were to all go through for the next few months was a sad one,* but we all came out with a feeling of hope far greater than we had ever had before. We shall all be stronger for the experience in the years to come. President Kennedy left us a little of his courage and we lost not only a fine president but a friend we will never forget and always admire." (Emphasis added)

"The ordeal we were to all go through for the next few months was a sad one"?

I thought these notes were contemporary to the assassination? And why weren't they used for his book or documentary?
Oops.

Photo of USSS Agent Frank Kenney, Oregon Senator Maurine Neuberger and President John F. Kennedy – September 1963 [Archives of Special Agent in Charge Frank J. Kenney, with permission of Michael Wood]

CHAPTER TEN

Nixon and the Secret Service Mole

Author Anthony Summers wrote, " ... the Secret Service ... was not uncontroversial during the Nixon presidency ... The service allowed itself to be used for political and private purposes, such as spying on Nixon rivals like Edward Kennedy and George McGovern, or surveilling his own brother Donald." The *New York Times* would write of Nixon's "perversion of the Secret Service." Former White House deputy counsel Edward Morgan has claimed that Nixon tried to convert the Secret Service into his personal "secret police." John Erlichman recalled, "I was concerned about it. The Secret Service turned the president down very seldom. They were very willing to please."[1]

Probably the agent most "willing to please" Nixon was agent Robert Newbrand. Newbrand guarded Chief Justice Earl Warren during the Warren Commission investigation along with fellow agent Elmer Moore, as former agent Rufus Youngblood told me. Bob Newbrand also had guarded JFK, as Gerald Blaine confirmed. Mamie Eisenhower even attended Newbrand's wedding![2] Interesting background, to say the least.

A rare photo of Secret Service agent Robert Newbrand (Truman-Nixon agent Art Godfrey in background):

But that is far from the end of the story:

Date: Thursday, September 7, 1972 – 4:47pm – 6:15pm
Participants: President Nixon, Bob Haldeman, Alexander Butterfield
Location: Oval Office

Within an hour of the shooting of Alabama Governor George Wallace on May 15, 1972, in Laurel, Maryland, President Nixon had ordered Secret Service protection for Senator Edward Kennedy. Kennedy had <u>agreed to the protection</u> on "a temporary basis." On June 5, Kennedy had

1. *The Arrogance of Power: The Secret World of Richard Nixon*, p. 247.
2. UPI wire photo dated 10/13/54.

formally requested that the Secret Service protection be removed. "He doesn't like to have to explain to his children who those men with guns are hovering around everywhere," his press secretary, Dick Drayne, explained. But as Kennedy increased his campaigning during the fall on behalf of Democratic presidential candidate George McGovern, Secret Service protection was seen as prudent. Kennedy's mother, Rose, reportedly had called President Nixon to express her concerns for her son's safety. When protection was resumed, she wrote Nixon to thank him for his personal intervention.[3]

Nixon and White House Chief of Staff H.R. "Bob" Haldeman saw an opportunity for gathering political intelligence that they might be able to use if Kennedy ran for president in 1976. Their plan involved planting a Nixon loyalist, Robert Newbrand, in Kennedy's protection detail in the expectation that Newbrand would pass on useful information to the White House. Newbrand was a retired Secret Service agent who had been part of Nixon's protection detail in the Eisenhower administration and had been called on from time to time in Nixon's White House as what Alexander Butterfield called a "sort of utility man."

Secret Service protection for Kennedy resumed on September 8 and ran until just after the election, on November 8, 1972.

It is unclear what, if anything, Newbrand passed along to the White House about Kennedy; after this September 7, 1972, conversation was declassified in the 1990s, former Deputy Chief of Staff Alexander P. Butterfield told the *Washington Post* that he did not believe any compromising information about Kennedy ever came out of the Secret Service.[4]

> **President Nixon:** Now, the other thing that I want understood, have you covered with him the business of the [Edward] Kennedy coverage?[5]
>
> **Alexander Butterfield:** Yes.
>
> **Bob Haldeman:** Yes.
>
> **President Nixon:** What man have you--have you assigned a man to him?

---

3. George Lardner, Jr., "Nixon Ordered Spy Placed in Sen. Kennedy's Secret Service Detail," *Washington Post*, 8 February 1997, p.A06.

4. Maxine Cheshire, "Kennedy Dismisses Guards," *Washington Post*, 9 June 1972, p.B1; "Kennedy Guard Lifted at Request of Senator," *New York Times*, 10 June 1972, p.13.

5. Kennedy was widely rumored to be having an affair with 28-year-old New York socialite Amanda Burden. Maxine Cheshire, "Burdens Seek Quick Divorce," *Washington Post*, 8 August 1972, p.B1. Burden was also a close friend of Kennedy's sister and brother-in-law, Jean and Steve Smith. Maxine Cheshire, "Does the G.O.P. Bug Danny Boy?," *Washington Post*, 5 June 1973, p.B3.

Butterfield: Yes. It's all taken care of, sir. [Unclear.]

President Nixon: That they all--and they all know that [unclear].

Haldeman: And I'll talk to [Robert] Newbrand and give him--I just want to get him one [unclear].

Unclear exchange.

President Nixon: But he's not [unclear], as I understand.

Haldeman: [Unclear.]

President Nixon: [Secret Service Director James J.] Rowley is not to make the assignment. Does he understand? Rowley [unclear].

Haldeman: He's to assign Newbrand.

President Nixon: Does he understand that he's to do that?

Butterfield: He's effectively already done it. And we have a full force assigned, 40 men.

Haldeman: I told them to put a big detail on him [unclear].

President Nixon: A big detail is correct. One that can cover him around the clock, every place he goes.

Laughter obscures mixed voices.

President Nixon: Right. No, that's really true. He has got to have the same coverage that we give the others, because we're concerned about security and we will not assume the responsibility unless we're with him all the time.

Haldeman: And Amanda Burden can't be trusted. [Unclear.] You never know what she might do. [Unclear.]

President Nixon: OK. Fine. Incidentally, I want it to be damn clear that he requested it.

Butterfield: [Unclear.]

President Nixon: He requested it. [Unclear] because of threats. In other words, of course, that builds the son of a bitch up. And I wanted to be sure that we didn't [unclear].

Edit. Butterfield exits and White House Press Secretary Ron Ziegler enters to discuss an upcoming cruise on *Sequoia*, the presidential yacht. Once he leaves, the President resumes discussing the Secret Service detail on Senator Kennedy.

President Nixon: I just wondered how you handled the--how you told Rowley you wanted Newbrand.

Haldeman: I told Alex [Butterfield] to tell Rowley that Newbrand was to be put in charge of the detail. That I'm having Alex do.

President Nixon: Yeah.

Haldeman: So that it's a routine--he handles, deals with the Secret Service.

President Nixon: And Rowley doesn't [unclear] Rowley doesn't bitch, now. [Unclear.]

Haldeman: He won't bitch.

President Nixon: And you'll talk to Newbrand?

Haldeman: And I'll talk to Newbrand and tell him how to approach it, because Newbrand will do anything that I tell him to.

President Nixon: He will go on [unclear].

Haldeman: [with Nixon acknowledging] He really will. *And he has come to me twice and absolutely, sincerely said, "With what you've done for me and what the President's done for me, I just want you to know, if you want someone killed, if you want anything else done, anyway, any direction--"*

President Nixon: The thing that I [unclear] is this: we just might get lucky and catch this son-of-a-bitch and ruin him for '76.

Haldeman: That's right.

President Nixon: He doesn't know what he's really getting into. We're going to cover him, and we are not going to take "no" for an answer. He can't say "no." The Kennedys are arrogant as hell with these Secret Service. He says, "Fine," and he should pick the detail, too.

Haldeman: Then you go on the basis of, what? Kennedy may throw it out. But if he does, that's fine.

President Nixon: That's OK.

Haldeman: It doesn't matter.

President Nixon: That's going to be fun.

Haldeman: *Newbrand will just love it.*

President Nixon: *Sure. Also, I want you to tell Newbrand if you will that [unclear] because he's a Catholic, sort of play it, he was for Jack Kennedy all the time. Play up to Kennedy, that "I'm a great admirer of Jack Kennedy." He's a member of the Holy Name Society. He wears a St. Christopher [unclear].*

Haldeman laughs. End of tape.

Needless to say, Newbrand was a bad seed. But this wasn't his first rodeo, so to speak.

Backing up a bit for some more historical context:

Nov. 9, 1963 – Miami Police tape-record a conversation in which an extreme right-wing political organizer accurately predicts the assassination of President John F. Kennedy just as it was to happen 13 days later. The man said the President would be killed by shots fired "from an office building with a high-powered rifle."

Then he dropped his tape-recorded bombshell.

> **Somersett**: . . . I think Kennedy is coming here on the 18th . . . to make some kind of speech. . . I imagine it will be on TV.
>
> **Milteer**: You can bet your bottom dollar he is going to have a lot to say about the Cubans. There are so many of them here.
>
> **Somersett**: Yeah, well, he will have a thousand bodyguards. Don't worry about that.
>
> **Milteer**: The more bodyguards he has the easier it is to get him.
>
> **Somersett**: What?
>
> **Milteer**: The more bodyguards he has the more easier it is to get him.
>
> **Somersett**: Well, how in the hell do you figure would be the best way to get him?
>
> **Milteer**: From an office building with a high-powered rifle. How many people does he have going around who look just like him? Do you know about that?
>
> **Somersett**: No, I never heard he had anybody.
>
> **Milteer**: He has about fifteen. Whenever he goes anyplace, he knows he is a marked man?
>
> **Somersett**: You think he knows he is a marked man?
>
> **Milteer**: Sure he does.
>
> **Somersett**: They are really going to try to kill him?
>
> **Milteer**: Oh, yeah, it is in the working. Brown himself, Brown is just as likely to get him as anybody in the world. He hasn't said so, but he tried to get Martin Luther King.

After a few more minutes of conversation, Somersett again spoke of assassination.

Somersett: . . . Hitting this Kennedy is going to be a hard proposition, I tell you. I believe you may have figured out a way to get him, the office building and all that. I don't know how the Secret Service agents cover all them office buildings everywhere he is going. Do you know whether they do that or not?

Milteer: Well, if they have any suspicion they do that, of course. But without suspicion, chances are that they wouldn't. You take there in Washington. This is the wrong time of the year, but in pleasant weather, he comes out on the veranda and somebody could be in a hotel room across the way and pick him off just like that.

Somersett: Is that right?

Milteer: Sure, disassemble a gun. You don't have to take a gun up there, you can take it up in pieces. All those guns come knock down. You can take them apart.

Before the end of the tape, the conversation returns to Kennedy.

Milteer: Well, we are going to have to get nasty. . .

Somersett: Yeah, get nasty.

Milteer: We have got to be ready, we have got to be sitting on go, too.

Somersett: Yeah, that is right.

Milteer: There ain't any countdown to it, we have just got to be sitting on go. Countdown, they can move in on you, and go they can't. Countdown is all right for a slow prepared operation. But in an emergency operation, you have got to be sitting on go.

Somersett: Boy, if that Kennedy get shot, we have go to know where we are at. Because you know that will be a real shake. . .

Milteer: They wouldn't leave any stone unturned there. No way. They will pick up somebody within hours afterwards, if anything like that would happen, just to throw the public off.

Somersett: Oh, somebody is going to have to go to jail, if he gets killed.

Milteer: Just like Bruno Hauptmann in the Lindbergh case, you know.

The entire tape-recording lasts roughly a half-hour and much of it is either garbled or irrelevant. Each voice is distinctly unique. Somersett spoke his words quickly, infusing each syllable with a thick Southern accent. Milteer's high pitched, effeminate voice dilutes the deadliness of his words.

Kennedy came to Miami Nov. 18, 1963 for the Inter-American Press Association convention at the Americans. The Secret Service, alerted about the tape by Miami authorities (and certainly by the FBI who received the information directly from Somersett), abandoned a planned motorcade. Instead, the President helicoptered to Miami Beach.

Incredibly, none other than Bob Newbrand, the local Secret Service spokesman, said: "I know for sure we didn't put him (Milteer) under surveillance. *We were never that much involved with that.* If anybody made a threat we wouldn't put him under surveillance, we'd lock him up! [Emphasis added]"

Clearly, the Secret Service dropped the ball in a major way here. In addition, Newbrand is dead wrong. As I reported in chapter two of my first book, SAIC of PRS (the intelligence branch) Robert Bouck told me that he was aware of the Milteer threat before the assassination, as Secret Service documents also confirm. With this in mind, it is striking that, of all people, it is Newbrand who is called to "put out the fire," so to speak. From JFK to Teddy, he was there.

NIXON MAKES RADICAL CHANGES

Nixon saw to the retirement or dismissal of the top five Secret Service officials-Chief James J. Rowley: replaced by H. Stuart Knight, former SAIC of the V.P. LBJ Detail[6]; Deputy Director Rufus W. Youngblood[7]; ASAIC of White House Detail William L. "Bill" Duncan, who was the advance man for JFK's Fort Worth stop 11/21- 11/22/63[8]; SAIC of WHD Robert H. "Bob" Taylor, who dated back to Nixon's Vice Presidential days[9]; and Assistant Director Thomas L. "Lem" Johns[10]:

WASHINGTON (UPI) — Robert H. Taylor has been ousted as head of the White House Secret Service detail, a spokesman acknowledged Monday.

Sources said Taylor, 46, was removed because of friction with Presidential Assistant H. R. Haldeman. They said the rift began about the time of the November election and peaked several weeks ago during the funeral for former President Lyndon B. Johnson.

Nixon Chief of Staff H.R. Haldeman's fingerprints were on all of these dismissals. In addition to Taylor and Johns, Youngblood, Rowley

---

6. HSCA testimony of Rowley, 9/78 (audiotape); Author's interview with Rowley, 9/27/92; Author's interviews with Knight, 10/22/92 & 2/8/94; See also *The Secret Service: The Hidden History of an Enigmatic Agency* by Philip Melanson (2002), pp. 105, 186 & 221, and *New York Times*, 10/23/73.

7. *Confessions of an Ex-Secret Service agent*, p. 45. Author's interviews with Youngblood, 10/22/94 & 2/8/94 (same dates as Knight) See also *The Arrogance of Power: The Secret World of Richard Nixon* by Anthony Summers, page 247, and *Washington Post*, 10/19/71.

8. A. Dale Wunderlich, a PRS agent who went to Dallas after the assassination re: the investigation, and William L. Duncan now are leaders of an established executive protection firm as of 2003 (although Duncan appear to have left the company around 2001). Both gentlemen sat for videotaped oral histories in 2005 for the Sixth Floor Museum; Rush (Venker), p. 58; see also *Fort Worth Press*, 11/22/63 – captioned photo of Duncan.

9. Rush (Venker), pp. 56-58, 149; *Protecting the President* by Dennis McCarthy, pages 198, 201-202; *The Secret Service: The Hidden History of an Enigmatic Agency* by Philip Melanson (2002), pages 105 and 221; see also *The Flying White House*, pp. 260-261.

10. New revelations from his 2013 DVD *Lem Johns: Secret Service Man;* author's interview with Johns.

151

and Duncan were victims of Haldeman's wrath.[11] Nixon agent Marty Venker wrote: "The agents used to joke that if anybody ever started shooting at the President, Haldeman better duck because a Secret Service bullet might find him."[12] Fellow Nixon agent Dennis McCarthy wrote: "The agents' animosity toward Haldeman was so violent that they talked among themselves about "getting" Haldeman. More than once, I heard frustrated members of the White House detail say that if there was ever a gunfight around the President, Haldeman better get his ass down in a hurry or he might catch a stray bullet from a Secret Service gun."[13]

Mike Endicott, who served on the WHD during the Nixon era, wrote in his book *Walking With Presidents* (pp. 67-68): "Special Agent In Charge Bob Taylor was in serious negotiations with the senior White House Staff concerning the placement of agents alongside the limousine during the inaugural parade ... He understood the desire of the White House Staff not to have agents riding the rear bumper of the limo, but Taylor knew he needed to have his agents close enough to respond in the event the situation required it. Taylor agreed to have the agents walk parallel to the limousine near the crowd during the initial phase of the parade. He told Chief of Staff H.R. Haldeman he would keep open the option of using agents in their traditional positions on the rear bumper, near the rear doors, and next to the front fenders of the limousine if the situation dictated ... Taylor directed agents to move to their normal positions ... I gained a lot of respect that day for Taylor when he would not relent to the demands of Haldeman." See for yourself:

11. *Confessions of an Ex-Secret Service Agent*, pages 45, 58, 149; *The Secret Service: The Hidden History of an Enigmatic Agency* by Philip Melanson (2002), pp. 105, 186 & 221; See also *The Arrogance of Power: The Secret World of Richard Nixon* by Anthony Summers, page 247, and *Washington Post*, 10/19/71.
12. *Confessions of an Ex-Secret Service Agent*, page 46.
13. *Protecting the President*, page 202.

Strangely, Nixon's favorite limousine during his administration was the refurbished Kennedy death limousine[14]:

In this rare document from his Vice Presidential days during the Eisenhower era, Nixon shows his respect for the Secret Service:

---

14. *Confessions of an Ex-Secret Service Agent* by George Rush, p. 176.

UNITED STATES SECRET SERVICE

FOR ADMINISTRATIVE USE ONLY

Vol. No. 20 - No. 48   5-29-58

THE CHIEF SAYS:

Following are excerpts from a talk by the Vice President before the National Press Club in Washington, D. C., on May 21:

"Now, turning to some specific comments with regard to people who were on this trip, may I mention one group which seldom gets mentioned and get their pictures in the paper usually only when their backs are to the camera. I speak of the Secret Service. In both Peru and in Venezuela there was a very small number of Secret Service men. And I think that one of the greatest tributes to the Secret Service and the performance of these men is the fact that where there was a possibility that someone might have been injured--despite the provocation, in neither of these countries was anybody killed nor seriously injured. The greatest credit goes not to me, not to the members of our party, but to the Secret Service who showed tremendous restraint, who took a great deal of abuse, and who handled themselves magnificently.

"Of course, I have a personal interest--the Secret Service is there to protect me. I didn't want to get killed. But, on the other hand, as most of you can imagine, there were the international repercussions and the national repercussions, in the event that one of them had found it necessary to use a weapon. You can see what the results would have been from the standpoint of the United States. "

I have also been told personally by many members of the party, including the press, of the excellent work of the agents.

Vice President Nixon had reason to appreciate the efforts of the Secret Service: they literally saved his life on 5/13/58 in Caracas, Venezuela from a violent mob – agents John "Jack" Sherwood, H. Stuart "Stu" Knight (later Director during the Nixon presidency), Robert H. "Bob" Taylor (later special agent in charge during part of the LBJ and Nixon eras), Wade J. Rodham (more on him elsewhere in this book), Howard D. Grubb, Ernest I. "Ernie" Aragon, Andrew P. O'Malley, Emory P. Roberts (later infamous during the JFK and LBJ eras, rising to Inspector during the Nixon era), Charles E. "Chuck" Taylor, Harry B. Hastings, Leroy M.

"Roy" Letteer, and John E. Schley. [15] Agent Stu Stout is also credited with being on this trip.[16] The Secret Service learned a lot from this trip about what to do, protection-wise, and what not to do, as well.[17] Proper pilot and lead cars were used afterward during motorcades, as well as (often quite a few) motorcycle officers to lead and clear the way for the official limousine.

That said, the Secret Service could also annoy Nixon, as revealed in this April 17, 1972 memo from Nixon to Haldeman following the Canadian trip: "The situation in Canada was intolerable," Nixon wrote. "[Robert H.] Taylor insisted on sitting on the jump seat where he could have just as easily sat in the front seat because there were only two in the front seat. The jump seats were constructed in such a way that they bent completely back on both Pat (Nixon) and me so that in her case she had to put her legs over on the other side, and I, of course, was totally uncomfortable all the way." Looking forward to a trip to the Soviet Union, he wanted better arrangements. He did not want "some interpreter or some Secret Service man sitting on my lap." Author Anthony Summers reported, "Often genial with those who guarded him, Nixon could also be irrationally unpleasant."[18] Vice President Walter Mondale told agent Mike Endicott that "Nixon was evil, evil," a remark that Endicott took umbrage with.[19]

When Nixon became enmeshed in the Watergate crisis, "[he] sometimes liked to be taken on long drives around Washington," journalist James Carney wrote. "In the privacy of his limousine, he would discuss Watergate with his closest advisers. It never occurred to him to be concerned that his Secret Service bodyguard ... heard everything from his perch in the front seat."[20] It was the Secret Service who installed the Oval Office taping system that led to Nixon's downfall. Alfred G. Wong, the former head of the Technical Security Division (TSD) for the Secret Service at the White House, was in charge of installing the listening devices. Wong was a Chinese-American originally from the New York office.[21] Wong and his cohorts had the perfect intelligence network to eavesdrop on all of Nixon's official, and unofficial, business. From the *Washington*

15. *Looking Back and Seeing The Future*, page 68.
16. *The Advance Man* by Jerry Bruno and Jeff Greenfield (1971), page 80.
17. Discovery Channel documentary *Inside The Secret Service* (1995).
18. *The Arrogance of Power: The Secret World of Richard Nixon*, p. 434.
19. *Walking With Presidents* (2008), pages 302-303.
20. *Time* magazine article by James Carney entitled "The Bodyguard: Shadows and Shields," 7/27/98. See also *Extreme Careers-Secret Service Agents: Life Protecting the President*, p. 52.
21. Re: Wong and background: 3 HSCA 418, 422; RIF# 180-10089-10262: 9/20/63 Secret Service Protective Survey Report; RIF#154-10002 10419: 2nd New York trip; 3 HSCA 358; Youngblood LBJ Library oral history, 12/17/68, p. 41; *Looking Back And Seeing The Future*, p. 134.

Post, 7/17/73: "Reliable government sources said yesterday that Alfred Wong, the former head of the technical services division for the Secret Service at the White House [On JFK's 9/24/63 Milford, PA trip], was in charge of installing the listening devices. Wong had recommended James W. McCord Jr., who was later convicted in the Watergate case, for McCord's position as head of security at the President's re-election committee. Secret Service agents Louis B. Sims and Raymond C. Zumwalt, both presently assigned to the technical services division at the White House were in charge of maintaining the elaborate eavesdropping operation at the White House and changing the tapes, according to the sources."

Former agent Darwin Horn wrote the author on 1/7/04: "Al Wong was Chief of Security for the Supreme Court." John Ready, the agent in charge of JFK's area of the limousine in Dallas, later guarded the tapes.[22] In fact, even Secret Service agents Marty Venker and Dennis McCarthy voiced their suspicions about the taping system. In particular, Mr. Venker believed "Deep Throat" to be a Secret Service official.[23] Actually, in June 2005, 91-year-old former FBI agent W. Mark Felt, who retired in 1973 as Associate Director (the no. 2 man), revealed himself to be "Deep Throat." But this does not rule out Secret Service agents who either helped in Nixon's downfall or, at the very least, had compromising information.

Author Anthony Summers reported, "A former member of the Executive Protection Service, the uniformed branch of the Secret Service, told the author that the president's tapes were in fact insecure, that duplicate copies existed. The Secret Service had its own microphone, in multiple White House locations, as part of the protection system, and these made Nixon's privacy additionally vulnerable ... some Secret Service agents involved with the taping were also former FBI agents, and Hoover aides were able to gain access to the tapes."[24]

As the Nixon tapes demonstrate, the President urged aide Charles Colson to have the Secret Service spy on Democratic opponent George McGovern in 1972. Confidential information was picked up by an agent on McGovern's detail and promptly passed on to the White House.[25] The House Judiciary Committee, which had voted on five articles of impeachment against President Nixon during the Watergate crisis, stated that Nixon had "repeatedly engaged in conduct violating the constitutional rights of citizens ... misused ... the Secret Service ... to conduct or continue

22. 3/1/78 HSCA interview with John Ready.
23. *Confessions of an Ex-Secret Service Agent*, p. 149; *Protecting the President*, pp. 30-31.
24. *The Arrogance of Power*, p. 535.
25. *The Arrogance of Power*, p. 411.

electronic surveillance or other investigations for purposes unrelated to national security ..."[26]

H. R. Haldeman stated, "In all those Nixon references to the Bay of Pigs [on the Watergate tapes], he was actually referring to the Kennedy assassination."[27]

Regarding Agent Art Godfrey, author Anthony Summers, who also interviewed the agent (as did I on two occasions), wrote, "Godfrey ... had been unusually close to both Nixon and [Bebe] Rebozo. After retiring in 1974, he had visited the disgraced president at San Clemente and watched the Grand Prix with him at Long Beach. Rebozo even asked Godfrey to work for him. As late as 1994 Godfrey was a member of the February Group, an association of diehard Nixon loyalists."[28] Other agents seemed unusually close to Nixon, including Ron Pontius who, like Godfrey, was a veteran of the Kennedy years.

Former agent Walt Coughlin described President Nixon as "A quiet, bright, shy recluse."[29] For my taste, this is an excellent summation of the 37th president.

MEMBERS OF THE PRESIDENTIAL PROTECTIVE DIVISION (AND RELATED AGENTS) DURING THE NIXON AND FORD ADMINISTRATIONS[30]:

ALBERT ANGELONE, J. ANTONELLI, Kissinger detail WILLIAM BACHERMAN, JOHN H. BAFFA, KEN BALGE, JERRY O. BALL, RICHARD F. BARBUTO, Assistant Director DAN BARTON, ROBERT W. BATES, JAMES M. BEARY, JR., GERALD BECHTLE, VP Ford Detail HUBERT BELL, MICHAEL R. BEST, Assistant Director LILBURN "PAT" BOGGS, THOMAS J. BONDURANT, VP Ford Detail JOE BOWLES, WILLIAM H. BRAWLEY, VP Ford Detail BOB BROWN, P. HAMILTON BROWN, WARNER BROWN, LARRY BUENDORF, VP Ford Detail BILL BURCH, Assistant Director of Protective Intelligence JAMES T. BURKE, MICHAEL O. BURNS, ELMON L. BURTON III,

26. *The Arrogance of Power*, p. 474.
27. *The Ends of Power* by H.R.Haldeman, pp. 68-69.
28. *The Arrogance of Power: The Secret World of Richard Nixon*, p. 247 (See also photo section re: picture of Godfrey).
29. E-mail to author 2/28/04.
30. Not including numerous field office agents. Based on numerous sources, including countless interviews with former agents, Secret Service shift reports and other documents, and many books cited in the introduction. Thanks especially to the Richard Nixon Presidential Library and the Gerald Ford Presidential Library, especially the documents pertaining to an 8/1/72 reception President Nixon had for the entire PPD and their wives, as well as a 8/19/74 reception President Ford had for the entire VPPD and their wives.

VP Ford Detail AL BUSKIRK, Kissinger detail JAMES CANTRELL, DAVID CARPENTER, A. CARR, JOHN E. CARRELL, JR., VP Ford Detail DOUGLAS CARVER, ROBERT M. CAUGHEY, VP Ford Detail DENNIS CHAPAS, RICHARD O. CHEADLE, DENNIS CHOMICKI, VP Ford Detail PAUL CIATTI, BOBBY F. COATES, Inspector HENRY COHEN, JIM CONNOLLY, ARTHUR L. COPELAND, VERN COPELAND (First Lady Detail), GEORGE W. COSPER, VP Ford Detail ROGER COUNTS, VP Ford Detail DICK CRABTREE, VP Ford Detail DENNIS CRANDALL, DAVE CRISP, WILLIAM C. DAVIS, VINCENT L. DEBENEDETTO, LUBERT F. BERT" DE FREESE, ROBERT DEPROSPERO (ATSAIC VP Ford detail), CLIFF DIETRICH, ALLAN G. DILLON, LEONARD D. DRY, ASAIC (responsible for the Nixon family details) WILLIAM L. DUNCAN, VP Ford Detail DAVID DUNN, LEONARD EGAN, BILL EBERT, MICHAEL ENDICOTT, VP Ford Detail TOM FARRELL, PATRICK J. FINNERTY, STEVE GARMON, DON GAUTREAU, VP Ford Detail ED GERMAN, VP Ford Detail GENE GIBSON, DONALD GLEASON, JOEL K. GLENN, ARTHUR L. GODFREY, ATSAIC DAVID B. GRANT, JOHNNY GRIMES, RICHARD W. GROSSENBACHER, PAUL G. GRUMMON, Kissinger detail NED HALL II, ROBERT C. HALL, CLIFFORD W. HAMILTON, JAMES M. HARDIN, VP Ford Detail STEVE HARRIS, W. RICHARD HARTWIG, VP Ford Detail TOM HEALY, VP Ford Detail JIM HENDERSON, Assistant Director CLINTON J. HILL, JAMES C. HOLT, HENRY HOOPER, WILLIAM E. HUDSON, VP Ford Detail JIM HUSE, ANDREW M. HUTCH, KENNETH D. IACOVONI, JOE J. INMAN, ROBERT JAMISON, GARRY M. JENKINS, Assistant Director THOMAS L. "LEM" JOHNS, RICHARD JOHNSEN, VP Ford Detail TIM JOHNSON, VP Ford Detail WILLIS JOHNSON, DALE L. JUNE, RAYMOND C. KALINOWSKI, VP Ford Detail BOB KANTOR, DALE KEANER, VP Ford Detail TOM KEELEY, SAIC 1973-1978 RICHARD E. KEISER, G. KENDALL, VP Ford Detail JACK KIPPENGER, CHARLES E. KORFF, Chief H. STUART "STU" KNIGHT, J. KRAJEWSKI, VP Ford Detail PAT LA BARGE, VP Ford Detail DENNIS LACEY, JERRY M. LAMB, RICHARD LEFLER, TOM LIGHTSEY, VP Ford Detail BOB LIPPENCOTT, WILSON "BILL" LIVINGOOD, VP Ford Detail BEN LOCKETT, WAYNE F. LORENZ, JAMES D. LOVELL, VP Ford Detail ERNEST LUZANIA, CLARENCE "BUCK" LYDA, JR., JOHN MAGAW, SAIC Intelligence Branch JAMES MASTROVITO, VP Ford Detail JIM MATICIC, VP Ford Detail FRANK McAFEE, VP Ford Detail KEITH McATEE, CHARLES W. McCAFFREY, RICHARD A. McCANN, DENNIS V.N. McCARTHY, VP Ford Detail TOM McCARTHY, VP Ford Detail GARY McDERMOTT, PATRICK E. McFARLAND, ROBERT T. MELCHIORI,

JACK MERCHANT, LEWIS MERLETTI, VP Ford Detail GARY MILL-
ER, MICKEY L. MILLER, VP Ford Detail RICHARD MILLER, STE-
PHENSON C. MILLER, JAMES MITCHELL, EARL MOORE, VP Ford
Detail FRED MOORE, ED MOUGIN, VP Ford Detail BOB NELSON,
WILLIAM NELSON, JOSEPH D. NOVAK, JR., ANDREW A. O'CON-
NELL, ERNEST E. OLSSON, JR., VP Ford Detail JOHN PARKER, JER-
RY PARR (ATSAIC, ASAIC VP Agnew Detail, DSAIC of VP Ford
detail), JOSEPH J. PEREZ, VP Ford Detail JACK PERRY, JOE PETRO
(VP Ford detail), STEVE PETRO, HUGH N. PETTIT, JOHN PFORR
(VP Agnew detail), VP Ford Detail NANCY PHILLIPS, VP Ford
Detail ED POLLARD, RONALD M. PONTIUS, WILLIAM C. POTTS,
LAURENCE QUIMBY (Chief, Executive Protective Service), TOM
QUINN, DAVID RAY, VP Ford Detail JACK RAY, VP Ford Detail
JIM RAY, Kissinger detail SAIC JOHN D. "JACK" READY, DOTSON
REEVES, FRANK A. RENZI, RICHARD REPASKY, MACK RICHARD-
SON, Tricia Nixon detail leader CHARLES W. "CHUCK" ROCHNER,
ANNIE M. ROGERS, DENNIS G. ROSDAHL, Chief JAMES J. ROW-
LEY, Assistant Director of Protective Forces PAUL RUNDLE, DAVE
SALEEBA, VP Ford Detail JEFF SALTER, LEE R. SCHAR, DONALD R.
SCHWARTZ, driver/ Special Officer HANK SCHWOBEL, MICHAEL
J. SHANNON, DENNIS P. SHAW, Special Officer WILLIAM SHELL-
HAMMER, LOUIS B. SIMS (Technical Security Division), SAIC of
Protective Operations JOHN SIMPSON, GEORGE A. SNOW, ROBERT
SNOW, VP Ford Detail GARY SPECTOR, BRIAN L. STAFFORD, VP
Ford Detail KELLEY STANARD, RICHARD STEINER, B. STERNBERG,
LARRY A. STEWART, R. STOKES, VP Ford Detail JOE STROMICK,
SAMUEL SULLIMAN, VP Ford Detail JIMMY TAYLOR, SAIC 1968-
1973 ROBERT H. TAYLOR, VP Ford Detail BOB TEATER, RICHARD
W. TERRY, VP Ford Detail BILL THIEL, Julie Nixon detail leader
HAROLD G. "HAL" THOMAS, CHUCK VANCE, MARTY VENKER,
LEROY J. WAGNER, NORMAN G. WALLACE, EDWARD P. WALSH,
J. BRANCH WALTON, IRVINE D. WATKINS, DOUGLAS A. WEAVER,
MYRON I. "MIKE" WEINSTEIN (Assistant Director Inspection),
THOMAS WHAN, VP Ford Detail BILLY WILLIAMS, CARL M. WIL-
LIAMS, GARNETT S. WILLIAMS, FRANK C. WILSON, SAIC Techni-
cal Security Branch AL WONG, VP Ford Detail LYLE WORKMAN,
DALE WUNDERLICH, Assistant Director RUFUS W. YOUNGBLOOD,
ATSAIC CHARLES T. "CHUCK" ZBORIL, VP Ford Detail JIM ZLO-
TO, RAYMOND C. ZUMWALT (Technical Security Division)

CHAPTER ELEVEN

THE AGENT WHO DESTROYED KENNEDY'S BRAIN AND WAS TIED TO NIXON'S WATERGATE

MIKE MASTROVITO

Former agent James "Mike" Mastrovito, who passed away 11/24/2006, was quite an enigma – according to his obituary: "He retired in 2004 after a career of some 50 years in law enforcement and intelligence, as an employee of the FBI from June 1958 until June 1959; U.S. secret service from July 1959 until July 1979. At the time of his retirement from secret service he was special agent in charge of the Intelligence Division at Secret Service Headquarters in Washington, DC. He had served in this Division continuously since 1964. He retired again in 2004 after working as an independent contractor with the CIA and had resided in foreign countries for 20 years prior to his 2004 retirement." As Mastrovito later wrote on his blog from 5/27/05: "On April 1, 1997, I was interviewed telephonically by a representative of the Assassination Records Review Board (ARRB), concerning my years with the U. S Secret Service Intelligence Division, when I was the custodian of the Kennedy Assassination file. The report of this conversation is noted in the

ARRB file number MD 261, pages 1892 and 1893…I will make some comments and corrections to this report as it appears that at the time of the interview some of my statements were misconstrued." Quoting from the ARRB interview: "From 1960 to 1962, Mastrovito was on the White House Detail. In the summer of 1962, Mastrovito was in the USSS field office in Charleston, West Virginia. After the assassination, he was called to headquarters. He became a Deputy in the Intelligence Division (formerly Protective Research Section PRS) for 10 years before becoming the director of the Intelligence Division a few years before he retired.[1] He worked with Walter Young, who replaced Robert Bouck. According to Mastrovito, Bouck moved out of PRS in the reorganization of the Intelligence Division after 1963. When Mastrovito took charge of the JFK Assassination file, it consisted of 5 or 6 file cabinets of material. After Mastrovito finished "culling" irrelevant material, the collection was down to one five-draw file cabinet. Mastrovito guessed that his purging of extraneous material took place around 1970. He said that the extraneous material consisted of records of 2000-3000 "mental cases" who called the Secret Service after the Kennedy assassination to claim responsibility for the shooting. Mastrovito offered that Robert Blakey questioned him about this destruction of documents and threatened legal action. Mastrovito pointed out that Chief Rowley's August 1965 memo directed him to remove irrelevant material.

Blakey had obtained index cards from the Secret Service for what were then called "White House cases" and/or CO2 cases. These cards had been sent to the Warren Commission in a card index file. From these cards, Warren Commission members had requested specific Secret Service reports. Blakey had also sought specific files based on his examination of these index cards. Apparently, Mastrovito had destroyed some files that Blakey had wanted to see. Mastrovito decided which files to keep and which files to destroy." Mastrovito later commented: "In regard to my "culling" of the files, further explanation may be helpful. A CO-2 number was assigned to the assassination as soon as it occurred and until the Warren Commission issued its final report, all information and material pertaining to the assassination in any way was given this sole number. Thus, much extraneous information, such as tips and "confessions" by mental cases was placed in this file. The "culling," did not destroy all of these reports. Those "culled" were given separate file numbers and many of these cases were eventu-

---

1. Mastrovito's position as head of the Intelligence Branch of the Secret Service is duly noted in former agent Mike Endicott's book *Walking With Presidents* (2008), page 202.

ally destroyed in accordance with the official retention and destruction schedule of the Secret Service. Professor Blakey did request certain files of persons whom had been given the original assassination number, but were subsequently given separate numbers and had been destroyed, and I recall explaining to his staff in detail why these files no longer existed as I had made the decision that they did not belong in the JFK Assassination File."

Back to the ARRB interview: "Mastrovito said no one had access to the assassination file except people in the Secret Service. Some reports were copied for the FBI and the Warren Commission. Mastrovito said protective surveys were not in the assassination file but were kept in the operations division.

Mastrovito said that a "CO2" number referred to Intelligence Division or PRS numbering. He speculated that a "CO-S" would go directly to the Chief's office. CO2 cases did not go to the Chief's office unless there was a particular or special reason for the Chief's attention." Mastrovito later interjected: "I tried to explain that threat cases had historically been given file numbers by headquarters rather than the field offices. In the early days of the Secret Service, the CO-2 cases were directed from headquarters and given the Chief's office designation. Later, with the advent of the Protective Research Section, which was renamed the Intelligence Division, the CO-2 numbering system was retained. Cases did not go directly to the Chief's office, nor originate in that office."

Back to his ARRB interview: "Mastrovito mentioned that Thomas Kelley was an Assistant Director of the Secret Service when Mastrovito knew him. Kelley interviewed Oswald in the DPD jail. Mastrovito used to kid Kelley because he never wrote a final report on the case." Later, Mastrovito noted: "In regard to my comment that I had kidded Assistant Director Kelley for never having written a final report in the Assassination case, I note that AD Kelley wrote detailed reports regarding his participation in the interviews with Lee Harvey Oswald. There was no need for him to write a closing report as the FBI took over the investigation. This was a private joke between the two of us, as he, being my boss, was always requesting reports from me."

Once again, back to the ARRB interview: "I asked Mastrovito if he had viewed or obtained any artifacts while he was in charge of the assassination file. Mastrovito replied that he had received a piece of President Kennedy's brain. Mastrovito offered that this item was contained in a vial with a label on it identifying its contents. The vial was the size of a prescription bottle. Mostrovito did not remember if it was glass or plastic. The vial was from the Air Force (sic) Institute of Pathology. (Armed Forces Institute of Pathology) Mastrovito said this vial from the AFIP lab came into his possession "about 3 or 4 years later." i.e. after the assassination.

(Then Mastrovito said it was about "1969 or 1970") The label said the vial had been sent from the autopsy at Bethesda; there was no other explanation with it. Mastrovito said he could not see what was special about the portion in the vial. I asked Mastrovito who gave him the vial, and he replied that his supervisor, Walter Young (first Chief of the Intelligence Division), gave it to him when he (Young) resigned from the Secret Service. Young had apparently received it from someone at AFIP. Mastrovito offered that Walter Young died last year. Mastrovito said he destroyed the vial and its contents in a machine that destroys food." Mastrovito later commented: "I have been asked several times about my decision to destroy the piece of the President's brain. I make no apologies for this decision. In view of what is being offered for sale on e-Bay these days, I believe I made the correct one."

Picking up from his ARRB interview: "Mastrovito offered more information about Secret Service records as follows: He said that after the assassination, the Secret Service change its policy regarding its records in presidential libraries. Before November 1963, the Service had sent its records to the federal records centers and to presidential libraries. That is, Secret Service criminal files were available to the public, for example, in the FDR library and the Truman library. After the assassination, the Secret Service recalled its criminal files from the Truman library saying that the agency wished to review them in light of the assassination. Instead of returning these files to the Truman library as promised, as Mastrovito put it, "the Secret Service kept the files, and we destroyed them." In those days, according to Mastrovito, the feeling at the Secret Service was that people's criminal files should not be available to the public. The Secret Service also recalled selected files from the FDR library.

Mastrovito was quite agreeable to the suggestion of future contacts from me, and he provided his travel itinerary and telephone numbers for the next several months."

Mastrovito later maintained his own blog where he wrote the following on 5/29/2005: "I retired in 2004 after a career of some fifty years in law enforcement and intelligence, as an employee of the FBI, the Secret Service and as an independent contractor with the CIA. I have created this site to address reports appearing on the internet in which I am mentioned. I will make comments and corrections to these reports as I believe are needed. These reports pertain to NSA watchlists, the "CIA" Crowley files, the JFK Assassination and the Watergate affair.

I will make no additional comments regarding any of these subjects. I do not intend to join the long list of those who have shamelessly profited from books, articles and media appearances as a result of the information that they were privy to during their government careers." This can be taken as a direct slap in the face to fellow former agents Clint Hill and Gerald Blaine.

I contacted Mastrovito's residence while he was still living in 2005. The former agent did not wish to be interviewed and, as noted above, passed away later on the next year. However, I was pleasantly surprised by being contacted out of the blue by Mastrovito's daughter Michele Beard in 2012. She wrote the following on 4/22/12: "I was going through some of his boxes…he told me the "brain" story after he retired completely from work the year before he died. I came across some documents in boxes last night that may or may not be sensitive. One is a copy, with a cover letter, of the doctor's notes/reports from Parkland in Dallas to the head doctor in Bethesda the day after the assassination…What do you think? Should I turn these over to the Secret Service? I really don't know if there are already copies of these that are public information….I have a lot of photos that I am sure you would find interesting…I found a file called "Kennedy Shooting Photos and Evidence Photos." Most are stamped on the back as being made and developed by the Dallas Police Department. I can scan some for you later."

However, when I wrote back expressing interest, she never responded back and ceased contact with me.

Returning to her father, regarding his role in Watergate, James M. Mastrovito wrote: "The final report of the Watergate Commission, Vol. 1, was released in 1974. The report runs 761 pages in its pocketbook edition. The final 29 pages, although not a part of the official report, consist of a Minority Report authored by Senator Howard Baker and his staff relating to alleged CIA involvement in Watergate. On the final page of the Minority Report, and the last page of the entire Watergate Report, is a sole paragraph which reads:

> Michael Mastrovito of the Secret Service should be interviewed concerning his Agency communications on June 17, 1972. Agency documents indicate that Mastrovito agreed to downplay [James]

McCord's Agency employment; that Mastrovito was being pressured for information by a Democratic state chairman; and that Mastrovito was advised by the CIA that the Agency was concerned with McCord's emotional stability prior to his retirement.

This paragraph has been mentioned in at least two books and has been referenced on the internet, and in the past I received inquiries from investigative reporters. Obviously, the paragraph infers that I and the Secret Service may have had further information relating to Watergate, or worse, may have been involved in it. I was never called to testify and I was not even given the courtesy of a phone call from either Michael Madigan or Howard Liebengood, staff lawyers for Senator Baker who authored this report, to advise me that my name was being included in their final paper.

When the Watergate incident occurred, early in the morning of June 17, 1972, I was in charge of the Protective Intelligence unit of the Secret Service in Miami Beach, Florida in support of the protection of dignitaries for the Democratic National Convention which was held in Miami Beach later that summer. I had been there since late May in liaison with all police agencies, the FBI and the CIA. The CIA chief and I met frequently. This was not a new assignment for me as I had served in the same capacity for the Republican National Convention in Miami Beach in 1968.

The paragraph in question results from a phone conversation I had with the CIA chief held later in the morning of June 17, 1972. I had been advised by my Headquarters in Washington of the general details of the incident and that James McCord was one of those arrested. I knew little of McCord, had never met him, and did not know where he had been working. The chief and I agreed that it was a stupid operation and we discussed McCord's involvement. The chief did not tell me at this time that others arrested also had CIA connections. Following our conversation the chief sent a classified cable to his Headquarters reporting our conversation. I have never seen the cable, thus, I have no knowledge of what other comments he made regarding me. Obviously, the Minority Staff took out of this cable only what they felt was pertinent for their interest and wrote the paragraph about me.

The final section of the Minority Report is entitled, Action Required, and a sub-section is entitled, Miscellaneous. In their haste to conclude their Minority view, the authors threw in my name in this sub-section to juice up their position that further investigation needed to be conducted. Obviously, nobody else agreed with their politically inspired Minority Report, because no further investigation was ever made. To be the only name mentioned four times in one paragraph on the last page of this long report has been quite upsetting for me. If I had been called to testify, under oath or not, I would have responded to the three insinuations in this paragraph as follows:

In response to: "Mastrovito agreed to downplay McCord's Agency employment":

My answer: I made no such agreement. I told the CIA chief that the Secret Service convention advance group would make no comments regarding Watergate from Miami Beach, and that any statements would be made by our Public Affairs office in Washington. I also told the chief that it was well known that McCord had worked for the Agency (indeed, at his arraignment later in the day of June 17, 1972, McCord's previous Agency employment was publicized). There would have been little reason for me to make a futile attempt to downplay McCord's Agency employment. It appears to me that the chief was trying to impress his headquarters that he was attempting to keep the lid on McCord's previous employment.

In response to: "Mastrovito was being pressured for information by a Democratic State Chairman":

My answer: I personally was not pressured by any Democratic official. I told the CIA chief that the Democratic Party was naturally upset that some of the Watergate perpetrators had come from Miami. I told him that Dick Murphy, the Chairman of the Democratic National Convention had been in touch with our Miami Beach office (not me), and that he wanted assurances that the Secret Service would keep him updated.

In response to: "Mastrovito was advised by the CIA that the Agency was concerned with McCord's emotional stability prior to his retirement":

My answer: The CIA chief did make that comment to me. My reaction was to laugh, knowing that this was his attempt to cover the Agency's backside. I also recall making a flippant comment to him on the order of "McCord must have been nuts to get involved in this mess."

As I stated above, I never saw the cable which the chief sent to his Headquarters following our phone conversation, therefore, I do not know what other comments he made in this message. Obviously, he was under a lot of pressure, thus, his comments regarding our conversation were crafted to his advantage. I do find it shoddy tradecraft that he used my true name in a classified cable.

Senator Baker made the following statement which is printed on the back cover of the pocketbook edition of the Watergate Report:

"We aspire...to write a report that will stand as an important document in the political history of the Nation."

Unfortunately, his Minority Report degrades the overall Report and will confuse historians in the future, plus, of course, give food for thought for the conspiracy theorists. To quote Robert Novak in his column Of March 27, 1975,"Senator Baker insinuated much, but proved nothing. And by hinting at revelations that he could not produce, Baker seriously damaged his own credibility."

I might not entirely agree with Novak's assessment that Baker damaged his credibility. Senators always seem to have a way of slithering out of problem areas. But if he did not damage his reputation, he sure cast suspicion on mine. I have no other information relating to Watergate. I had none when it occurred, and I have none now. But unfortunately for me, my name will always be associated with this sordid affair due to the Star Chamber mentality of Senator Howard Baker and his staff. Shame on them."

Returning to Mastrovito's CIA connections, two people connected to JFK's Texas trip also went on to have careers in the CIA: LBJ's Secretary Marie Fehmer, who became the first woman officer of the CIA[2], and Secret Service agent Roger Warner.[3] Interestingly, former agent Gerald Blaine of *The Kennedy Detail* infamy also later worked on a project with the CIA after his time with the Secret Service was over.[4] Three other prominent agency officials had OSS/CIA connections: Deputy Chief Paul J. Paterni was a member of the OSS, the predecessor of the CIA, during WWII and served in Milan, Italy with fellow OSS men James Jesus Angleton, and Ray Rocca, later liaison to the Warren Commission.[5] Chief Inspector Jackson Krill also had an OSS background[6], as did Treasury Secretary C. Douglas Dillon.[7]

It is no wonder why Nixon aide Charles Colson said that the Secret Service was infiltrated by the CIA[8], a sentiment also expressed to me by intelligence operative Gerald Patrick Hemming.[9] Author Philip Melanson

2. *Today* show 1/12/89: interview with Fehmer.
3. Warner revealed this fact via his personal Facebook profile!
4. *The Kennedy Detail*, page 348.
5. Julius Mader, *Who's Who in the CIA* (Berlin: Julius Mader, 1968); *Cloak and Gown*, p. 363; Burton Hersh, *The Old Boys: The American Elite and the Origins of the CIA* (New York: Scribner's, 1992), p. 182.
6. *Who's Who in the CIA*; HSCA RIF# 180-10074-10394(interview with SA Robert Jamison); Rowley Oral History, Truman Library, p. 31; *The Joplin Globe*, 1/22/00.
7. Numerous, including: http://www.newyorker.com/magazine/2011/03/14/wild-thing-louis-menand
8. *Miami News* 6/25/74.
9. *Survivor's Guilt*, page 214.

wrote in his 1984 book *The Politics of Protection*: "Traditionally, though secretively, the Service has received training and equipment from the CIA … Although the precise nature and extent of Secret Service dependence upon CIA remains top secret, it is surely important given the Service's limitations of personnel and resources."[10]

Bernie Malone, Rowley's cousin, wrote to me on 12/31/16:

> "James J. Rowley was my cousin, he was very close to my mother. He absolutely had nothing to do with the assassination, he protected and personally cleared all presidential trips starting with FDR and never lost a president [until JFK]. Eventually he became director of the Secret Service during the Kennedy years & during that time as you would expect of a director, the field work was delegated to other senior Secret Service Senior members, especially during Kennedy's campaign for re-election.
>
> I can assure you, if he were in Dallas that day, he would have not allowed that motorcade to travel through that ambush with all those open windows, he certainly would not have approved of the suspicious actions of the agents in charge, those agents would not have been called off the back of the limo. There were agents that you have mentioned who were involved, most likely through LBJ.
>
> As far as the other agent's, they were understaffed, worked long hours with little sleep and many did not approve of JFK's infidelity, regardless, they were in no condition to protect the president that day. James Rowley was turned down by Congress to allocate the much-needed funds for the Secret Service, they were understaffed & this was a disaster waiting to happen. James Rowley was in Washington DC on the day of the assassination and this was a perfect opportunity for the conspirators to take control of every detail before, during & after the assassination. I don't believe the regular Kennedy detail was involved with the possible exception of Greer.
>
> This is why I believe James Rowley allowed his ass to get grilled during the Warren Commission, he did not throw the men he knew were not responsible under the bus. I personally believe he realized that this was something much bigger than him. The one positive thing that came out of this tragedy is The Secret Service received the funding to expand and change how presidents would be protected in the future. The Secret Service Training Center is named after my cousin James J. Rowley."

10. *The Politics of Protection*, page 42. Technical dependency on the CIA: CIA Memo 6/5/73, discovered by Philip Melanson.

CHAPTER TWELVE

THE SPECIAL AGENT IN CHARGES (SAICs) OF THE WHITE HOUSE DETAIL (WHD), LATER KNOWN AS THE PRESIDENTIAL PROTECTIVE DIVISION (PPD), 1901-2017

Without question, the Special Agents (SA's) of the White House Detail (WHD), now known as the Presidential Protective Division (PPD), are the crème de la crème of the agency – the elite corps. These are the brave men and women assigned the special duty and honor of protecting the nation's President. These men and women are there to protect by law and after paying their dues in field offices catching counterfeiters and standing post whenever a president or dignitary visits their local jurisdiction.

However, the men who provide the top leadership to these agents are perhaps, other than the Directors, in the most pressure-packed positions: they are only as good as the success of the mission performed by the agents under them. With a few notable exceptions, the lion's share of this small and distinguished group has gone largely unnoticed and unreported through the many decades they have been of service to the country. Here, then, is a first time listing of all the known agents who comprise the Special Agent in Charges (SAICs) of the White House Detail (WHD), later known as the Presidential Protective Division (PPD), 1901-2017. There is precious little information, official or otherwise, concerning the top agents that protected our presidents. The Secret Service, officially speaking, would never release this information (I know – I asked). Going through official channels can often lead nowhere, as can be seen this official response I received regarding JFK:

Dear Mr. Palamara:

Mr. Jerry Bechtle forwarded your letter dated December 17, 1997, to the Secret Service for response.

In regard to your question concerning the protection of President Kennedy, the Secret Service does not consider it appropriate to comment on issues of this nature.

Thank you for your interest.

Sincerely,

H. Terrence Samway
Assistant Director
Office of Government Liaison
and Public Affairs

The following is based on many years of dogged research via books, rare documents, agent interviews, and news releases, also helped along by an AP news excerpt that helped piece together the number of top agents, at least up to the end of the 20th century:

The Associated Press, 7/18/98: "[Larry] Cockell is one of only 24 special agents to be in charge of the presidential protective division since it started in 1901 and is the first black to hold the job."

1. Joseph E. Murphy (Teddy Roosevelt [1901]-Taft eras)
2. Dick Jervis (Wilson era)
3. Col. Edmund W. Starling (Wilson-FDR)
4. Michael F. Reilly (1943-1945)
5. George C. Drescher (SAIC 4/12/45-5/3/46; nephew Earl L. Drescher became the deputy chief of the Executive Protective Service in the late 1970's)
6. James J. Rowley (1946-Sept. 1961)
7. Gerald A. Behn (Sept. 1961-Jan. 1965)
8. Rufus W. Youngblood (1965)
9. Thomas "Lem" Johns (Fall 1965)
10. Clinton J. Hill (Approx. 1966-1968)
11. Robert H. Taylor[1] (LBJ & NIXON: 1968-Feb. 1973)
12. Richard E. Keiser (Feb. 1973-1978; Nixon, Ford[2], Carter)
13. John R. Simpson (Carter; 1978-1979)
14. Gerald S. Parr (Carter-Reagan; 1979 early 1982)
15. Robert DeProspero (Reagan, Jan. 1982-approx. April 1985)
16. Ray Shaddick (Reagan/ Bush; 1985-1989)
17. John W. Magaw (Bush; approximately 1989-1992)
18. Rich "Skip" Miller (Bush/ Clinton; approximately 1992-1993)
19. David Carpenter (Clinton; 1994-1995)
20. Don Flynn[3] (Clinton)
21. Lewis C. Merletti (Clinton)
22. Brian L. Stafford (Clinton)
23. Larry Cockell (Clinton)
24.[4] Carl Truscott (Bush)
25. Eddie Marinzel (Bush)
26. Nick Trotta (Bush)
27. Don White (Bush) [photo not available]
28. Joe Clancy (Obama; 2/1/09-6/30/11)
29. Vic Erevia (Obama; 2011-2013)
30. Robert Buster (Obama; 2013-2015; assistants: Thomas Rizza, Kimberly Tello)

1. Taylor passed away 3/12/81 at the age of 54: *New York Times*, 3/14/81.
2. Keiser was not on the 9/5/75 California trip where Lynette Alice (Squeaky) Fromme, a member of the Charles Manson family, tried to assassinate President Ford because he had come down with a severe attack of hiccups – *Newsweek*, 9/15/75.
3. Flynn passed away 1/19/14 at the age of 61
4. As you will notice, if the 1998 AP story is to be believed, I am one agent off the mark of 24 to this point. However, after extremely diligent research and consultation with former agents, it is truly a mystery as to who the missing agent is, assuming the veracity of the exact number (24) as quoted in the article.

Members of the Presidential Protective Division (and Related Agents)
During the Administrations of Presidents Carter and Reagan[5]:

WILLIAM ALBRACHT, REGGIE BALL, CLIFF BARANOWSKI, JOHN
BARLETTA, HUBERT T. BELL (SAIC of VP Bush detail), THOM-
AS BLECHA, BARNEY BOYETT (VP Mondale detail), LARRY BU-
ENDORF, AL BUSKIRK, SHAWN CAMPBELL (Nancy Reagan de-
tail), JOE CARLON, DAVID G. CARPENTER, DENNIS CHOMICKI,
LARRY COCKELL, JOHN F. COLLINS, ROGER COUNTS, HAROLD
CREAMER, H. DOUGLAS CUNNINGHAM, LARRY CUNNINGHAM,
VP Mondale detail DAVID CURTIS, SAIC ROBERT L. DEPROSPE-
RO, KEN DE ROBERTS, JOHN DESMEDT, GARY DE YULEA, LARRY
DOMINGUEZ, PETE DOWLING, WINFIELD ERICKSON, DENNIS FA-
BEL, DONALD A. FLYNN, STEVE GARMON, MARY ANN GORDON,
VP Detail DAVID GRANT, KEVIN GREBA, BILL GREEN, RICHARD
J. "DICK" GRIFFIN, JOHNNY GUY, STEVE HARRISON, ROBERT
HOGAN, TED HRESKO, JIM HUSE, JIM KALAFATIS, ROB KASDON,
SAIC RICHARD KEISER (1976-1978), PAUL KELLY, Director H.
STUART "STU" KNIGHT, ERNEST KUN, JAMES LE GETTE, ERIC
LITTLEJOHN, DOUG LAIRD, JOHN MAGAW, MIKE MADDALONI,
EDDIE MARINZEL, JACK MASTRANGELO, DANIEL MAYER (VP
Bush detail), TIMOTHY MCCARTHY, DALE MCINTOSH, LEWIS C.
MERLETTI, RICH S. "SKIP" MILLER, RUSSELL MILLER, GARRICK
NEWMAN, GEORGE OPFER (First Lady detail), SAIC JERRY PARR,
JOSEPH PETRO, TOM PETRO (brother of Joe), JOHN PIASECKY, VP
Bush detail ED POLLARD, TOM QUINN, ROBERT G. REESE, RICH-
ARD REPASKY, BARBARA RIGGS, LEE R. SCHAR, GEORGE SCHMAL-
HOFER, DON SCHNEIDER, STEVE SERGEK, SAIC RAY SHADDICK,
WALT SHEPPARD (VP Bush detail), SAIC and Director JOHN R.
SIMPSON, PATRICK SULLIVAN, WILL SLADE, CARL SMITH, JACK
SMITH, ROBERT SNOW, DANNY SPRIGGS, BRIAN L. STAFFORD,
PHIL STRUTHERS, DICK SUEKAWA, ROBERT B. SULLIMAN, JR.,
VP Detail WOODY TAYLOR, GREY TERRY, GENE THOMPSON,
KAREN TOLL, JOE TRAINER, NICK TROTTA (Uniformed Division
and PPD-1988), CARL J. TRUSCOTT, DREW UNRUE, FRAN UTEG,
JIM VAREY, MARTY VENKER, JANE VEZERIS (Public Affairs), ED
WALSH (Protective Research), BOB WANKO, Special Officer BOB
WEAKLEY, MYRON I. "MIKE" WEINSTEIN (Assistant Director In-
spection; Protective Intelligence; Deputy Director), BILL WEISS,
FRED WHITE (Assistant Director – Administration), GARY WI-

5. Not including numerous field office agents. Based on numerous sources, including countless
interviews with former agents, Secret Service shift reports and other documents, and many books
174 cited in the introduction.

ESTRAND, DALE WILSON, KENT WOOD, JIM YAROSH, RAY YON-
KUS, MIKE YOUNG, CHARLES T. ZBORIL

Some of the Reagan detail (including Danny Spriggs, Bob Wanko, Tim McCarthy, Jerry Parr, Joe Trainer, Ray Shaddick and Robert DeProspero) with President Reagan:

CHAPTER THIRTEEN

PRESIDENT REAGAN'S NUMBER ONE AGENT ROBERT DEPROSPERO: SIMPLY THE BEST

People often ask me, "Vince, who are your favorite agents?" Here are the Secret Service agents I hold in highest regard and who fascinate me the most:

1. Robert DeProspero (SAIC President Reagan era 1982-1985);

2. Gerald Behn (SAIC President Kennedy-President Johnson eras 1961-1965);

3. Jerry Parr (SAIC President Carter-President Reagan eras 1979-1981);

4. Dan Emmett (CAT or PPD, President George H.W. Bush-President George W. Bush eras; rose to ATSAIC);

5. Joe Clancy (SAIC and current Director, President Obama era)

Even though I may be the harshest critic of the Kennedy Detail, I have a lot of respect, admiration for and fascination with Jerry Behn, who served from FDR (1939) to LBJ (1967) and was widely respected and admired by all of his colleagues. He was not in Dallas and I hold no suspicion toward him. He was, forgive my fan boy dialect, a cool looking dude who seemed to know what he was doing and had the respect and know-how to carry out his duties. If Behn had been in Dallas, I believe the outcome for President Kennedy would have been much better. I spoke to Behn three times on 9/27/92 and the information I gleaned from the cordial former agent was of extreme importance to my work. Behn passed away on 4/21/93. I spoke to his daughter Sandra and wife Jean later on, as well.

Rare and unpublished photos of Gerald Behn and his family + one of Behn as a young boy.[1]

Jerry Parr was one of the true heroes of the Secret Service, protecting President Reagan by pushing him into the limousine on 3/30/81 as assassin John Hinckley took aim at the President (agents Ray Shaddick and Tim McCarthy hold "honorable mention" status for their valor and performance on this date, as well). Simply put, if Parr did not make the decision to take a wounded President Reagan to George Washington University Medical Center, Reagan would have perished. *Washington Post* reporter and all around good guy, Del Wilber, wrote the definitive book on the Reagan assassination attempt, *Rawhide Down* (I have spoken to and corresponded with Del many times). Parr himself, who I had the pleasure of speaking to in 1995, wrote a great book called *In The Secret Service* (written with the help of his wonderful wife Carolyn, whom I had the pleasure of having some social media contact with). Sadly, Jerry passed away on 10/9/2015.

---

1. Graciously provided by a relative of Behn's.

The great Jerry Parr with President Reagan:

Dan Emmett wrote what I consider to be the best Secret Service memoir *Within Arm's Length* (I am mentioned on the cover of the original edition of Dan's fine book). Dan was praised by fellow agent Dan Bongino for his teaching skills when Emmett was an instructor[2], saying Dan was "as tough a human being as I had ever encountered," as Dan has a fine reputation for teaching many agents who went on to careers in the Secret Service. A former Marine and CIA agent, Dan's career in the Secret Service spanned 21 years protecting three presidents (four, if you count being a young post stander with President Reagan). I have spoken to and corresponded with Dan many times; great guy.

Current Director and former Obama SAIC Joe Clancy is another terrific role model for anyone aspiring to be a Secret

Agent Dan Emmett:

2. Dan Bongino's *Life Inside The Bubble* (2013), page 20.

Service agent. This gentleman just exudes charisma and toughness. Tough as nails, incorruptible, and a practicing Catholic, Director Clancy inspires anyone interested in the Secret Service.

Director Clancy:

Then, there is "Bobby D" (here pictured with President Reagan).

Robert DeProspero (full name Robert Lee DeProspero, a.k.a. Bob, Bobby, and Bobby D) is arguably one of the most respected protection agents the United States Secret Service has ever been honored to employ.[3] Agent Joe Petro said Bob was "as good a protection agent as the Secret Service has ever had."[4] Jerry Parr said: "I was blessed with great deputies… Bob DeProspero on PPD."[5]

3. See, for example, the book *Standing Next To History* (2005) by former Secret Service agent Joseph Petro, pages 140-142, 202-204, & 206-207.
4. *Standing Next To History* (2005), page 141.
5. *In The Secret Service* (2013), page 189.

Bob graduated from West Virginia University (WVU) with a Bachelor's Degree (BS) in physical education in 1959 and a master's degree (MA) in education in 1960[6] and later joined the United States Secret Service (USSS), serving from 1965-1986.[7] He was the Special Agent In Charge (SAIC) of the Presidential Protective Division (PPD) during a large part of the President Reagan era (January 1982 to April 1985), succeeding Jerry S. Parr.[8] Parr chose an excellent replacement: DeProspero was the perfect agent to head Reagan's detail in the wake of the assassination attempt. Fellow former agents Walt Coughlin, Jerry Kivett, Howell Purvis, Robert Snow, Darwin Horn, Mike Maddaloni, and a host of others waxed on about DeProspero's virtues to me in unique interviews that I conducted between 1991 and 2007. Walt wrote the following: "Have known Bobby for many years. Very disciplined – no nonsense guy-wrestled [at] West Va. U. Very good protection guy – Bobby is respected." Former agent Mike Maddaloni wrote, "Bobby D was ... very quiet, short in stature, but a weightlifter who was very powerful." Former agent Bob Snow wrote the author: "I know Bobby De. He was one of the best." Former agent Jerry Kivett wrote the author: "I served on occasions with Bob ... and have high regard for [him]." Former agent Howell "Hal" Purvis likewise wrote, "He was a dedicated agent and well respected by his peers ... I thought he was the best." Former agent Bob Ritter wrote: "DeProspero had a reputation of being an effective and fair supervisor, who elicited the best from those under him. With a poker face and reserved demeanor, DeProspero kept his subordinates guessing. He said little, but when he did – you listened. Never knowing for sure where they stood with DeProspero, most agents gave more than they might have otherwise. DeProspero's managerial style presented no problem for [me]; [I] always gave [my] best."[9]

DeProspero devised several very important and innovative security measures during his time in the Secret Service (while SAIC of PPD) that are used to this very day: the "hospital agent" (stationing an agent at the nearest primary trauma hospital on a presidential movement),[10] to

---

6. Please see: http://alumni.wvu.edu/awards/academy/1995/robert_deprospero/
7. 6/14/05 e-mail from George D. Rogers, Assistant Director, Office of Government and Public Affairs, to Vince Palamara.
8. Please see: *New York Times*, 1/4/82 and *Washington Post*, May 15, 1998, page A01.
9. *Breaking Tecumseh's Curse* (2013), page 432.
10. *Standing Next To History* (2005), page 141. See also *Syracuse Herald Journal*, 4/10/85: "AN AWESOME JOB – Agent was willing to die to keep Reagan alive WASHINGTON (AP) As the man who walked one step behind President Reagan for 4 years, Robert L. DEPROSPERO began every day knowing he could be called upon to place his body between the president and a bullet. There never was any doubt that he'd do it. "I always felt I was the guy," he said." Also, please see: *Philadelphia Inquirer*, 6/27/98; *New York Times*, 5/19/82; *Frederick Post*, 4/3/84.

which he received from the agency, among his many other awards, the prestigious Special Recognition for the Establishment of the Presidential Trauma Protocol[11], as well as the creation of magnetometer (metal detector) checkpoints to screen every individual who could get a view of the president, earning yet another agency award, Special Recognition for Improved Security Measures.[12]

As a result of his outstanding achievements as SAIC of PPD, DeProspero was appointed assistant to the director in the Office of Training[13], directing both a 20 million dollar expansion of the physical training facility and the administration of literally hundreds of courses[14].

The tremendous influence of DeProspero's time and talents in the Secret Service can still be felt today: not only have many of the assistant directors, deputy directors, and even some directors of the Secret Service (Lewis C. Merletti, Brian L. Stafford, Barbara S. Riggs, Stephen M. Sergek, George Opfer, and David G. Carpenter, to name a few) come out of DeProspero's PPD[15], Robin L. Deprospero (Philpot), whom I have spoken to and corresponded with, is currently the chief of the Personnel Security Branch, Special Investigations and Security Division, of the Secret Service, extending the proud legacy of the Deprospero family from the 1960's through and including the millennium and beyond.[16]

DeProspero can be seen holding onto the rear handrails of Reagan's limousine (along with George Opfer, head of Nancy Reagan's detail), during the January 1981 inaugural.[17] A light-hearted moment: during Reagan's attendance at the 1984 Olympics, Reagan turned to the unmoving, stern-faced DeProspero and said "Gee, Bobby, mine is ticking."[18]

Robert L. DeProspero also served in the U.S. Air Force from 1960-63, then went on to teach biological sciences and coach football and wrestling at Madison High School in Vienna, Va.

---

11. http://alumni.wvu.edu/awards/academy/1995/robert_deprospero/
12. *Standing Next To History*, page 141; see also: http://alumni.wvu.edu/awards/academy/1995/robert_deprospero/
13. *Standing Next To History,* page 202; excerpt from DeProspero retirement party as shown in the AFAUSSS newsletter (Bob is listed as ATD: Assistant To the Director) – see: http://robertdeprospero.blogspot.com/
14. http://alumni.wvu.edu/awards/academy/1995/robert_deprospero/
15. *Standing Next To History*, page 203; personal research of the author.
16. http://wvutoday.wvu.edu/pdf/Sep171998.pdf   See   also: http://a257.g.akamaitech.net/7/257/2422/01jan20061800/edocket.access.gpo.gov/2006/pdf/E6-13942.pdf
17. See the video *Inside The Secret Service*, Discovery Channel, 1995, as well as photo section of former agent John Barletta's 2005 book *Riding With Reagan*. See also the You Tube video I made that I gave to Bob himself, as well as his daughter Robin: https://www.youtube.com/watch?v=66g3hb-n2HG8
18. *Bucknell World*, 9/04: http://www.bucknell.edu/Documents/BucknellWorld/BWSept04.pdf

DeProspero joined the U.S. Secret Service in 1965 and was first assigned as a special agent in the Washington Field Office with subsequent assignments in the White House Detail and the Protective Support Division.

In 1973, he was promoted to assistant to the special agent in charge of the Vice Presidential (Agnew) Protective Division. As he moved up the ranks in the Secret Service from 1975-82, he held many positions including assistant special agent in charge of the Washington Field Office, inspector in the Office of Inspection and deputy special agent in charge of the Presidential Protective Division.

DeProspero took charge of the presidential detail in 1981 just months after the attempted assassination of President Ronald Reagan and was appointed special agent in charge of the Presidential Protective Division in 1982.

During his tenure in that role, he was responsible for planning, organizing, coordinating and directing the protection of the President of the United States and members of his family at all times and under all conditions. DeProspero was also responsible for providing protection during one of the Secret Service's largest and most complex security operations – the 1984 Presidential Campaign. He accompanied President Reagan on some of 500 domestic trips and 60 visits to foreign nations.

As a result of his numerous achievements, DeProspero was appointed assistant to the director in the Office of Training. DeProspero retired from the Secret Service in March of 1986. During his 20 years with the Secret Service, he made many significant and innovative improvements regarding protective measures. He spent more time than any other agent protecting officials including Dwight Eisenhower, Lyndon Johnson, Nelson Rockefeller, Edmund Muskie, Spiro Agnew, Gerald Ford, Jimmy Carter and Ronald Reagan.

Among his many awards are: U.S. Treasury Department Albert Gallatin Award, Special Recognition for the Establishment of the Presidential Trauma Protocol and Special Recognition for Improved Protective Security Measures. He was named the Outstanding West Virginia Italian-American in 1985 and was inducted into the WVU School of Physical Education Hall of Fame in 1992.

On 4/10/11, I received the shock of my life and a most pleasant surprise – Bob DeProspero himself wrote to me out of the blue: "Vince, I have been watching your work for many months. Am impressed with your research, accuracy and willingness to "tell it like it is."In retrospect, should have talked to you instead of Del [Wilber]. Bob DeProspero."[19]

19. DeProspero is mentioned in both Del Wilber's book *Rawhide Down* and former agent Bob Rit-

Unbeknownst to Bob at the time, it was I who started his Wikipedia page (since amended by others)![20]

In later correspondence, Bob filled in more details, based on my questions: "On November 22, 1963, I was a biology teacher, football coach, and wrestling coach at Madison High School in Vienna, Virginia. I heard the report of the shooting of President Kennedy while driving home from wrestling practice. The occurrence had all to do with my career in the USSS. If you recall part of the Warren Commission resolution was that the Secret Service should hire 200 more agents. I had boys on my football team and wrestling team whose daddy's were active agents and they immediately recruited me. I finished that school year in May and was in the USSS in June. I also had a young female student who was my lab assistant whose uncle was Stu Knight who later became Director of the Secret Service. I was [later] on the [Vice President Spiro] Agnew detail the whole time Agnew was in office. I was a shift leader under Sam [Sulliman] and also John Simpson. Clint [Hill] did not stay very long after Agnew became VP, but I knew Clint from having worked on the LBJ White House Detail in the early 1960's."[21] One of Bob's students, Hany Hasny, wrote to me the following: "He was my wrestling coach when I was in 8th grade. He coached us at Robinson High in Fairfax, Virginia, where his son, Bobby, was a standout wrestler. He is a man of unforgettable disposition. Tremendous presence, but no pretension. Very humble and understated. Soft spoken. I knew he was Reagan's top secret service man, but I was too young to appreciate what that meant in terms of the science he made of his work."[22]

In later correspondence, Bob filled in more details of his background: "Entered the Service in June 1965 and was assigned to the Washington Field Office (WFO). I went to Gettysburg on a temp [assignment] to the Eisenhower Detail in September (legislation passed to protect former Presidents), then permanent assignment to the White House when LBJ was there. I was thrown to the "4 winds" during the 1968 campaign. Rockefeller, Muskie, McGovern and then permanent assignment to VP Agnew at the end of the campaign. 1968 was long before rotations so most of us left home and did not come back until the end of the campaign except for brief visits."

Regarding the attempted assassination of President Reagan on March 30, 1981, I asked Bob where he was that day and here is his response: "John

ter's book Breaking Tecumseh's Curse.
20. https://en.wikipedia.org/wiki/Robert_DeProspero
21. In the 2011 DVD Lem Johns: Secret Service Man, a Secret Service shift report for the LBJ Ranch is shown depicting, among other agents, Bob DeProspero.
22. Online message 4/19/13.

Simpson and I quickly made our way (on foot) from the White House to the hospital. After double checking the security that had been established at the hospital and enhancing it somewhat, I relieved Jerry [Parr, the SAIC]. I stayed with the president while he was in intensive care. As a matter of fact the famous notes he wrote like "Could we take that scene over?" and "all in all I'd rather be in Philadelphia" he would pass to me and I would give them to the doctors. I don't remember how long I remained on duty but it was probably through that night and most of the next day."

Agent Don Cox wrote me on 9/28/2008: "I worked with (Danny) Spriggs and Bill Green on campaigns. Both, as you know, were at the Hilton [on 3/30/81]. Green, I believe, did the advance and Danny was doing Protective Intelligence. There was a Special Officer named Bob Weakley that was driving the spare limo. He deserves a lot of credit. When the call came out to divert to GWU hospital Weakley was the one that heard the transmission and peeled off from the motorcade to lead the limo to GWU. Another friend, Shawn Campbell, was with Mrs. Reagan at the time."

Robert DeProspero (behind Reagan).

Bob and I continue to correspond since and I have become Associate Producer of a major forthcoming documentary on his life and career called *The Man Behind The Suit*. In addition, his daughter Robin, currently in the Secret Service, contacted me via e-mail and phone in order to give me the honor of adding my praise of her father ("as the foremost civilian literary expert on the U.S. Secret Service") to the written nomination of a very prestigious award Bob received!

Former agent John Barletta wrote to me on 11/18/11: "What a world of difference from protecting Jimmy Carter to Ronald Reagan. That being said, I would have taken the bullet for President Carter just as I would have for President Reagan. It is the job – protecting the presidency no matter who holds the office."

The official poster of the upcoming documentary I am an Associate Producer for, *The Man Behind The Suit*:

CHAPTER FOURTEEN

LEADING CIVILIAN LITERARY SECRET SERVICE EXPERT

To date, my research has been quoted in over 120 books (1992-2017 and counting), in newspapers, in magazines, in journals, on the radio, on television, on DVD, all over the internet, and on several forthcoming documentaries, mainly in regard to my specific JFK assassination research. However, the notable Secret Service related items would have to include the History Channel's *The Men Who Killed Kennedy* (DVD) in 2003 (I was labeled a "Secret Service expert"[1], as I also was on the cover of former agent Dan Emmett's 2012 book *Within Arm's Length* and in Vincent Bugliosi's[2] books *Four Days In November* from 2007 and 2013's *Parkland*, the book based on the movie of the same name), Philip Melanson's 2002 book (later updated in 2005 and recommended by JFK era agent Tony Sherman to myself) *The Secret Service: The Hidden History of an Enigmatic Agency*, Gerald Blaine's 2010 book *The Kennedy Detail* (wherein I am mockingly labeled a Secret Service "expert," which I wear as a badge of honor coming from his ilk), Gerald Blaine and Clint Hill's C-SPAN appearance in November 2010 (on DVD and YouTube), Clint Hill's later appear-

---

1. I was also seen on this program by former JFK agent Larry Newman, as well.
2. Author Vincent Bugliosi wrote the author on 7/14/07: "I want you to know that I am very impressed with your research abilities and the enormous amount of work you put into your investigation of the Secret Service regarding the assassination. You are, unquestionably, the main authority on the Secret Service with regard to the assassination." I am also mentioned on 16 pages (text, footnotes, and disc) of his 2007 book *Reclaiming History*.

ance on C-SPAN by himself in May 2012 (also on DVD and YouTube), the forthcoming documentary *A Coup In Camelot* (which debuted at The Texas Theater in 2014), the forthcoming documentary *King Kill '63* (which also debuted at The Texas Theater in 2014), and the forthcoming documentary on Secret Service agent Bob DeProspero entitled *The Man Behind The Suit* (I am Associate Producer), among others. In fact, it was Bob's Secret Service daughter Robin that (also) called me a leading civilian literary Secret Service expert, which I consider a counter to Blaine's mocking tone. That said, I have perspective and am grounded firmly in reality – within the same week of that high honor, a failed attempt at yet another interview with former JFK era agent Larry Newman ended with him saying I was "crazier than a shit house rat"... so I am more humble than you think.

With all that in proper perspective, here are a few more gems calling on my expertise and opinion.[3]

I am quoted several times in a major article on the United States Secret Service in *COINage* magazine (February 2010 issue), the leading coin collector journal, available at newsstands, super markets, bookstores, etc. around the USA and many foreign countries. I am quoted along with best-selling author Ronald Kessler (whom I have corresponded with) and official Secret Service spokesman Malcolm Wiley. The article is entitled "The Secret Service Division: Will the Agency Continue to Fulfill its Dual Role?" (Protection and investigating counterfeiting). The article was written by Dom Yanchunas (who interviewed me at length via phone in November 2009). The cover of the magazine has the tag at the top: "The Secret Service's New Role?" and is the lead-off article in the magazine.

For those who missed it, here are the pertinent excerpts:

> Vincent Palamara, a longtime independent researcher of the Secret Service, said those [*counterfeiting*] cases should be sent to some other agency. "It's time for the Secret Service to devote itself solely to protecting the president and the dignitaries," Palamara said. "If we were having this conversation 10 or 15 years ago, I would say yes, everything's fine---but this is the post-9/11 world. When we switched from Bush to Obama, with the hate groups and the racial thing, the threat levels have increased.

---

3. I even made a major *Politico* article about Hillary Clinton's major best-selling book *Hard Choices* (that, as noted earlier, does not mention her uncle Wade) – "Another reviewer, Vince Palamara added, "I am very impressed with this book so far; much better than her previous books. Hillary is a force to be reckoned with."

http://www.politico.com/story/2014/06/hillary-clinton-book-review-amazon-107664#ixzz-40mIKitEY

Good investigative agents make good protective agents," [*official Secret Service spokesman* **Malcolm**] Wiley said. It's important for the nation that the Secret Service focuses its resources on ensuring that no harm comes to the president, said Palamara, who has interviewed at least 80 former agents on subjects including the assassination of President John F. Kennedy. He said Secret Service and other federal officials exaggerate the symbiotic relationship between bodyguard duty and monetary responsibilities. "They are two things that are really apples and oranges," Palamara said.

"It would be appropriate for the Treasury Department to take it [*counterfeiting investigations*] over," Palamara said. "That would help with counterfeit currency [investigations] because you would have people who are solely doing that."

The Secret Service teaches agents both specialties [*protection and counterfeit investigations*] at its training facility in Beltsville, Maryland, and in 136 field offices. Still, demonstrating talent for one task will prompt the agency to assign certain personnel more work in one area versus the other, Palamara said. For the anti-counterfeiting division, "it would be someone who had a college degree in finance or something, or someone who is just very good at investigations," he said. "The people with the military background are the type that gets sent over to the protective end of things."

Palamara said the anti-counterfeiting instruction is sometimes wasted. "A lot of Secret Service officers never even use that training if they go over to protecting the president and stay there," he said. [Note: Prominent agents Art Godfrey, Emory Roberts, and Robert DeProspero are just some of the noteworthy agents who stayed in protection their whole career. In fact, former agent Walt Coughlin wrote in a letter to myself: "The reality is the most respected [agents] are those who were good [at] both protection and field work – took lots of transfers and paid the "full price." ... Most of the protection only guys never left D.C. and there was some resentment about that. Never enough to affect friendships but it was there."]

He [*Palamara*] would expect the Secret Service, like any bureaucratic agency, to protect its turf if anyone in Washington tries to split it up. "There's no way they're going to take this lying down," he said. "There would be tremendous fighting. But in their heart of hearts, they must know that this is a totally different world than it was in the '60's, '70's and even the '80's.... Everybody thought it was heresy when the Secret Service was removed from the Treasury Department [*when they were transferred to the Department of Homeland Security*], but everybody survived.

2009 GAWKER ARTICLE: *WHAT HAPPENS WHEN YOU TWEET OBAMA DEATH THREATS?*

"A little over a week ago, we introduced you to Jay Martin, the man who very explicitly wished death upon Barack Obama via Twitter. He has disappeared from the Internet. What happened to him?

Conservative blogger Solly Forrell, and 19 year-old Washington state resident Jay Martin were two idiots whose outrage over the health care vote on March 21st inspired them to tweet Obama Death threats. (Martin tweeted: "If I lived in DC i'd shoot him myself…Point Blank. Dead Fucking Serious." Read all his death tweets here.) Martin's Twitter account is now down, and he hasn't responded to our emails. Solly Forrell's last tweet was a few hours after he threatened Obama. The Secret Service reportedly began investigating both of them shortly after their threats. So, are they, like, in Guantanamo Bay now or what? *We emailed Secret Service expert Vince Palamara – who's interviewed dozens of former Secret Service members and been in History Channel documentaries and everything! – and he explained what likely happened to Jay Martin.*

How seriously would the Secret Service have taken Jay Martin's tweets?

The Secret Service investigates any/ all threats, even ones allegedly made in jest.

Would they treat a threat on the Internet differently than one directly sent to the White House?

They treat the internet just as importantly as they do a person writing a "snail mail" letter to the White House. In fact, one can argue that the internet is even more threatening, because a vile and threatening blog or message can impact and influence other like-minded persons.

Last week, ABC reported that Martin was "under investigation" by the Secret Service. How does the Secret Service conduct their investigations?

Quickly and discreetly: they don't like a lot of publicity, to ward off copycats. They will consider the motive, means, and opportunity – and mental state – of the person or persons and weigh the consequences accordingly. If the person making the threat does not have the means to carry it out (a young school child or a handicapped invalid), that is taken into due account. Also, if the person is adamant that their threat was not to the level of what it might

[have] inferred, they will take that into proper consideration. I would almost guarantee that Jay Martin would have been visited. An arrest would be the judgment of the agents and their investigation.

What kinds of penalties or consequences does Jay Martin face?

Five years in prison, perhaps more, if weapons or planning were in the works. [If the threat was determined to be less serious] a "watch list" would be made up of those individuals or groups that warrant monitoring of some fashion, especially when a dignitary is visiting a certain region, as well as periodic checks whenever the chief executive is in the region.

So, that's what you get if you post Obama death tweets. Jay didn't seem like the kind of guy with an elaborate plan to assassinate the president, so we're guessing he got a knock on the door from some Secret Service agents, a slap on the wrist, and will now have a big black van parked outside his house whenever Obama comes to town. If you're reading this, Jay, we'd love to hear about how all this worked out for you!"

VOICE OF AMERICA NEWS 3/12/15:

Vincent Palamara, an author who has written about the history of the Secret Service, says that while lapses of professionalism are not new at the service, morale has plummeted and cases of misconduct have risen since the agency was transferred to the Department of Homeland Security – an agency with a history of bureaucratic dysfunction.

"Ever since they switched to Homeland Security, what's happened is they're under this big monstrous bureaucracy and consequently some things are getting swept under the rug," he said.

I mentioned agent Bob DeProspero very favorably when I spoke to the Chief White House correspondent for Voice of America, telling him that an advisory committee of former highly esteemed Secret Service agents and officials would be a big help to augment Director Clancy in his quest to clean house and tighten the Secret Service ship in the midst of a few embarrassing headlines lately. Bob would be my number one choice by far. Others would include Jerry Parr, Dan Emmett, Joe Petro, Eddie Marinzel, Nick Trotta, Lew Merletti and David Carpenter.

WND 12/7/14 SECRET SERVICE EXPERTS WORRY ABOUT OBAMA'S SAFETY

NEW YORK – Two leading Secret Service experts are worried about the safety of President Obama because of mounting disclosures of misconduct and lapses in protection.

Dan Emmett, a former Secret Service agent with first-person experience in the presidential security details of former Presidents George H. W. Bush, Bill Clinton and George W. Bush, told WND the "office of the presidency for the last couple of years has not been as secure as it has been in years past."

"This goes back to a complete failure in leadership from the director's seat all the way down to middle management," said Emmett, the author of the 2014 book *Within Arm's Length*.

"It's not out of question that a Secret Service agent, or even two or three, might get drunk and act stupid on a trip, but it was beyond imagination during my career that a supervisor would get drunk and act stupid on a trip," he said.

Vincent Michael Palamara, who claims to have interviewed more Secret Service former agents than any other researcher, said he has confidence in the new acting Secret Service director, Joe Clancy, but "unless Clancy can clean up the Secret Service fast, President Obama is going to continue to be at risk."

Palamara, a leading expert on the Secret Service lapses surrounding the JFK assassination, has devoted a page of his blog to tracking the Secret Service under President Obama, with a recent focus on Clancy's background and experience in the Secret Service.

Emmett noted that some of the Secret Service agents involved in the Cartagena, Colombia, prostitute scandal and other incidents were supervisors at the GS-14 level or even higher.

"I've been very critical of the Secret Service with impropriety after impropriety over the last couple of years, and I have no dog in the fight," he said. "I'm just calling them as I see them. When the leadership is not good, the troops do not perform up to standard."

Emmett also expressed hope the Secret Service was "on the road to recovery" with the appointment of Clancy.

"There cannot be a worse tragedy for the nation than losing a president," he stressed. "We must make sure that never happens again."

Secret Service leadership failures

Clancy replaced Julia Pierson after she resigned in the wake of a disastrous appearance before the House Oversight and Government

Reform Committee Sept. 30 in which she was grilled for more than three hours over two security breaches.

The first breach was an incident that occurred at the Centers for Disease Control and Prevention headquarters in Atlanta on Sept. 16 when Secret Service agents allowed a security guard armed with a gun and three prior assault convictions to ride an elevator in close proximity to President Obama.

It was followed by a second incident three days later in which Omar Gonzalez, a knife-wielding Iraq War veteran, jumped the White House fence and entered the East Room before he was tackled by an off-duty security agent.

Palamara, author of the 2013 book *Survivor's Guilt: The Secret Service and the Failure to Protect President Kennedy*, told WND that Clancy has a short time to reestablish discipline in the Secret Service detail assigned to protect the president.

"Clancy was appointed to clean house," Palamara said. "You read between the lines and now, I believe, you are going to see a culture that that is ship-shape now.

"What's been going on with the Secret Service is disgraceful, with these drinking forays, the partying with prostitutes, and the fence jumpers who get into the White House. This is gross negligence, tremendous incompetence, and it worries me."

Mark Sullivan, the director of the Secret Service who preceded Pierson, was forced to resign Feb. 22 after six Secret Service agents were forced to resign over reports they partied with prostitutes in Cartagena in advance of a presidential visit.

Avoiding repeat of history
Palamara told WND he is concerned that patterns of Secret Service misconduct he has documented in JFK's Secret Service detail prior to the assassination are being repeated in Obama's presidential detail.

"Many in the Secret Service in the JFK era did not like President Kennedy's womanizing or his position on civil rights, or maybe his policies toward Cuba," he said. "But here, with President Obama, the Secret Service is supposed to be apolitical, but the agents are human beings."

Palamara pointed out the Secret Service can put the safety of the president at risk by not taking actions they should be taking.

"Secret Service agents can let things happen when they start not liking or caring about the president," he explained. "It's inactions as well as actions that can put the president at risk."

He compared the Secret Service under Obama to the Secret Service under President George W. Bush.

"You didn't hear about these kinds of Secret Service scandals with President George W. Bush," he said.

"I think what the scandals under Obama are really revealing is Secret Service discontent with the president. The Secret Service agents are trained far better than they were in the Kennedy days. And as far as I'm concerned, even by 1963 standards, President Kennedy should have lived, had the Secret Service been doing their job the way the Secret Service should have been doing their job as they were trained to do."

Palamara fears the Secret Service's failure to protect JFK could repeat itself.

'Stand down'?

Palamara contends in his book *Survivor's Guilt* that contrary to the conclusions of the Warren Commission, President Kennedy did not order Secret Service agents to stay off the presidential limousine, and he did not insist that police motorcycles ride behind the limo to keep open his direct access to the crowd along the motorcade route.

"The story that JFK had ordered Secret Service agents to stay off the back of the limousine was a creation of Secret Service agents that wanted to take the onus of the assassination off their backs to place the responsibility on the back of the dead president who couldn't defend himself," he maintained.

Palamara pointed out that photographs of the presidential limousine in Dallas on Nov. 22, 1963, show Secret Service agent Clint Hill rode the back running board several times along the route before the motorcade entered Dealey Plaza.

"It's the other way around than most people understand," he said. "By law, it's the president who takes instructions from the Secret Service, not the other way around. President Harry Truman was famous for saying the only boss a president has is the Secret Service."

Palamara pointed out that even agent Clint Hill, the Secret Service agent who jumped on the back of the limo after JFK was shot, said in an interview that President Kennedy could tell the Secret Service what he wanted done, but that did not mean the Secret Service was going to obey.

In an interview for the Sixth Floor Museum in the Texas School Book Depository building in Dallas, recorded on Nov 18, 2010, Hill said he "had been told" JFK preferred the Secret Service not be on the back of the limo. Despite this, he noted his responsibility was to protect Mrs. Kennedy, and "four or five times as we drove down Main Street, I got on the back of the president's car, on the left side, to be in close proximity to Mrs. Kennedy, in case anybody tried anything."

Palamara also documented in his book that in a motorcade in Tampa, Florida, Nov. 18, 1963, only a few days before the assassination in Dallas, Secret Service agents rode on or near the rear of the presidential limousine. Agents also walked on either side, while police motorcycles drove alongside and in front of the presidential limousine, not just behind the limo as was the case in Dallas.

"The Secret Service was in big trouble after the JFK assassination," Palamara pointed out. "The Secret Service lost the president, and the JFK detail was worried about their reputations, their jobs and their pensions."

Palamara's breakthrough came in 1992, when he talked with Gerald Behn, the special agent in charge of the White House detail at the Kennedy White House.

"Behn told me JFK never ordered the Secret Service off the back of the limo, and that opened the floodgates," Palamara said. "Subsequent to that, all the Secret Service I interviewed about the JFK trip to Dallas told me the same thing."

Palamara's conclusion was clear.

"JFK's assassination was either attributable to gross negligence or worse on the part of the Secret Service,' he said. "At the very least, by standing down with security in the Dallas motorcade, the Secret Service left JFK a sitting duck."

Palamara referenced the 1963 film taken of the JFK motorcade departing Love Field in Dallas on November 22, 1963, in which Secret Service agents Henry J. Rybka and Donald Lawton express shock at being ordered off the riding stations on the rear bumper of JFK's limousine.

On pages 234-235 of his book, Palamara establishes that Secret Service agent Emory Roberts rose up in his seat from the Secret Service car following the JFK limousine from Love Field, shouted and used hand gestures. He ordered Rybka to fall back from the rear area of JFK's limousine, causing a perplexed Lawton to also fall back from the car, raising his arms several times in disgust.

"There were several Secret Service agents protecting JFK that I have on the record stating they were angry at JFK," Palamara said, including Roberts in this list. "Various of the agents have told me JFK was a 'procurer of prostitutes,' and that 'any president who treats the office this way doesn't deserve to be president.' And these are the guys assigned to protect the president? I don't think so."

Palamara also notes (page 233) that Roberts shift participated in the "infamous drinking binge in Fort Worth" that kept Secret Service agents on the presidential detail out most of the night be-

JFK motorcade in Tampa, Florida, Nov. 18, 1963, with Secret Service agents Chuck Zboril, (left, and Don Lawton, right, riding on or near the back of the presidential limousine.

fore JFK was assassinated. Roberts shift was accused of being "the worst offender," because they were the only ones assigned to the 8 a.m. to 4 p.m. shift with JFK on Nov. 22, 1963.

Rybka and Lawton, two agents Palamara believed took seriously their responsibilities to protect JFK, ended up being left behind at Love Field.

"JFK was the ultimate Secret Service scandal – they lost the president," Palamara said.

"So far what has happened to President Obama is silly stuff in comparison – Obama left the White House before the armed intruder jumping the fence got into the East Room, and he rode an elevator with an armed security guard with an assault record who evidently had no ill intent toward the president.

"Let's just hope Clancy can set the Secret Service right before all that changes," he said in conclusion.

Emmett disagrees

Emmett takes issue with Palamara's conclusion that there was any malice on behalf of the JFK Secret Service detail that led them to "stand down."

But there's no disagreement that the Secret Service failed, he said.

"Vince continues to assert the obvious and attempts to prove what has already been proven, that the Secret Service was responsible for the death of JFK," Emmett said. "This is like saying that the sun came up today. Everyone knows that."

Emmett said the failure of the Secret Service on Nov. 22, 1963, "had nothing to do with hangovers or whether JFK did, or did not order the agents off the limousine – an event I have always been skeptical about."

"Further, it was not due to any Secret Service conspiracy. JFKs death was due to the failure of PPD [Presidential Protection Detail] to take appropriate action as the result of a complete lack of training, especially drivers' training," he said.

"The entire day was lost when the day began, taking the president out into the downtown streets of Dallas in an open-top limo" he insisted. "As someone who drove POTUS for one year, I can attest that driving slowly in a straight line while under fire was the reason JFK died."

Emmett said the first round through the back was survivable and had the driver, William Greer, begun evasive maneuvering subsequent to looking back to see Kennedy had been hit, it is unlikely the head shot would have occurred.

He said, also, the detail leader, Roy Kellerman, riding in the front passenger seat of the JFK limo, looked around to see the president had been hit in the back.

"Had he acted properly by moving to the rear seat and pulling JFK down, history would have been significantly different," he said.

Emmett summed up his argument as follows: "JFK died because PPD agents of the day never trained. Had the Secret Service agents in JFK's era trained as today's agents, JFK would have survived Dallas. While each was a dedicated and devoted public servant, none was any more capable of reacting properly on that day than a group of insurance salesmen with guns. They simply had no idea what to do, other than Clint Hill, who responded more out of natural instinct than training."

Emmett argues that the problems in the current Obama-era Secret Service began after 9/11 when the Secret Service was moved from Treasury to DHS, and a large number of additional agents were hired.

"After 9/11, we got agent candidates at the academy that were so substandard they never would have been hired before," he said. "I watched the quality of a class of 24 agents in training that would produce before 9/11 about 18 super-solid future agents and about six that were average, to a class of 24 agents in training after 9/11 that would produce about eight agents that were average and 16 who were sub-standard."

He said many of these agents are now managers.

Political correctness also is to blame, Emmett said.

"Barack Obama was going to have a female Secret Service director and that was the end of the story," he said.

"Julia Pierson was a fine agent. We came on the job together, and I consider her to be a friend. But she was not director material. When she got the position, I feared it would not end well, because she lacked a strong sense of being a leader."

He said the Secret Service "is filled with great managers and she was probably a great manager."

"But just because you keep being promoted does not make you a good leader."

Emmett faulted Pierson for delegating without going out into the field to see in person what was happening.

"You can't sit in your office on the eighth floor, do nothing but hold meetings, and expect that everything is going to go well," he said."

OCTOBER 2014 VANITY FAIR ARTICLE COULD THE SECRET SERVICE HAVE SAVED JFK?[4]

As agent John Norris explained in Bill Sloan's book *J.F.K.: Breaking the Silence* and in an interview for Vincent Michael Palamara's book *Survivor's Guilt: The Secret Service and the Failure to Protect President Kennedy:* "Except for George Hickey and Clint Hill, [many of the others] just basically sat there with their thumbs up their butts while the president was gunned down in front of them.... Agent Gerald Behn, the head of the White House detail, who was not in Dallas that day, told one writer, "I don't remember Kennedy ever saying that he didn't want anybody on the back of his car."

THE ARRB FINAL REPORT GIVEN TO PRESIDENT CLINTON:

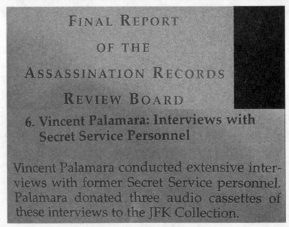

FINAL REPORT

OF THE

ASSASSINATION RECORDS

REVIEW BOARD

6. Vincent Palamara: Interviews with Secret Service Personnel

Vincent Palamara conducted extensive interviews with former Secret Service personnel. Palamara donated three audio cassettes of these interviews to the JFK Collection.

4. http://www.vanityfair.com/news/politics/2014/10/secret-service-jfk-assassination

ACKNOWLEDGMENTS

I want to thank, first and foremost, my wonderful wife Amanda Palamara for all her understanding and inspiration. I would also like to thank my mom Patricia Palamara and my father Guido Palamara for their unique inspiration for all I do, as well as my highly intelligent brother Tom Palamara. Special appreciation goes out to Deb Galentine and Michael Wood for their gracious help and support. In addition, former agents Darwin Horn, Frank Stoner, Gerald Behn, Walt Coughlin, Abraham Bolden, Sam Kinney, Robert DeProspero, and Dan Emmett were of particular help.

I would also like to thank all the following people I interviewed and/or corresponded with for this book, as well as for my previous two books. Here is the complete listing-

Secret Service agents (+ officials, surviving family members and other important people) contacted by the author [Note: not including countless authors, researchers, staff of presidential libraries and the National Archives, other library staff members, and the members/staff of the Warren Commission, HSCA and ARRB. This list also does not include many unsuccessful contacts and attempts through the years via phone and letters]:

1. Gaspard d'Andelot "Don" Belin (General Counsel/ Acting Secretary of the Treasury, JFK-LBJ era)

2. . James J. Rowley (FDR-Nixon)

3. Neighbor of the late Paul J. Paterni

4. Michael W. Torina

5. Gerald A. Behn (FDR-LBJ) + widow, daughter, relatives, and next door neighbor

6. Floyd M. Boring (FDR-LBJ) + relatives

7. June Kellerman, widow of the late Roy H. Kellerman (FDR-LBJ) + daughter (via Harold Weisberg)

8. Arthur L. Godfrey (Truman-Nixon)

9. The family of the late Stuart G. Stout, Jr. (FDR-LBJ era)

10.   Jerry S. Parr (JFK-Reagan) + wife

11.   11. JFK aide David F. Powers

12.   12. Maurice G. Martineau (FDR-Nixon era) + son

13.   Larry Newman

14.   John D. "Jack" Ready

15.   Clinton J. Hill (Ike-Ford)

16.   Gerald S. Blaine (Ike-LBJ)

17.   Talmadge W. Bailey

18.   Rufus W. Youngblood (Truman-Nixon)

19.   Robert I. Bouck (FDR-LBJ)

20.   DNC advance man Martin E. "Marty" Underwood

21.   Robert E. Lilley + granddaughter

22.   Winston G. Lawson (Ike-Reagan)

23.   Abraham W. Bolden, Jr. (Ike-LBJ) + family

24.   William "Tim" McIntyre

25.   Samuel A. Kinney (Truman-LBJ) + wife and relatives

26.   Donald J. Lawton + nephew

27.   Uniformed Division John F. Norris

28.   Relative of the late Wade Rodham

29.   Jerry D. Kivett

30.   Press Secretary Pierre Salinger (via reporter Roger Peterson)

31.   White House photographer Cecil Stoughton

32.   Son of the late White House photographer Robert Knudsen

33.   Charles T. Zboril + wife

34.   Anthony Sherman

35.   Lynn S. Meredith

36.   Radford W. Jones

37.   Samuel E. Sulliman

38.   Darwin David Horn, Sr.

39.   James R. "Jim" Goodenough

40.   Ronald M. Pontius

41.   Helen O'Donnell, daughter of the late JFK Chief of Staff Kenneth P. O'Donnell

42.   Frank G. Stoner (FDR-Nixon)

43.   Gerald W. "Jerry" O'Rourke

44.   Vincent P. Mroz (Truman-Nixon)

45.   J. Walter Coughlin

46.   Bill Carter

47.   J. Frank Yeager

48.   Florida Congressman Samuel Melville Gibbons

49.   Dan Emmett (Reagan-Bush 43)

50.   Bob Ritter

51.   Photographer Tony Zappone (re: 11/18/63 Tampa)

52.   DNC advance man Jack Puterbaugh

53.   Robert R. Snow

54.   Gerald Bechtle + son

55.   Assistant Director of Public Affairs H. Terrence "Terry" Samway

56.   Ernest E. Olsson, Jr.

57.   Kenneth S. Giannoules

58.   Thomas L. "Lem" Johns

59.   Winston J. "Winnie" Gintz

60.   Paul S. Rundle

61.   Forrest Verne Sorrels

62.   Frank D. Slocum

63.   Kenneth J. Wiesman

64.   Joseph Paolella

65.   Dale Keaner

66.   Ed Morey

67.   Kent D. Jordan

68.   Percy Hamilton "Ham" Brown/ AFAUSSS

69.   Special Officer Stanley B. Galup

70.   Relatives of the late W. Arnold Landvoigt

71.   Dale Wunderlich

72.   Wilson "Bill" Livingood

73.   John Joe Howlett

74.   Assistant Director of Public Affairs George M. Rogers

75.   DPD motorcycle officer Samuel Q. Bellah

76.   Richard Greer, son of the late William R. "Bill" Greer (Truman-LBJ) + friend

77.   Robert A. Steuart

78.   H. Stuart "Stu" Knight (Truman-Reagan)

79.   Tampa PD motorcycle officer Russell Groover

80.   AP photographer Henry Burroughs

81.   Dallas Morning News reporter Kent Biffle

82.   Texas Highway Patrolman Milton Wright

83.   Son of the late Lt. Colonel George Whitmeyer

84.   O'Neal Funeral Home driver Aubrey Rike

85.   Reporter Jack Moseley

86.   Daughter of the late James "Mike" Mastrovito

87.   Family of the late William C. Davis

88.   Niece of the late Dan Moriarty

89.   Son-in-law of the late Rudolph "Pete" McDavid

90.   Granddaughter of the late Jack Willard

91.   Family of the late Mike Reilly

92.   Family of the late Kenneth Hale

93.   Family of the late Schuyler Donnella

94.   Relative of John "Jack" Joseph Giuffre

95.   Nephew of Bill Duncan

96.   Intelligence operative Gerry Patrick Hemming + daughter

97.   Friend of the late James K. "Jack" Fox

98.   Charles J. Marass

99.   C-130 crew member Vincent J. Gullo

100.   Rex W. Scouten

101.   Richard E. Johnsen + son

102.   Family of the late Thomas B. Shipman

103.   Son of the late FBI agent Francis X. O'Neill

104.   FBI agent Don A. Adams

105.   John Carman

106.   Friend/ executor of the late Andrew M. Hutch

107.   Family of the late Henry J. "Hank" Rybka

108.   Donald A. Stebbins/AFAUSSS

109.   Son of the late Harry D. Anheier

110.   Nephew of the late Dennis R. Halterman

111.   Robert L. DeProspero (LBJ-Reagan) + friend/former
student

112.   Robin DeProspero-Philpot

113.   Daughter of the late Roy Leteer

114.   Mike Wood, relative of the late Frank Kenney

115.   Nephew of the late former agent James M. Hirst

116.   Friend of Victor Gonzalez

117.   Friend of Paul Landis

118.   Howell "Hal" Purvis

119.   Don Cox

120.   Norman Katz

121.   Earl L. Drescher

122.   John Barletta

123.   William M. McCord

124.   Relatives of the late George J. McNally

125.   Tom Heuerman

126.   Mark Harmon

127.   Ned Hall III, son of the late Ned Hall II

128.   Grandson of the late White House Police Captain Herbert L. Marcey

129.   Mike Maddaloni

130.　　Eve Dempsher, Secret Service secretary

131.　　Friend of the late John E. Campion + John's niece

132.　　Parkland Hospital Dr. Charles Crenshaw

133.　　Parkland Hospital Dr. Malcolm Perry

134.　　Parkland Hospital Dr. Ronald Coy Jones

135.　　Parkland Hospital Dr. Paul Peters

136.　　Parkland Hospital Dr. Donald Seldin

137.　　Parkland Hospital Dr. Donald T. Curtis

138.　　The widow of Texas Highway Patrolman Hurchel Jacks

139.　　Parkland Hospital Dr. Robert N. McClelland

140.　　Parkland Hospital Nurse Patricia B. Gustafson (Hutton)

141.　　Parkland Hospital Dr. Adolph Giesecke

142.　　DPD Stavis Ellis

143.　　Mrs. Billie Martinets

144.　　Parkland Hospital Dr. William Risk

145.　　Parkland Hospital Dr. William Osborne

146.　　Parkland Hospital Dr. Donald Jackson

147.　　Dr. Boris Porto, son of Parkland Hospital Dr. Lito Porto

148.　　Parkland Hospital Dr. Earl F. Rose

149.　　Methodist Hospital Dr. Gerard Noteboom

150.　　William A. Harper (Harper fragment)

151.　　FBI agent Cortlandt Cunningham

152.　　DPD Marion Baker

153.　　Gary Beckworth, son of the late Congressman Lindley Beckworth

154.　　Bethesda Hospital Chester Boyers

155.　　Bethesda Hospital Richard Lipsey

156.　　Bethesda Hospital Jerrol Custer

157.　　Bethesda Hospital John T. Stringer, Jr.

158.　　FBI agent James W. Sibert

159.　　Widow of the late Layton Ledbetter, Bethesda Hospital

160.　　Bethesda Hospital Don Rebentisch

161.   Bethesda Hospital Dr. James J. Humes

162.   Bethesda Hospital Paul K. O'Connor

163.   Bethesda Hospital Jan Gail "Nick" Rudnicki

164.   Eyewitness Beverly Oliver

165.   Eyewitness Ed Hoffman

166.   Eyewitness Mary Moorman Krahmer

167.   Ruby Stripper Shari Angel

168.   Oswald friend Palmer McBride

169.   Alleged LBJ mistress Madeleine Duncan Brown

170.   White House reporter Sarah McClendon

171.   Family of the late Dick Metzinger

172.   Family of the late Harry T. Donaghy

173.   Dennis David

174.   Family of the late Elliot C. Thacker

Index